Literature, Religion, and Postsecular Studies
LORI BRANCH, SERIES EDITOR

PURITANISM *and* MODERNIST NOVELS

From Moral Character to the Ethical Self

 Lynne W. Hinojosa

THE OHIO STATE UNIVERSITY PRESS • COLUMBUS

Library of Congress Cataloging-in-Publication Data
Hinojosa, Lynne W., 1966–
  Puritanism and modernist novels : from moral character to the ethical self / Lynne W.
Hinojosa.
    pages cm. — (Literature, religion, & postsecular studies) Includes bibliographical ref-
erences and index.
  ISBN 978-0-8142-1273-8 (hardback) — ISBN 978-0-8142-9378-2 (cd)
  1. Modernism (Literature)—Great Britain. 2. English fiction—History and criticism. 3.
English fiction—Irish authors—History and criticism. 4. Puritan movements in literature.
5. Christianity and literature. I. Title.
  PR478.M6H56 2015
  823'.91209112—dc23

                        2014027044

Cover design by Mary Ann Smith
Text design by Juliet Williams
Type set in Adobe Sabon
Printed by Thomson-Shore, Inc.

9 8 7 6 5 4 3 2 1

For Mom and Dad
Victor
Miriam and Monica

⊘ CONTENTS

❧ ACKNOWLEDGMENTS

S CHOLARSHIP is always produced in community, and I am deeply thankful to be part of a wonderful community of teacher-scholars at Baylor University. I offer my thanks especially to my Baylor colleagues Andrew Wisely, David Lyle Jeffrey, and Ralph Wood for their helpful comments and suggestions on the manuscript. Pericles Lewis and Elizabeth Newman each generously read various chapters and offered helpful comments. I also thank and remember with much admiration and affection my late colleague, Susan E. Colón, who read many pages and evaluated ideas with me, offering encouragement and wise advice. I thank the Young Scholars in the Baptist Academy organization and the members of our 2009 meetings who read the very first pages of the project. The Honors Program and Honors College at Baylor University, as well as Baylor's Institute for Faith and Learning, all supported my research at the British Library. I am very grateful to Thomas Hibbs and the Honors College at Baylor for granting me a research leave to work on the book.

Parts of the book have already appeared in print. My thanks go to the editors at *Christianity and Literature* and the *Journal of Modern Literature* for allowing material they originally published to appear in Chapters Two and Five of this book, respectively.

Finally, I would like to thank my friends and family, both extended and immediate, all of whom have been so supportive. My daughters, Miriam and Monica, bring joy and delight every day. My husband, Victor, has sacrificed a great deal to support my work, more than I even know, all the while encouraging me. I cannot thank him enough for this and for so much more.

PART ONE

Theory and Context

CHAPTER ONE

From Moral Character to the Ethical Self

W HEN TEENAGER Briony Tallis, the central figure in Ian McEwan's 2001 novel, *Atonement,* submits the first draft of her novella to the new literary magazine, *Horizon,* she thinks the following about novelistic form:

> What excited her about her achievement was its design, the pure geometry and the defining uncertainty which reflected, she thought, a modern sensibility. The age of clear answers was over. So was the age of characters and plots. Despite her journal sketches, she no longer really believed in characters. They were quaint devices that belonged to the nineteenth century. The very concept of character was founded on errors that modern psychology had exposed. Plots too were like rusted machinery whose wheels would no longer turn. A modern novelist could no more write characters and plots than a modern composer could a Mozart symphony. (265)

Briony reaches this position through a conversion into what she thinks is adulthood. When she sees from a window a scene at a fountain in which her sister undresses in front of a male friend and then submerges herself into the fountain waters for unknown reasons, Briony seems to sense a significant change in her outlook. She recognizes she does not understand all that happened, that her perceptions are limited in getting at the truth of what she has witnessed. She self-consciously moves from her earlier childhood mode of writing plays and fairy tales in order to give the viewer or reader a moral lesson, to what she sees as a more mature epistemological uncertainty. From now on, she thinks, "There did not have to be a moral. She need only show separate minds, as alive as her own, struggling with the idea that other minds were equally alive" (38). If she "write[s] the scene three times over, from three points of view," highlighting the incompleteness of any one perspective of reality, she thinks she will produce an "amoral" novel (38).

Later, however, the editor of *Horizon*, presumably Cyril Connolly (who edited the journal from 1940 to 1949), writes Briony back with a rejection letter, albeit with much interest in her talent and detailed suggestions for revisions. Briony's novella, it turns out, has been rejected precisely because it does *not* have enough plot and character development:

> Our attention would have been held even more effectively had there been an underlying pull of simple narrative. Development is required. // So, for example, the child at the window whose account we read first—her fundamental lack of grasp of the situation is nicely caught. So too is the resolve in her that follows, and the sense of initiation into grown-up mysteries. We catch this young girl at the dawn of her selfhood. One is intrigued by her resolve to abandon the fairy stories and homemade folk-tales and plays she has been writing (how much nicer if we had the flavor of one) but she may have thrown the baby of fictional technique out with the folktale water. For all the fine rhythms and nice observations, nothing much happens after a beginning that has such promise. . . . This static quality does not serve your evident talent well. (294–95)

The editor's letter goes on to suggest that not only are plot and character development the qualities most readers desire to have in stories but also these are the essential elements that make stories what they are:

> In other words, rather than dwell for quite so long on the perceptions of each of the three figures, would it not be possible to set them before us with greater economy, still keeping some of the vivid writing about light and stone and water which you do so well—but then move on to create some tension, some light and shade within the narrative itself. Your most sophisticated readers might be up on the latest Bergsonian theories of consciousness, but I'm sure they retain a childlike desire to be told a story, to be held in suspense, to know what happens. . . . Simply put, you lack the backbone of a story. (296)

No matter how sophisticated writers become in describing and representing the complexities of human beings, the editor implies, readers still have
a "childlike" desire for storytelling: plots with conflicts, suspense, movement, moral and spiritual development, in which they can trace the shades
and nuances of human beings living the realities of life. According to the
editor, Briony has perhaps been too much influenced by Virginia Woolf
(295).

Those who have read *Atonement* know how differently and more
complicated Briony's "final" 1999 draft of the story turns out, fifty-nine
years after that initial rejection. With typical postmodern self-reflexivity,
McEwan wants readers to consider Briony's changing choices as a novel-
writer and in the process to consider what it is that novels are supposed
to do, what they actually do, what is supposed to happen to the reader
through the process of reading, and what the writer's responsibilities are
to the reader, to truth, and to justice.[1]

Briony struggles as a writer in 1940, in the middle of World War Two,
the event that leads to the supposed divide between modernism and postmodernism. Briony's rejection of stories meant to serve a clearly discernable moral purpose and her dismantling of all novelistic conventions
in her novella reenacts what modernist novelists did as they reacted to
nineteenth-century novelistic conventions. When Briony composes her
final draft in 1999, presumably she has been exposed also to postmodern thought and novels, and thus her last draft becomes a contemporary
statement (but perhaps not McEwan's) on the novel's role in human life
and on the legacy of both modernism and postmodernism. In the end,
as James Phelan notes, the novel constructs a novella "along modernist
lines" but also "simultaneously question[s] such a construction" (334).

In their experimentation with novels, modernists raised questions
much like Briony did with her novella: Is there such a thing as human
"character"? Are novels supposed to lead readers to a discernable moral
lesson? If so, how and what? Do human beings "develop" morally or otherwise in "plots"? What are the moral obligations of the writer to imitate
"reality"? Or are all novels already and always a lie? Are novels political?
Do novels do anything? Do they matter? According to McEwan's novel
and his character Briony, the legacy of modernism still lingers, and such
questions about the novel's relation to morality have not resolved themselves. In fact, novelists today must grapple with these questions if they

---

1. For more on *Atonement* and modernism, ethics, and literary history, see: Phelan,
Cormack, Finney, D'Angelo, and also Hidalgo.

are to be taken seriously. The publication of *Atonement* in 2001 suggests there is much more to be said about the innovations modernist writers brought to the tradition of the British novel. *Puritanism and Modernist Novels* analyzes and historicizes early modernist treatments of morality and character in novels.[2] It also reflects on the value of modernism's contributions in these areas: Is it even possible to create an amoral novel? What does life look like if one abandons the notion of moral character? To what extent were these actually the goals of modernist novelists?

This book examines four early modernist novels: Oscar Wilde's 1891 *The Picture of Dorian Gray*, E. M. Forster's 1908 *A Room with a View*, James Joyce's 1915 *A Portrait of the Artist as a Young Man*, and Ford Madox Ford's 1915 *The Good Soldier*. It posits that in many ways "modernism" develops as a reaction against "Puritanism." Denoting various things, "Puritanism" is most generally tied to concepts of morality and moral character by modernists. Yet the attempted rejection and supersession of Puritanism may be much more pronounced in the literary criticism responsible for constructing modernism as a literary period than it is in the actual novels produced by the authors studied here. While these authors certainly wanted to escape some of the confining moral effects attributed to Puritanism in their own contexts, they also knew to various degrees that historical Puritanism and the concepts of morality and moral character could never be completely superseded or escaped, both in the novel and in British society. When the American novelist, Marilynne Robinson, in her 1998 essay "Puritans and Prigs," states that Puritanism "appears to me to have died early in this century" (*Death* 150), she is not referring to the extinction of Nonconformist Christianity or versions of Puritanism that continue to be practiced today. Rather, she refers to the cultural forces in the early twentieth century, including literary criticism, that denigrated a stereotypical "Puritanism" and thought it should be surpassed, buried forever. Much of Robinson's work has involved recovering a more charitable sense of what Puritanism was in North America, especially via John Calvin, while exposing the ways in which it has often been stereotyped by those promoting some other ideology. This book participates in that kind of work. Less concerned to recover an accurate sense of what Puritanism actually was in early modern England, however, this book focuses on the ways in which the British novel tradition and

---

2. I use the term "early modernism" to denote the last decade of the nineteenth century and the first two of the twentieth. Christopher Butler coins this term in *Early Modernism: Literature, Music, and Painting in Europe, 1900–1916* (Oxford: Oxford UP, 1994).

especially the early modernist novel in England contributed to (or did not contribute to) this stereotyping and dismantling of Puritanism.[3] It analyzes why the dismantling was deemed necessary and what the results of these attempts were, focusing especially on the concepts of morality and moral character.

To pursue these claims, I first develop a theory of the novel that shows how the novel is inextricably informed by the narrative of moral development emphasized in early modern Puritan hermeneutics and Bible-reading practices. I generally define Puritan hermeneutics as "typological reading," an interpretive practice chapter 2 outlines more fully. Puritan hermeneutics is a foundational influence in the English literary tradition and should be studied for its role in novels just as much as other narrative influences such as romance, myth, or historiography. Often overlooked in novel studies and generally ignored in modernist studies,[4] Puritan hermeneutics shaped the novel in early modernity, including its overarching narrative form as well as the expectations readers and writers had both for the characters' moral and spiritual transformation and for their own reading experience. Remnants of such hermeneutics continue to shape novels throughout the tradition to the present day, a fact *Atonement* self-reflexively highlights as it wonders if the novel can ever be amoral.

This book argues that the relation of the British novel tradition to Puritan biblical hermeneutics is a dialectical one. While the novel remains embedded in Puritan hermeneutical assumptions and practices, the truth of Puritan beliefs about history, God, and the self are increasingly questioned in modernity, such that escape from "Puritanism" becomes the plot movement of many novels. The modern novel's characters often feel trapped by a Puritan-like narrative with its moral and spiritual categories and strive to escape them to achieve moral and spiritual freedom. This dialectical impulse of the novel—in which fictional escape from the Puritan narrative is constitutionally dependent upon the historical reality of Puritanism's remaining existence in society, novel, and self—is what I call the "novelistic narrative." This narrative becomes a dominant force in modernity that shapes how modern subjects view themselves. Over the course of its history, the novel helps create "Puritanism" into a stereotype and "escape" into a modern longing. Additionally, the novel helps shift Puritan typology, with its deep

---

3. For a thorough study of the treatment of Nonconformity in Victorian novels, see Cunningham, *Everywhere Spoken Against.*

4. For a partial treatment in modernist studies, see William J. Scheick, *Fictional Structure and Ethics: The Turn-of-the-Century English Novel* (Athens: U of Georgia P, 1990).

religious bases in the Bible-reading practices of the church, toward mere "typecasting," with its shallow moral bases in "secular" society. Puritan or Nonconformist churches continue to exist and influence society, while the hermeneutics of typology and typecasting continue to shape the novel. Assuming that fiction and history mutually inform each other, then, this book asks: To what extent do we see the world and act in the world as if life were a novel?

The late nineteenth and early twentieth centuries are an especially crucial period to study in this light. In these decades, late Victorian and early modernist writers and artists engaged in a full-scale, overt critique of Puritanism and what they perceived to be its continued prominence in England, both in novels and in society. Modernist experimentation with novelistic characterization was at heart a dismantling or inversion of both the Puritan hermeneutical principles they saw shaping the novel and the Puritan practices and influences they felt dominated social morality. Modernists especially focused on the nature of the human subject or self, and they inverted the Puritan conception of the self with its focus on moral character to explore what I call an "ethical self." Yet in their desire to escape "Puritanism" and "morality," early modernists, because the novel itself is integrally formed by it, remained dialectically tied to Puritan hermeneutics. Analyzing this factor helps show how the ethical and religious stances embodied in modernist novels are often more complicated than has been traditionally thought.

Although colloquially one might view the words "moral" and "ethical" as synonymous, this book uses them to denote different types of human subjects that novels are seen to create. In doing so, it follows the usages delineated by Andrew Gibson, who draws his distinction of the terms "morality" and "ethics" from Geoffrey Harpham, Drucilla Cornell, and Emmanuel Levinas. "Morality," according to Gibson, is tied to particular cultures and conventions and is always "interested," involving judgment and definition. It is part of the historical world that cannot be escaped. "Ethics," on the other hand, is "a kind of play within morality" which "holds it open, hopes to restrain it from violence or the will to domination" (*Postmodernism* 15). Even though it is always determined by morality, "ethics" involves indeterminacy and is always "disinterested." It is the "excess that cannot be known positively within any given system of morality, the aporia that limits any attempt to collapse the good into positive knowledge" (16). It does not involve categories, codes, principles, or anything that is "assumed to be knowable prior to ethical relation, prior to the immediate encounter with what is outside us" (16). For

Levinas the encounter with what is outside is the encounter with the face of the Other. In this space, something "ethical" occurs that precedes articulation of moral categories and judgments as well as knowledge itself.

Puritanism and Modernist Novels attaches the term "moral" to the "Puritan self"—an increasingly fictionalized representation of the Puritan type within the novel tradition who is thought to be sovereign, rational, and overly concerned with moral and spiritual development, moral categories, and moral judgment. My use of the term "Puritan self" is at times associated directly with Puritan Christians but also at times is generalized to denote any sort of subject considered to be hindered and limited by its attention to moral categories. The "ethical" is what a character becomes or finds when he purportedly escapes the Puritan narrative of morality to exist outside its limits. Because the word "aesthetic" is so often used by modernists to talk about escaping or transcending the moral realm to achieve a "higher ethics," this book might have contrasted Puritan "moral character" with the modernist "aesthetic self." As Lee Oser argues in *The Ethics of Modernism,* for modernists "ethics is itself a form of aesthetics" (7), and the "modernist body" is an "aesthetic body" (9). Oser associates the "higher ethics" of modernists with a "refined self-consciousness" and creative power (16). In general, however, it seems to me that for many modernists, this "ethics" based on the "aesthetic" involves becoming and being a certain sort of subject who exists and has certain types of experiences outside Puritan social morality more than it involves developing formal theories of beauty, ethics, or aesthetics. The modernist use of the word "aesthetic" is more often related to the experience of escape and the "ethical" described here, although this is not true in every case. The relation of the "aesthetic" to what I am calling the "ethical" varies within specific texts and authors and so is worked out more over the course of the book.

The term "Puritan" always has two points of reference. It refers to the historical early modern Puritan cultures and Bible-reading practices from which the novel emerged in England and which survived historically into the late nineteenth century and beyond. It also refers to a fictionalized Victorian Puritanism seen to be dominant in the social morality with which modernist novelists engaged but that may have been quite different from what Nonconformist Christianity actually was and continued to be. Both early modern Puritan hermeneutics and novelistic fictionalized Puritanism shape both the novel and society throughout modernity. This doubled sense of Puritanism binds together history and fiction in novels as well as form and content. It forms the basis of the novelistic narrative of confinement and escape that becomes such a powerful grand narrative of modernity.

All four of the modernist authors treated in this book—Oscar Wilde, E. M. Forster, James Joyce, and Ford Madox Ford—are well aware of the hermeneutics of the British novel tradition, and they play with this in their novels. This book argues that the traditional notion of "modernism" as a radical break with the past, an escape from the old Victorian moralities and social categories, a replacement of Christianity with art, is itself generated from within the novelistic narrative. Current branches of literary criticism continue to perpetuate this narrative in which freedom from Puritanism (and, more broadly, Christianity) is achieved and elevated as a superior—and secular—experience. For example, Stephen Kern in his recent book, *The Modernist Novel: A Critical Introduction,* sees modernism as primarily a movement to replace religion with art. Although his argument is quite helpful in showing how "modernism was a subversion and reworking of nine master narratives and an unqualified celebration of a tenth," what he terms the artistic narrative, Kern most forcefully highlights "religion" as the most central narrative that is overcome (44): "Modernists lined up to subvert religion and especially its churches and the narrative that defined its historical role" (211). Kern also argues that modernist novels "characterized religion as dogmatic, vengeful, fraudulent, inhibiting, and potentially violent" (211). In the end, Kern lauds the artistic achievements and bodily returns of those modernists who were "alienated from conventional society but at home in the house of fiction" (215). But Kern does not consider the moral status of these modernist projects. As a consequence, he advocates the aesthetic or ethical achievements of modernism, as so many do, without considering the ramifications of this position. While a few novelists did reject religion as fiercely as Kern describes, many others saw the relationship between art and religion to be much more complicated. They saw limitations in the idea that one could escape all moral and religious hindrances to become an ethical (or aesthetic) self.

The breakdown of moral and social categories and the progress of various social and political movements obviously began or continued in many arenas in the modernist period, but nonetheless remnants of Puritanism and morality have never disappeared and continue to remain embedded in novels, society, and our views of ourselves and others. In many ways modernism as an aesthetic movement in art and literature was conceptualized according to the logic of what Marilynne Robinson has called "the myth of the threshold." To Robinson, this myth involves narratives that are based on

> the idea of a historical threshold—before we thought thus, and, now, in this new age of comprehension, we, or the enlightened among us, think otherwise. There are any number of thresholds, which initiate any number of new conceptual eras. And in every case there is a statement about the past as seen from the vantage of a fundamentally altered present. (*Absence* 5)

Robinson sees this pattern of debunking and rebelling against the past originating in Darwin, Nietzsche, and Freud (*Absence* 20–21). The myth of the threshold can be a condescending posture and method: "To have stepped over a threshold that separates old error from new insight" is to assume one has a firmer grasp of truth and reality on one's own side of that threshold (*Absence* 20). Returning to some of the novel's historical roots, then, complicates how we view modernist novels and negates the idea that there was a threshold modernists crossed. In the end, *Puritanism and Modernist Novels,* as well as the novels it treats, asks whether such a grand narrative of historical escape from moral categories and types is limited in outlook and thereby continues to limit our ability to engender societal, cultural, and historical change. After all, as this book argues, the dismantling of moral categories itself relies on creating an ultimate stereotype—the Puritan. This is an irony central to the British novel tradition.

This book's theory of the dialectical relation of both the novel and modernism to religion and morality renders the relation of both fields to secularism much more complicated and contributes to ongoing interdisciplinary scholarship on the secularization narrative of modernity.

A primary reason Puritan biblical hermeneutics has largely been neglected in novel studies is that for so long the novel has been seen as a secular genre. Pericles Lewis summarizes the pattern well:

> Theories of the novel have tended to emphasize the process of secularization. The most common narrative describes the rejection of earlier, religious narrative forms (especially the epic, but sometimes the saint's life or the spiritual autobiography), in which events fall under the sway of supernatural forces, such as gods or monsters, in favor of naturalistic techniques of description and subject matter from the empirically observable world. Versions of this story appear in the works of Walter

Benjamin, Erich Auerbach, Mikhail Bakhtin, and Ian Watt, but the most succinct account appears in Georg Lukács's classic study *The Theory of the Novel* (1916), which describes the novel as "the epic of a world that has been abandoned by God." Lukács's interpretation has contributed to secularist assumptions of many influential recent studies of the European novel, from Fredric Jameson's *The Political Unconscious* (1981) to Franco Moretti's *Modern Epic* (1994). (23)

The most interesting trend to note is that all of the "secularist" critics mentioned, with the exception of Auerbach, are Marxist in critical orientation. Michael McKeon should of course also be added to this list of dominant theorists and historians of the novel who are Marxist (and in turn, two non-Marxists, Northrop Frye and Margaret Doody, should be added to such a list of major theorists). The relation of Marxist literary history to narratives of secularization within novel theory, as well as the relation of Marxism to narratives of secularization generally, is a topic that could and should be pursued more. While the main aim of this book is different, it briefly addresses the connection of Marxism to the view of the novel as secular.

Viewing the novel through a narrative of secularization obscures the significance of "religious" influences on the novel (and in the strict Marxist case, it reduces any religious influences to a sort of false ideology).[5] To cite a few examples, of all the excerpted essays in McKeon's 947-page anthology, *Theory of the Novel: A Historical Approach*, the Bible is indexed on only two pages, and "Christianity," "Puritan," and "Protestant" on none. In Franco Moretti's huge two-volume edited anthology, *The Novel* (2006), which totals 1,866 pages, the Bible is only indexed on two pages. Yet Puritan religious influences on the novel are the very same influences that provided the historical soil out of which Hegelian and Marxist dialectic later emerged. At one level, it seems entirely natural to view the novel through a lens of dialectical history and form. Bakhtin's theory of heteroglossia and dialogism, Watt's theory of the emergence of realism, and McKeon's dialectical strands of romantic idealism, naïve empiricism, and extreme skepticism, for example, all resonate with what we sense and detect in the novel and its history. The novel does actually appear to be dialectical in nature.[6] Yet this book argues that Puritan

---

5. The term "religion" is ridden with difficulty. For an argument that says "religion" is an empty term without any "essence," see William T. Cavanaugh, *The Myth of Religious Violence: Secular Ideology and the Roots of Modern Conflict* (Oxford: Oxford UP, 2009).

6. William B. Warner describes the Marxist affinity for the novel's form thus: Marx-

hermeneutics are also dialectical. Puritan reading practices and theories of history and the self do not involve exactly the same theory of dialectical synthesis as Hegel later formulated it, but they embody a dialectic of a different sort that becomes embedded in the novel. Chapter 2 describes more specifically this Puritan dialectic that in turn helps shape both the novel and Hegelian and Marxist dialectic.[7]

In analyzing the relation of the novel to Puritan hermeneutics I do not claim to offer what McKeon calls a "grand theory" of the novel. In fact, in order to see what can be learned about the modernist novel, religion, and morality, I am only considering one influence on the novel among many others that have been and should continue to be analyzed—romance, historiography, philosophy, print culture, science, politics, to name a few areas. Likewise, the influence of many later cultural developments on the modernist novel could be treated and are not, such as Darwinism or positivism. Even so, this study adds new insight and challenges for existing grand theories of the novel, for it addresses the influence of Puritan Bible-reading practices and hermeneutics on the novel in new ways.[8]

Currently, modernity's narratives of secularization are being challenged and scrutinized within many disciplines. In literary studies, such work generally involves rethinking literature's relation to religion and secularism and its role in bringing spiritual experience to its readers.[9] Scholars in novel studies and in all period studies, including modernist studies, are also increasingly opening such questions. A Spring 2011 conference at The Center for the Study of the Novel at Stanford, for example, focused on the question "Is the Novel Secular?" In addition to McKeon, however, only a few scholars have drawn direct connections between the emergence of the modern novel and the Bible.[10] Only a handful has

---

ists seem drawn to the "way the novel anticipates at a cultural level those achievements toward which [M]arxism aspires at the level of both knowledge and politics. The novel does a detailed analysis of the social; it is cast in the form of purposive progressive historical narratives; the novel achieves immense popularity in the modern period" (62).

7. Northrop Frye makes a few brief connections between biblical narrative and hermeneutics and Hegel and Marx in *The Great Code: The Bible and Literature*.

8. McKeon's own grand theory in *The Origins of the English Novel, 1640–1700* treats more thoroughly than any other account the historical context of Puritanism and Bible-reading.

9. For an introduction to these topics in literary studies, see the exchanges in the following: *New Literary History* 38 (2007): 607–27; *Religion and Literature* 41:2 (2009); and *Christianity and Literature* 58:2 (2009).

10. As this book was being prepared for publication, Norman Vance's *Bible and Novel: Narrative Authority and the Death of God* appeared (Oxford: Oxford UP, 2013). See also

specifically analyzed the early modern novel's engagement with Puritan hermeneutics.[11]

In modernist studies, the most pertinent recent book to examine secularization and religion is Pericles Lewis's 2010 *Religious Experience and the Modernist Novel*. Lewis argues that shifts in social thought about religion in the early twentieth century influenced novelists to experiment with novelistic form and to think about religious experience in new ways. Rather than deepening the secularization process, modernist novelists actually combated the results of it in their own ways as they sought new modes of spirituality and the sacred. Lewis's analysis is profoundly helpful as it draws parallels on questions of religious experience between high modernist novelists (Woolf, Kafka, Proust, Joyce, and Henry James) and sociological thinkers (William James, Freud, Weber, and Durkheim). *Puritanism and Modernist Novels* also analyzes shifts in novels in the modernist period that are linked to changes in religious understanding. In part these changes, as Lewis's book shows us, are shaped by the emergence of anthropology, psychology, and sociology as disciplines, by new trends in philosophy, and by other wider cultural discourses. This book analyzes some of these larger discourses of the late nineteenth and early twentieth centuries.

However, in addition to seeing novelistic treatments of religion as shaped by discourses outside the novel, this book argues that the tradition of the novel is itself constituted by the questioning of religion, particularly its Protestant and Puritan varieties. As Valentine Cunningham has said, central to the novel is the "struggle with Christianity—with the Christian narrative, the Christian plot" ("The Novel" 39). Even novelists in Southern Europe who are Catholic are "members of the large Protestant family of fiction, formally speaking" (39). I concur with Cunningham's revision of Lukács's famous phrase: rather than being the epic of a world abandoned by God, instead the "Novel is the Epic of a world . . . having everything to do with God and also trying to do without that God, and not just any God, but rather the God of the Protestant Reformers and the Protestant Bible translators" (40). The novel is simultaneously shaped by Puritanism while attempting to escape Puritanism. This novelistic dia-

Frei, Preus, Prickett (all), Frye, and also Knight and Woodman. More commonly, critics link spiritual autobiography and biblical narrative rather than the novel outright. See, for example, Starr and also Henderson.

11. See Hunter, Korshin, Damrosch, Qualls, Seidel (all), and also Cunningham (all). For studies of typology in literature more generally, see Bercovitch and also Miner.

lectic makes it difficult to categorize the genre within a secular–religious dichotomy.

A central argument of this book examines the theories of the self that are created in novels and potentially replicated in novel readers. Marxist, secularist novel theory relies on the idea that the novel is the genre of modern individualism, which, linked to Protestantism, also produces an individualized sovereign mode of interpretation. While convincing to a large degree, this theory has its limits, for the impulse to escape such a view of the self, to achieve freedom from the dominant social and moral narratives, including the idea that the individual is sovereign, has also been present throughout the novel's history. While the Marxist focus on the novel's creation of the individual, sovereign ("Puritan") self is limiting, then, as it tends to limit the novel to this function, at the other end of the spectrum, a current branch of ethical criticism, here termed "New Ethical Theory," also tends to place certain limits on the novel. This school of criticism glorifies the modernist novel as a tool of moral (de)formation, such that the Puritan reading self—the sovereign individual—dismantles itself in the reading process, becomes freed of its previous moral and social knowledge and limitations and becomes an ethical self. Chapter 2 argues that this school of thought, while convincing to a degree, is also limited by its own origins in the "novelistic narrative." It even becomes problematic as it continues to adhere to an extreme form of sovereign individualism and interpretive authority. A central point of this book is that the ethical self is dialectically dependent upon the Puritan moral self for its own existence, and thus the idea that the former can completely escape the latter is always a fiction which is just as limiting as that from which the escape is sought.

Like the new ethical and Marxist novel critics, the modernists studied here each question the validity of the Puritan self on ontological, epistemological, and ethical grounds, and these questions shape how they rethink characterization, plot, and the moral and spiritual function of novels. Each of the modernist novelists studied here creates and experiments with the ethical self. Yet these authors are also aware of the limitations of this alternative self. They recognize to various degrees the dialectic of moral character and ethical experience, Puritanism and escape, embedded in the novel. The stances on religious and moral matters embedded in their novels, then, do not correlate with the rejection and supersession of Christianity and morality which modernism is so often seen as initiating. Of course, my study is limited to only four novels; other modernist novels will either support or challenge this theory to various degrees. Yet the four authors and novels treated here each have been seen by literary critics as narrating an escape from religion and hence also from conventional morality when in fact, something different may be going on.

All of the modernist questions about character, morality, and the human subject are joined to larger questions about the assumed historical context within which Puritan hermeneutics is practiced and believed. As they experiment with the human subject, modernists ask whether there is a grand narrative that shapes the universe and human history. They ask whether there is a God who directs history, creates human beings, has full knowledge of an absolute truth, and grounds a universal moral order. Their experiments with plots and endings have great implications regarding their hopes for human history and for the ability of humans to undergo positive change. Like McEwan's *Atonement,* this book considers the usefulness and effects of the ends to which modernist novels lead.

Chapter 2 develops more completely the theory of the novel's dialectical relation to Puritan hermeneutics only briefly outlined here. It offers short readings of Augustine's *Confessions* and Defoe's *Robinson Crusoe* to differentiate Puritan Bible-reading from what Puritan hermeneutics becomes in the novel. This chapter also delves into New Ethical Theory more fully. Chapter 3 provides a brief historical picture of the legacy of Puritanism in the late nineteenth and early twentieth centuries, using John Henry Newman's and Matthew Arnold's ideas about Puritanism as lenses for viewing the general milieu.

Historically, the Puritans were composed of a variety of Protestant groups. Also known as Nonconformists, these groups opposed the establishment of the Church of England (or Anglican Church) on theological, doctrinal, and political grounds. Andrew Cambers suggests that "Puritanism" should be conceived as "a broad religious culture, within which there were a range of subcultures that, although still recognizably and meaningfully puritan, sometimes pulled in different directions" (15). The dominant Nonconformist groups were the Congregationalists, Baptists, Presbyterians, and later the Methodists. By the late nineteenth century, these were still considered to be the primary Nonconformist denominations, although other smaller ones such as the Quakers and Unitarians were also considered to be Nonconformist. For Cambers, one practice that all Puritans would have recognized as central to their culture was "godly reading." Puritans were known for their intense Bible-reading and careful selection of nonbiblical texts. They felt reading could shape the reader spiritually and morally and was an ontological process that could potentially lead to the transformation of the reader. As chapter 3 shows, such practices and beliefs about reading continued to inform Nonconformist life in the late nineteenth century. They also continued to fuel debates over the merits of novel-reading and Bible-reading in the formation of souls, echoing concerns some Puritans had voiced from the beginning of the novel's history.

Nonconformists had a strong influence on Britain's culture and politics in the latter half of the nineteenth century, becoming leaders in Britain's world ascendency. Nonconformist thought on moral issues affected fiction, politics, drama, law, and family relations, among many other areas in English life. All of these influences often congealed into an exaggerated social stereotype that furthered the stereotyping processes of the novel. One does not have to go far in a study of modernism to find a negative comment about Puritanism. Some famous quips still shape current views, like H. L Mencken's secular view: "Puritanism. The haunting fear that someone, somewhere, may be happy," or G. K. Chesterton's Catholic one: "A Puritan is a person who pours righteous indignation into the wrong things." Such stereotyping of Puritanism was so prevalent that C. S. Lewis, in *The Screwtape Letters* (1940), ironically has the devil Wormwood declare to his student Screwtape: "The value we have given to that word [Puritanism] is one of the really solid triumphs of the last hundred years. By it we rescue annually thousands of humans from temperance, chastity, and sobriety of life" (47). Wormwood implies here that because no one wants to be identified as a Puritan, souls can easily but falsely be swayed by the devil into thinking they can live alternatively, in a realm outside virtue and moral character.

Many modernists, like George Bernard Shaw and D. H. Lawrence, both of whom have been called "anti-Puritan Puritans," struggled with their Protestant heritage.[12] Evidence of such a troubled relation can be seen in the writings of many modernist writers, especially the four treated in this book. Wilde, Forster, Joyce, and Ford each had a unique personal relation to Protestant Christianity and specifically Puritanism, which each respective chapter will outline. Often in these decades English Puritanism was associated with many things that needed to be escaped: sexual repression, rationalism, moral and spiritual asceticism, middle-class values, individualism, capitalism, close-mindedness, judgmentalism, and for the Irish, political oppression. For many, the primary benefit of escaping

---

12. See Gordon.

Puritanism was a supposed freedom from the moral limits placed on the body and sexuality. As seen in chapter 6, Friedrich Nietzsche's moral philosophy in large part was also a reaction against Protestant or Puritan-like morality. It provided for many modernist writers a means of rethinking Puritan morality and the self.

Of course, to sketch a full picture of Puritanism at the turn of the century one would need to take into account many thinkers, not all of whom can be treated here. Max Weber's famous formulation of Protestantism in his 1904–5 *The Protestant Ethic and the Spirit of Capitalism,* for example, has shaped and continues to shape views of Puritanism in literary and cultural studies and certainly should be studied for its influence on modernism. Similarly, William James, who famously focused on the nature of religious experience from a sort of meta-stance, helped ingrain ideas of religion's fictionality.[13]

As the book turns from the early modern period and a general theory of the novel in part 1 to readings of the four early modernist novels in part 2, it obviously skips over the intervening centuries. *Puritanism and Modernist Novels* essentially looks backwards to find the roots of trends found in the late nineteenth and early twentieth centuries. It sees what Puritanism became in the novels of a later time period and extrapolates back to offer hypotheses and a theory of the novel supported by some early modern examples and evidence, but that would need to be further tested and developed by others through more readings of particular texts and historical research. In this way, as it aims toward an audience in modernist studies, this book offers a theoretical account of Puritan reading and its influence on the novel rather than a detailed historical account. That said, a field of scholarship in the 1970s and 1980s to a large extent traced the influence of Puritan hermeneutics on the literary tradition both in the early modern period and in the intervening centuries, providing key studies of the missing historical trajectory.[14] Despite the fact that this field dissipated after the 1980s, more work could be done in these periods, and several scholars have recently picked up these threads of inquiry.[15] No one from this earlier phase to my knowledge extended their work to a significant degree into a study of modernism.[16]

---

13. Lewis treats both Weber and James in *Religious Experience and the Modernist Novel.*

14. See Korshin, Bercovitch, Hunter, Miner, Davis, Landow, and also Galdon.

15. See all of Seidel's work, and also Pettella.

16. Theodore Ziolkowski did some work in this period on typology in twentieth-century literature. See, for example, his essay in Miner.

Puritanism and Modernist Novels argues, then, that not only can an understanding of Puritan Bible-reading practices enhance our understanding of both the novel and modernism, but examining modernist novels can enhance our understanding of Puritanism's influence on the British literary tradition, social morality, and views of the self in modernity. Puritanism became more and more a fictional construct through the development of the novel over time, yet this construct in turn had great effects on historical reality and on how people viewed their lives. The novelistic narrative—the dialectic of Puritanism and escape—becomes a story that is simultaneously historical and fictional, a narrative within which people think and live. This theory may seem too ungrounded for some. Yet any study of the novel's influence on human reality necessarily blurs the boundary between fact and fiction as it also necessarily rests on one large assumption: novels affect their readers.

Each chapter in part 2 combines readings of "fiction" with readings of "history," giving a close reading of a modernist novel with new historical contextual research. Chapters 4 through 7 each read a modernist novel's engagement with Puritanism in its doubled history of the novel and the social contexts in which modernists were embedded. To my knowledge, these chapters contribute new insights to scholarship on the individual novels. Chapter 4 examines Oscar Wilde's *A Picture of Dorian Gray* in the context of late Victorian aestheticism and Nonconformist views of reading. It argues that Wilde understood the Puritan dialectic of the novel and that in fact, his novel is self-reflexively *about* that dialectic. Hegel's dialectical theory of tragedy provides a new way to interpret the novel's ending. Chapter 5 reads E. M. Forster's *A Room with a View* in the context of historiographical discourses of periodization that pit the Renaissance against the Medieval period. As historical periods were formulated and became part of historical discourse in the latter half of the nineteenth century, the Renaissance was narrated as a break with Medieval constriction and religion. Modernists in the same way narrate themselves as instituting a new Renaissance, a break with Victorian constriction and Puritanism. Forster consciously uses these period terms to structure the plot of his novel for similar purposes. Chapter 6 reads James Joyce's *A Portrait of the Artist as a Young Man* in the context of Nietzsche's moral philosophy. While there exists a multitude of studies on Joycean ethics, and several that connect Joyce to Nietzsche, there are more connections to make regarding Nietzsche's and Joyce's similar attitudes to Puritan morality. Chapter 7 reads Ford Madox Ford's *The Good Soldier* in the context of political debates regarding church, state, and morality in the 1900s and 1910s. While the references to religion in the novel are gaining increasing attention, connecting these to the novelistic narrative as well as to the ways in which this Puritan dialectic played out in public debates about marriage and divorce law is new. Like McEwan's *Atonement,* Ford's novel is self-reflexively *about* the effects of believing the self and the novel can be amoral.

CHAPTER TWO

Theory

Puritanism, the Bible, the Novel, Modernism

*T*YPOLOGY as a hermeneutical practice was the foundation of what seemed a unified worldview for the early modern Puritans.[1] It was a mode of reading applied to interpreting just about everything: the Bible, other written texts, history, the natural world, and the moral and spiritual character of the self. Puritan hermeneutics were dominantly shaped by John Calvin, who in turn was highly influenced by Augustine. According to Wesley Kort, Bible-reading for Calvin was central to the Christian life, such that doctrine and theology were meant to aid it, not be elevated above it (198). A seventeenth-century Puritan minister, Thomas Watson, in "How We May Read the Scriptures with the Most Spiritual Profit,"[2] described the centrality of the Bible to the Christian life:

> The Scripture is the compass by which the rudder of our will is to be steered; it is the field in which Christ, the pearl of price, is hid; it is a rock of diamond; it is a sacred Collyrium, or eye-salve; it mends their eyes

---

1. Some of the material in this chapter appeared previously in print as "Reading the Self, Reading the Bible (Or is it a Novel?): The Differing Typological Hermeneutics of Augustine's *Confessions* and Daniel Defoe's *Robinson Crusoe,*" *Christianity and Literature* 61:4 (2012): 641–65.

2. This chapter uses Watson's text as its primary example. Instructive guides for how to read the Bible could be found in any number of Puritan sermons and devotional texts. See also John Knott, *The Sword of the Spirit: Puritan Responses to the Bible* (Chicago: U of Chicago P, 1980).

who look upon it; it is a spiritual optic glass, in which the glory of God
is resplendent; is it the panacea, or universal medicine for the soul. (28)

Reading the Bible healed and reformed the Christian's will and soul. It
was the reader's guide to life and the vehicle by which he could recognize
the glory of God. The text was so central to all aspects of life for Puritans
that Watson argued: "Christians should be walking Bibles" (40).

Foundationally, St. Paul practices typological hermeneutics when
he reads portions of the Old Testament as prefiguring the New, as containing clues or patterns that foreshadow the later events of the New
Testament. Adam, for example, is a type that prefigures the antitype
Christ, but the latter is the perfected fulfillment of what was the imper-
fect imprint of the prior. This mode of relating Old Testament to New
acknowledges that both type and antitype are historical realities and
rests on the assumption that God works in history and has a plan for
it. God creates real things that prefiguratively signify other real things
later on in time that fulfill the purposes of His providence. Typological
interpretation is founded on the belief that, as Augustine said, "In the
Old Testament the New lies hidden; in the New Testament the Old is laid
open." In the biblical narrative, then, one can identify as one reads a pre-
ordained historical pattern in which types point to their future spiritual
fulfillment in Jesus, who enters history and transforms it.

Seventeenth- and eighteenth-century English Puritans saw their historical moment as typologically related to biblical history and therefore as
part of God's providential plan. As Paul Korshin says, English Puritans
"believed there were predictive connections between biblical times and
their own and they searched constantly for signs to justify their beliefs"
and their politics (3). Their present historical period was the postfigura-
tive antitype to Old Testament types: England was typologically related to
Israel and the Puritans to God's chosen people. In the Puritan view, God
created the larger historical pattern into which contemporary events fit,
and He inserted himself into that pattern, leaving clues or types by which
astute readers of history could see His presence and detect His actions.

Typological reading was also a means of understanding and order-
ing nature for the Puritans: they believed the material order reflected and
pointed to a spiritual order. If one meditated on the objects of creation
in which God placed signs and emblems to aid interpretation, one could
become more conscious of spiritual matters and read the place of one's
self and of the natural world within the larger order of Providence. The
ultimate significance of natural occurrences might be just as obscure to

the average human as the significance of historical events, but as William Cowper put it in a late-eighteenth-century poem, "God is His own interpreter, and He will make it plain."[3] In such a view, God is both creator and exegete.

This theology of reading nature had moral implications for human art. While some Puritans wrote novels, others were skeptical of fiction because the genre distorted the foundational idea that God both creates and interprets. In fiction, the human author creates the narrative and provides the clues for interpreting it, in essence usurping God's roles of creator and exegete of both history and nature (Hunter 116). For the Puritans only God could reveal correct interpretation, whether through the Holy Spirit or through other scriptures. As Watson says, "The Scripture is to be its own interpreter, or rather the Spirit speaking in it; nothing can cut the diamond but the diamond; nothing can interpret the Scripture but Scripture" (*Body* 31).

Puritan hermeneutics also adhered to the classical notion that love follows knowledge. In other words, only through gaining self-knowledge could one increase in love for God. Accurate self-knowledge involves both the recognition of one's sinful state in need of God's grace and the recognition of one's status as a creation of God for whom He has immeasurable love. For Calvin, according to Kort, "two bits of knowledge" are received while reading. The first is the "name of the one who has created everything," and the second is that "the One who created everything also redeems" (195). The individual reader begins to recognize his own moral and spiritual state as he identifies with characters or types within the biblical narrative. As he reads, the reader can see himself in a typological pattern: the Bible can read the self or bring self-knowledge as one places one's self into the narrative. One can identify with Adam in the garden, for example, or with the Israelites wandering in the wilderness, or with Jonah, too reluctant to do God's bidding. Watson describes this identification process thus: "Compare yourselves with the Word. See how the Scripture and your hearts agree; how your dial goes with this Sun. Are your hearts, as it were, a transcript and counterpart of Scripture? Is the Word copied out into your hearts?" ("How" 35).

Understanding the self's state through identification with a character type potentially could also lead to a reformation of the self as the reader then begins to identify with Christ, the antitype, sacrificing love of self in favor of love of God. Gaining self-knowledge occurs as the reader meets

---

3. The poem/hymn by Cowper is titled "God Moves in a Mysterious Way."

God in the text, with His grace guiding the reader into the Word. Kort argues that for Calvin, "Knowledge of God, like the power of the Holy Spirit, is related to the act of reading Scripture and not to be located prior to or apart from it" (193). In the movement between Old Testament and New, between identification with type and then antitype, the reader, directed by the Holy Spirit, comes to understand through the experience of reading both her distorted and divided, sinful "false self" and her "true self" found only in Christ and His love. The text speaks to and opens the inner self to gain new knowledge, to reorient its direction in life and for eternity. Such a hermeneutics argues that Bible-reading can lead to real change—to conversion but also to subsequent further change over the course of one's life—as God's grace opens the heart to new knowledge and to possibilities for love and forgiveness.

Yet this process must occur over and over again. Bible-reading is a habitual practice cultivated by Puritan believers and seen to be crucial to continued spiritual development. In believing Bible-reading could reveal the "true self" in such a manner, the Puritans assumed the presence of an inner conscience or soul in the reader, an interior space of moral and spiritual truth. Created by God, this inner space of truth is fully known only by God. Humans are created to be epistemologically limited. And because they are sinful, they need reformation continually and to read the Bible habitually in order to access such inner truth about themselves.

The repeated reading process of gaining self-knowledge and opening the self to God through love is a dialectical one. The reader moves between the here and now, what one knows (or thinks she knows), and the not yet, a future perfection that is currently not known but for which one must continually hope. The turning of the false self to the true self is a "personal divestment if not self-abnegation" that has to be repeated over and over again. A "negative relation must be clarified between what a reader knows and is and what is about to be received" (Kort 194). Typological bible-reading is dialectical, then, as the reader must constantly negotiate through God's guidance the old and new, the known and unknown. The time in which typological interpretation takes place is not linear but dialectical, moving back and forth between the now and not yet.

This dialectical movement of reading is a movement between reasoning about the present and envisioning a new future and a new self. Although Puritanism became stereotyped as both excessively rational and solely morally oriented, Puritan reading practices in actuality involved not only rational, moral evaluation but also aesthetic imagination and movements of the heart. Richard Baxter, another seventeenth-century Puritan preacher and theologian, describes proper Bible-reading as both rational and passionate as well as dialectical:

> In reading our understandings are oft illuminated with a heavenly light, and our hearts are touched with a special delightful relish of that truth, and they are secretly attracted and engaged unto God and are all the powers of our souls excited and animated to a holy obedient life.

Likewise, Watson's descriptions are dialectical: "Reading brings a truth into our head; meditation brings it into our heart; reading and meditation, like Castor and Pollux, must appear together" ("How" 24). Emotion and heart are just as crucial to the reading process as intellect and mind: "Leave not off reading the Bible till you find your hearts warmed. . . . Let it not only inform you, but inflame you," says Watson. The dialectical nature of typological bible-reading not only shapes the novel but also later on Hegelian and Marxist dialectic.

One potential reason Puritanism has been linked to a strict rationalism may be the large typological handbooks Puritans produced, the most famous of which is likely Samuel Mather's *Figures and Types of the Old Testament* (second edition, 1705). Puritan interpretation of the Bible at times focused obsessively on identifying the types and patterns embedded in the biblical narrative. Yet despite what seems to be an incredulous stretching at times of the possibilities of typological connection between Old Testament and New and a focus on the minutiae of the biblical text, reading was not considered an exact science or a completely rational activity by the Puritans. Knowledge of history, self, and God obtained through reading was often considered to remain epistemologically obscure and involved a nonscientific, poetic or aesthetic mode of reading led by the Holy Spirit.

Even Mather had much to say about the obscurity of the types and of the reading self: "There was and is a double use of Types and parables, and of that whole way of Argument by Similitude and Comparisons: They do both *darken* and *illustrate*; but if not explained, they are like a Riddle, they cast a dark mist and a cloud upon the thing" (9). For Mather, "the Apostle's definition of the type"—"a shadow of good things to come"—has three parts: 1) "some outward or sensible Thing, that represents some other higher thing"; 2) "There is the thing represented thereby, which is good things to come, which we call the Antitype"; and 3) "There is the work of the Type, which is to shadow forth or represent these future good things" (52). He likens the "general Nature of a Type" and its Antitype to: the shadow and its substance; the shell and its kernel; the letter and its Spirit or Mystery (52). Even though "it hath been the Goodness and Wisdom of God in all times and ages, to teach Mankind Heavenly things by Earthly; Spiritual and invisible things, by outward and visible," these teachings are not perfectly clear: they require special insight and knowledge given by the Holy Spirit (52). Just as the Antitype "infinitely transcends" the type, such that "no type could reach it" (57), similarly, no human interpreter can decode without God's aid the system of Types which He has created. In parallel, no human interpreter can decode his own inner self without God's aid. Christ, the antitype, is both now and not yet; he entered history but will come again to fulfill history. This future is unknowable fully in earthly life, and thus the habitual process of identification through Bible-reading is more poetic and uncertain than scientific or certain. Most significantly for this book's subsequent discussion, "identification" with a character in a text dos not involve rationally equating two things, but rather is a much more loose and fluid connection. There is a constant dialectical movement between recognizing the limits of one's self and opening up to what is new and beyond the self.

The self-recognition in light of God's grace that occurred in Puritan reading was also to be interpreted within a comprehensive view of reality. Ideally, the four traditional levels of interpretation—literal, allegorical, moral, and anagogical—seamlessly intersected with each other. Identifying with a type not only leads to a recognition of one's individual moral and spiritual state, then, but also of one's status as a human being within the teleological narrative of God's providential history, the ontological structure of God's creation, and the ethical order of God's people (the church). Bible-reading is a constant reminder to the reader of one's place in a narrative that moves in time (history) and has a context (creation) as well as a way to identify, reform, and instruct one's particular self in one's local context. For Puritans, then, there is a moral and spiritual order to the universe. This order manifests itself in creation, in history, and in the church. Bible-reading reminds the reader of his proper place within this order, and thus there is also a constant dialectical negotiation between one's own self and the larger realities in which the self participates. Bible-reading has implications for one's own particular story, but that story and the movement of the self ultimately only gain significance as they participate in the larger story of salvation history. The Puritan self formed through Bible-reading is simultaneously individual and communal.

Such hermeneutics and Bible-reading practices, among other forces, shaped greatly the form and content of early modern British novels as well as the expectations for moral and spiritual formation that readers had as they approached such texts. Korshin outlines how the genre of character books expanded in seventeenth-century England and became a staple of Protestant writing and a precursor to the modern novel (122). In such books characters represented virtues and vices and were to provide examples to readers of various moral states. As part of a whole "Christomimetic tradition" stemming from Thomas à Kempis's *Imitation of Christ,* which was reprinted often and very popular among Puritans, good characters were ones whose individual lives imitated Christ (Korshin 197). Through such literature, readers could identify moral types that then became prefigurative or predictive in their own imaginations. If one recognized the type, one could predict the course the future plot might take. Similarly, in the experience of reading, identifying one's self with a character type could illuminate one's own true self and prefigure the trajectory of one's own future. Tera H. Pettella in a recent study argues that early modern readers "read novels in much the same way they did their devotional texts" and that novel writers in turn used and modified the conventions of Puritan devotional texts in their novels (280).

The typological, dialectical process, in which the reader identifies with a character and thereby potentially gains self-knowledge and instruction, or even experiences reformation or conversion, shapes what early modern novels are and the moral and religious function they serve. In many ways, Puritan typology *is* the hermeneutics of the novel. Yet at this point, important qualifications need to be made to this claim, for obviously a novel is not the Bible.

The typological Bible-reading described above is certainly not a new thing that emerges with Puritanism in modernity. Typology is in fact an ancient way of reading the Bible that had existed for centuries and to which Puritans saw themselves returning. Augustine was a key influence as Puritan reformers reclaimed the Bible for the layperson. There are significant differences, however, in premodern and Puritan biblical typology compared to its novelistic variations. These differences manifest themselves in three interrelated ways. First, the nature of the individual self (reader) is ontologically different. For Puritans, the Bible-reader is an individual whose story is merely a part of a larger story of God's providential history, creation, and the church. Meaning comes in relation to community. In turn, the individual reader did not have final interpretive authority. In the novel, on the other hand, the individual reader remains solitary and is not necessarily connected to a larger sense of community or history. The reader is the sole interpretive authority. The second difference between biblical and novelistic typology has to do with the "religious" or "sacred" status of the text. The third difference has to do with the dialectical nature of the both the narrative and the reading process. Although interrelated, these three differences are discussed separately on a theoretical level next. After that, a brief comparison of Augustine's *Confessions* and Daniel Defoe's *Robinson Crusoe* shows the differences and similarities of typological Bible- and novel-reading. The final section of this chapter examines the parallels between Puritan hermeneutics and new ethical theory—a branch of current criticism of the modernist novel. All of these connections reveal how a study of the novel's Puritan roots might alter how we interpret texts in both novel and modernist studies.

The first difference between Bible-reading and novel-reading has to do with the nature of the individual self, ontologically, epistemologically, and ethically. Literary historians have traditionally assumed that Puritans read their Bibles in the same way novels are read—in solitude. Andrew Cambers affirms that contrary to such interpretation, Puritan Bible-reading was often practiced communally in the context of the church. While it is true that "books were central to godly culture" and Puritan self-identity and that "the image of the Puritan was intrinsically linked to that of the book," Cambers argues, the tradition of seeing Puritan reading practices as mostly individualized is simply not accurate (6). Instead, Cambers argues that "godly reading was a style of religious engagement with texts which was frequently oral and communal: to read among fellow believers was a key sign of evangelical religious identity" (9). "Belief," then, was "primarily socially constructed and maintained," and this fact casts "doubt on the common assumption that the Reformation ushered in an era of individualization and interiorization" (9). To Cambers, while recent historiography has expanded and refreshed our understanding of Puritan cultures, tying together ecclesiology, theology, and politics (13), scholars in literary studies, sociology, and cultural studies still tend to rely on Max Weber's "claims about the connections between Puritanism and the 'spirit of capitalism' and the emergence of modern Western culture" (15). In Cambers's view, this leads to an oversimplification of Puritan reading practices as "somehow crucial in the rise of silent reading and the development of interior religious belief and even of the self" (16). Puritans in some contexts practiced individualized reading, but it was neither the only mode of Bible-reading nor the dominant one. Reading one's place and limitations in the universe was practiced in the communal context of the church, and ideally the church congregation would interpret together God's word and the truths found therein, deciphering their relation to history and creation. The individual reader was not the sole interpretive authority. As Kort suggests, Calvin placed scriptural interpretive authority somewhere in between the tradition-based "authority of the church" and the authority of the individual reader of scripture (193). The Puritans identified themselves primarily as God's people, a group whose collective identity was ultimately more important than individual identity and whose history in fulfilling God's providential plan was more important than anyone's individual history.

In the end, then, much Puritan Bible-reading was more premodern (or Augustinian) and less individualistic than previously believed. Likely, it is the variation of Puritan hermeneutics involved in novel-reading, not in Bible-reading, which then engenders the modern mode of silent reading and interior self-examination that has for so long been attributed to Puritanism in general. The rise of individualized Bible-reading practices can be attributed not to the methods by which the Puritans read the Bible per se, but rather to what Stephen Prickett has called "the novelization of the Bible" or "biblical novelization" (*Origins* 267). That is, novel-reading practices, while emergent from and similar to Bible-reading practices, eventually in turn reshape Bible-reading practices in modernity. What becomes missing in novelistic typology are the very senses of communal identity that Cambers argues were foundationally constitutive of Puritan "godly" reading. In novelistic typology, the individual becomes the authoritative interpreter of spiritual and moral truth. The individual becomes sovereign. Over the course of the novel's history, this notion of the individual becomes stereotyped as "Puritan," yet this book argues that such a self is only one extreme of what might get produced in the dialectical movement of typological reading.

A second qualification to the claim that Puritan hermeneutics is the hermeneutics of the novel is to acknowledge that certainly not every novel or novelist consciously engages with the truth claims of Christianity or the biblical narrative and its consequent moral and spiritual categories. In this light I follow Korshin's caution that one should not read a novel typologically unless the author has placed obvious clues in the text that the novel should be read in this way (268). All of the novels treated in this book are full of such clues. I also wager, however, that if one were to examine the tradition in this light, more novels than expected would contain such clues, and remnants of Puritan typology and reactions to it could be detected in many stages of the British tradition. Additionally, there are novelists who employ aspects of Puritan hermeneutics while remaining ignorant they are doing so. Yet while typological elements in novels may become unhinged from their grounding in the biblical narrative, the text does not stop being "religious."

Novelists who self-consciously engage Puritan hermeneutics are well-aware of the typological practices of novel-reading, of the relation of the novel to the biblical narrative, and of their own role as a novelist in creating a new narrative. In many ways, the Puritan fear about fiction—that it places the human author in the position of God as both creator and exegete of "history"—is true and shapes novelistic conventions. Each novelist has to come to terms with his or her role as "God," either engaging the biblical narrative as "truth," self-consciously going against it, somehow doing some of each, or self-reflexively highlighting the fact that novels create their own grand narratives. Puritan typology is the hermeneutics of the novel, then, without necessarily the accompanying assumption that the biblical narrative is the truth of history or that there is a God who creates and interprets human history. The novel—even the modernist novel—cannot escape dealing with the biblical narrative and Christianity at some level, however, because Puritan hermeneutics is bound up in its very form and content.

The convention of the "novel-reading within the novel" scene reflects this inescapable yet potentially infinitely complex relation of novelist and novel to Puritan hermeneutics. In such scenes, a character is depicted reading a text, sometimes the Bible and often another novel, usually a romance. The narrative goes on to show how this reading shapes the character, whether for better or worse. From Crusoe's and Pamela's Bible-reading, to Catherine Morland's reading of gothic romance, to Emma Bovary's or Edward Ashburnham's reading of popular romance novels, to the intertextualities highlighted in many postmodern novels, such scenes are often used to ironize or satirize the typological effects of reading, calling into question Puritan concerns for the reader's moral and spiritual formation and the view of history in which such formation takes place. At the same time, however, these scenes also reinforce the fact that novels do work typologically and that it might very well matter into what grand narrative they are drawing the reader. Each of the texts analyzed in this book employs such scenes, from Augustine and Defoe to Wilde, Forster, Joyce, and Ford.

The novel through this self-reflexive ironizing calls into question the truth claims of all narratives, whether biblical or novelistic, while at the same time also allowing for the possibility that these narratives actually do contain truth that speaks to the inner soul or conscience. Within the confines of this project, then, the novel is "secular" in that it serves to fictionalize all forms of narrative, biblical and otherwise. It is also "religious," however, because it cannot escape the Puritan modes of interpretation and the possibility for moral and spiritual truth to be found within the narrative by the reading self. As the novel offers another grand narrative in place of the biblical one, it shapes its readers morally and spiritually, a "religious" function.

It seems that a crux of much current debate on secularization and religion has to do with how one theorizes the relation between form and content, in this case, between biblical narrative form and literary content. My view, that the embeddedness of typological hermeneutics in the novel, even though altered, might entail some level of break with Christianity but not with religion, would be countered vehemently by someone like Fredric Jameson. For example, when writing on Defoe in a contribution to Moretti's anthology, *The Novel,* Jameson states:

> I think that the debate as to whether Defoe himself was a Christian is misplaced: we have here rather the template for the organization of experiences in a new way, in which religious influence is itself a mere external and enabling condition. . . . To be sure, it is not wrong to say that the bildungsroman is then a secularization of this earlier, already secular "spiritual autobiography" of Defoe; but neither stage retains the meaning of the preceding one, but only the form. Thus it would be wrong to say that the bildungsroman is still religious in its (now secular) concern for the state of the individual soul: no, what is deployed now is a mere form that organizes its new social material in an analogous way. (102)

The secularism–religion dichotomy and the Marxist dialectic depend on this view. They depend on there being a complete and unbridgeable separation between form and content, between biblical narrative form and the social content of novels. They depend on viewing narrative form as something whose content can change over time so that the form loses its religious truth value. While that is a compelling way to see the history of the novel and of secular modernity, this book argues that the form and content of novels are inseparable because of the Puritan hermeneutics embedded in the novel. In Puritan Bible-reading, the form cannot be separated from the content, for there is only one grand story to be told, and it assumed to be both religiously true and capable of producing moral change in its readers. As Watson says, "The word written is not only a rule of knowledge, but a rule of obedience; it is not only to mend our sight but to mend our pace" ("How" 40). In the movement from Old Testament to New, the now and the not yet, the form is the content of the story and vice versa. In the dialectical process of reading a narrative, whether biblical or novelistic, "religious" truth and moral virtue are not separable; they are interpreted together in the act of reading. In novel-reading there is also one underlying "grand story" that potentially has analogous "religious" effects on the reader. This grand story of the novel also inspires change from an old self to a new, and even if "fictional," it implies a system of truth. This grand story of the novel is what I call in this book the "novelistic narrative."

In the end, despite the centrality of typology in the hermeneutics of novels, perhaps "secular" and "religious" are finally not the best terms for thinking about the novel. As Mark Knight and Thomas Woodman suggest in their introduction to *Biblical Religion and the Novel, 1700–2000,* there is something about the novel that is both "Christian and secularized": "The Protestant individualism of Crusoe and Pamela . . . is a religious as well as a secularized Protestantism" (2). Knight and Woodman highlight the paradox they see at the heart of the novel's form: "the more the fictional world of the novel expresses and embodies its religious roots, the deeper its thrust towards secularity appears to be" (5). This truly does seem paradoxical, but I am in full agreement. The more the novelist understands the Puritan hermeneutics at the root of the novel's form; the more he or she self-consciously explores, exploits, and reworks those principles; the more the fictionality of the author-made novelistic world is self-reflexively exposed in the novel's form; the more self-consciously "secular" or unmoored from the Puritan worldview, the biblical narrative, and God's authorship that text appears to be.

Better terms to encapsulate the nature of the novel may instead then be "belief" and "doubt"—belief and doubt regarding the "religious" truth of the grand narrative the novel presents, biblical, fictional, or otherwise; belief and doubt regarding the truth of the social-moral, ontological, and epistemological categories constructed in the novel; and belief and doubt regarding the self created in and by the reading process. A particular novel may lead the reader toward one end of the belief–doubt spectrum or the other, but within the tradition as a whole we can see novels that self-consciously respond with belief and doubt to the narratives and categories created in the Bible, in other novels, and in various social discourses.

This leads to our third and most significant qualification of the idea that Puritan typology is the hermeneutics of the novel. The dialectical movement of the character and reader—the nature of "conversion" or the turning of the self—shifts slightly. While identification between reader and character seems to be an obvious function of modern novels whose roots we can locate in Puritan Bible-reading practices, there has also always existed in the novelistic tradition the tendency to dismantle such character types, moral categories, and hermeneutics of the self. In this regard modernism's dismantling of the Puritan self is not necessarily a new thing. Indeed, a conventional form of irony within the novelistic tradition involves an inversion of Puritan hermeneutics. *Tristram Shandy,* for example, might be seen as a novel whose main motive is a dismantling of Puritan typology—the processes of typing, labeling, and identifying characters according to moral and spiritual clues, of reading the inner self, and of gaining certain knowledge about others.

Throughout the British tradition novelists have poked fun at Puritans. Interestingly, these negative treatments could come from other English Christians, especially the Anglicans and the Roman Catholics, or from doubters, agnostics, and atheists. Valentine Cunningham in *Everywhere Spoken Against* documents in great detail the overwhelmingly negative treatment of Nonconformity in nineteenth-century novels. James Munson argues many Victorian writers, including Trollope, Arnold, Dickens, Thackeray, Eliot, Bennett, and Gissing, were "hostile" to Nonconformists, stereotyping them as "narrow, ignorant, and provincial" (208). Even as it derives from Puritanism, the novel helps to stereotype the Puritan. This book argues that various modernist writers self-consciously understand and experiment with this fact, recognizing the inseparable connection of form and content, Puritan hermeneutics and novels.

Just as much as some novels create moral and spiritual character types who move in plots in order to gain moral and spiritual knowledge of themselves in a Puritan-like fashion, so just as much, other novels ironically attack this process, revealing typology's limitations and flaws. Just as Fielding's *Shamela* did with Richardson's *Pamela,* many novels become ironic or parodied commentary on earlier novels, the character typologies created therein by the "novelist-God," and the moralities promoted in the process. Frank Kermode's sentiment that "the history of the novel is the history of forms rejected or modified" (129), rings true, but I would add the caveat that the forms are only seemingly rejected or modified because the essential form always remains. Iris Murdoch's "the history of the novel is the history of anti-novels" also seems right (qtd. in Kermode 130).

Novelistic tradition, to sum up, is built on a dialectic of Puritan hermeneutics with its ironic dismantling, of belief and doubt. As Stephen Prickett has described modernity: "Whatever narratives of God might replace the medieval synthesis were henceforth to be either blindly fundamentalist . . . or fundamentally ironic" (*Narrative* 134).[4] The ironic deconstruction of Puritanism in the novel, however, is dependent upon Puritan hermeneutics for its own existence. This dependent and mutually constitutive relation is the dialectic of the novel—the novelistic narrative. Puritanism shapes the novel's form while a supposed escape from or dismantling of Puritanism shapes the novel's content. These dialectical elements are mutually constitutive of each other. In Puritan Bible-reading, the dialectical movement goes back and forth between the self's identification with a biblical type and what it thinks is self-knowledge and the giving up of self to God and the unknowable. In the novel, the dialectical movement goes back and forth between the social-moral categories of the novel that shape the self and the escape of the self into whatever it is that lies beyond and outside those categories.

One way to explain this dialectic of belief and doubt, "fundamentalism" and irony, confinement and escape, is to argue that the novelistic tradition records the separation of religion and morality in modernity. In Puritan Bible-reading, religion and morality are inseparable. Yet in modernity, as Alasdair MacIntyre argues, "morality" becomes its own unique category, separable from religion, in the period of roughly 1630 to 1850, in the wake of Enlightenment rejections of Christian and Aristotelian moral systems. When "morality" began to refer to "that particular sphere in which rules of conduct which are neither theological nor legal nor aesthetic are allowed a cultural space of their own," the "project of an independent rational justification of morality" such as what one sees in Kant or Mill, became the central concern of Northern European culture (39). However, without a universal narrative that implied a teleology, a sense of the categorical (the divine origins of the moral order), or a shared view of the human subject, this project was bound to be impossible (60). According to MacIntyre, Enlightenment theorists of a universal, rationally

---

4. For Prickett, "fundamentalism" can take many forms: Christian, Marxist, Freudian, and so on.

derived moral order ultimately failed because even though they rejected the shared background and foundation for moral order provided by religion, they themselves failed to provide for their own moral philosophies "any public, shared rationale or justification" (50). As a result, over time "moral judgments los[t] any clear status" and authority and became mere "linguistic survivals" from earlier times (60).

Following this logic, fragmented Puritan interpretative practices survive in the novelistic tradition and in social morality in modernity, but the accompanying biblical narrative within which such practices and categories are seen to be true increasingly loses its legitimacy.[5] As the assumed context of the church, creation, historical providence, and eternity is seen to be increasingly fictional, Puritan (among other) moralities separate from notions of religious truth. One way to view the modern novel, then, is that it depicts a world in which the Puritan typological methods still operate socially and morally but without necessarily the firm biblical narrative context in which they can be interpreted as representing the inner, religious truth about who a human being is or the truth about history. Puritan typology potentially becomes mere typecasting—a social and moral interpretive practice that seems unmoored from a religious foundation. Hence, Puritan typology also potentially becomes a set of social and moral interpretive practices and categories whose foundation and truth value can be constantly brought into question, ironized, dismantled. The novel ironically stereotypes Puritans even as it works to escape and dismantle typecasting processes. The conversion movement is not from false self to true self found in Christ who is both now and not yet, but from the false categories and narratives that society places on the self to the true self found in individual escape and freedom.

Although I use them in a different fashion, Ruth Benedict's anthropological terms are also useful in describing this dialectical relation of Puritan hermeneutics to its own ironizing in the novel.[6] Puritan hermeneutics and Bible-reading are practices of what Benedict calls a "guilt culture," which is "a society that inculcates absolute standards of morality and relies on men's developing a conscience" (222). Guilt cultures rely on "an internalized conviction of sin" as a sanction for good behavior (223). Thus, as Puritan Bible-reading reveals the truth within the soul, as it speaks to the conscience, the reader is shaped morally and spiritually and is reoriented toward becoming and doing good in the world and

---

5. For more on the breakdown of the biblical narrative, see Frei.

6. While Benedict's conclusions about Japanese culture have since faced significant criticism, her terms nonetheless remain useful to describe what is at work here.

loving God. For Benedict, guilt cultures are different than "shame cultures," which rely on "external sanctions for good behavior" (223). In other words, "shame" or judgment by one's society is the only impetus for good behavior. If "bad behavior does not 'get out in the world,'" the individual "need not be troubled" (223). Shame "requires an audience or at least a man's fantasy of an audience. Guilt does not" (223). In this light, the novel records the dialectic between what a Puritan guilt culture truly believes and the fragmentation of that guilt culture into a shame culture which is potentially seen as merely fictional. Put another way, novelistic tradition and form involves a dialectic of Puritan typology (religion conjoined with morality) and ironized social typecasting (mere modern morality), guilt and shame. As both the religious Puritan self with its conscience and social morality with its shame are discarded, some novelists promote the natural self—its passions, desires, and longings—in order to return the human to its body and away from both sets of moralizing abstractions. Escape to become an "ethical self" is one end of the dialectical movement of novels; adherence to the religious or social-moral or "Puritan" self is the other.

Not only did doubters, agnostics, and atheists attack and ironize Nonconformity in the novel, however, but so did Anglicans and Roman Catholics. This allies certain types of Christians with religious doubters and nonbelievers in helping to stereotype "Puritanism." These attacks on the Puritan within other branches of Christianity often centered on the interpretive authority given to the individual Bible-reader. They held in common with non-Christian critics a disdain for what they saw as the Protestant individual who assumes epistemological sovereignty. Chapter 3 treats this branch of criticism more fully by looking at some of John Henry Newman's ideas.

As mentioned, many Marxist theorists and historians of the novel focus on traits similar to those outlined here. Marxists are interested in how novels self-reflexively highlight the separability of the moral and spiritual categories and types used in a narrative from the actual material person or individual being depicted.[7] McKeon argues that the scientific revolution, the Protestant reformation, and the emergence of print culture all form a modern "condition of 'categorial instability'" according to which "traditional epistemological and social categories are conceived by contemporaries with a self-conscious detachment whose consequences

---

7. For an intriguing essay from this perspective, see Catherine Gallagher, "The Rise of Fictionality," in *The Novel,* ed. Franco Moretti (Princeton: Princeton UP, 2006), vol. 1, 337–63.

are far-reaching" (357). For him, the novel becomes uniquely suited to "mediate" the resulting questions of truth and virtue, "their separation from each other," and the instability and shiftiness of epistemological and social categories in relation to human "reality" (419). So far, this book agrees with McKeon as it argues that the novel records the separation of Puritan religion and social morality in modernity. As William Warner argued when McKeon's book first was published, however, the dialectical view of history to which McKeon adheres at times forces him to create a totalizing yet limited narrative about the novel's prehistory and its dramatic emergence. This book argues for a simpler model: novels and novelists who struggle with the relation of their characters to grand narratives and moral and spiritual categories, and theorists and historians of the novel who see the genre as embodying this struggle (or "categorial instability"), are all attuned, if only unconsciously, not to Marxism and the dialectical nature of history, but to Puritan hermeneutics and the Puritan dialectic of the novel.

One of the things Warner criticized was McKeon's idea that questions of truth and of virtue all manifest themselves dialectically. If this really was how history worked, these questions and answers would subsume each other while synthetically progressing toward something new, more complete, and unitary, "where difference arises out of simplicity within the womb of contradiction, undergoes a plural development to arrive as a simple unity at an ever more concrete totality" (Warner 71). According to Warner, even in McKeon's account this does not happen. Not all social and epistemological categories emerge dialectically dependent on each other, and certainly McKeon's theory does not cover all the historical possibilities for how to answer questions of truth. Warner agrees with McKeon's assessment that the novel is built on an exploration of ideas about truth and virtue, but rather than seeing this as a "dialectic" in which contradictory forms and categories move toward a foreshadowed Marxist telos, Warner suggests using a more basic formulation: that the novel takes up a particular "historically conditioned problematic of truth and virtue" (78). Questions of truth and questions of virtue have always been problematized in history, says Warner; the novel simply deals with a particular historical manifestation of such a problematic. These topics can certainly be explored in the novel without forcing them into a Marxist dialectical framework of history. For Warner, history is more contingent and the novel more heterogeneous, embodying a "complex plurality," than McKeon's dialectical view allows. Even though I also argue later against the idea that the novel is pluralistic, Warner's critique of McKeon helps shape my view. Specifically, this book argues that the novel takes up the "problematic" of the *seeming* separability of Puritan notions of truth (religion) and virtue (morality), but at the same time, as in Puritan Bible-reading, truth and virtue, religion and morality, are never entirely separable in the novel's form nor eliminated from its social contexts nor ever fully escaped. Although I do see the novel embodying a "dialectic," it is a Puritan one, not Marxist. One could say I am like McKeon forcing the novel into a different, totalizing, limited dialectical view of history—Puritan, biblical, typological, teleological. Importantly, however, I argue that the Puritan dialectic of belief and doubt, religion (typology) and social morality (typecasting), guilt culture and shame culture, confinement and escape, embedded in the novel is historically prior to and thereby at least in part constitutive of the Hegelian-like and Marxist-like secular dialectics that the novel is so often interpreted as embodying. The former novelistic narrative influences the development of the latter secularization narratives.

To McKeon and others, the novel seems to embody "the philosophy of the limit," the term Drucilla Cornell coined to replace the term "deconstruction." This is partially true, but the novel is also always more than this, for it also often adheres to notions of religious truth, despite all its questioning and dismantling. It embodies a moral position, despite its awareness of the separability of moral categories from reality. In these ways, the Puritan aspects of its form and content are never lost. In Puritan Bible-reading, the true and the moral are inseparable aspects of the self and of the text. Form and content are one thing. These hermeneutical unions always carry over into the novel, whatever the final stance the novel comes to embody. Thus, while I agree with McKeon that the novel records the separability of truth and virtue, religion and morality in modernity, it depicts neither McKeon's Marxist dialectical synthesis nor Warner's pluralization that are thought to constitute the movement of history. For even while the novel highlights the limitations of categories and the grand narratives that produce them in the face of human reality, in its form and content the spiritual and the moral always remain inseparable.[8] Every narrative created in a novel, however fictional, however self-consciously or skeptically ironizing, however believing or doubtful, nevertheless embodies connected notions of truth and morality that

---

8. My account that the "moral" and the "religious" are ultimately inseparable categories in the form of the novel, even as the novel depicts a world in which they seem separable, counters several recent studies which see novels as treating ethics (or the quest for "perfection") in purely secular terms. See for example, Stewart and also Andrew Miller.

exist in relation somehow to Puritan versions of those things. The novel records modernity's lasting struggle with the Puritan narrative of history and self.

AUGUSTINE'S *Confessions* and Defoe's *Robinson Crusoe* exemplify the differences between biblical and novelistic typology, respectively. One significant difference is that Augustine narrates his conversion as a dialectical process that occurs while reading yet continues throughout one's life as a Christian, while the narration of Crusoe's trajectory after conversion is not. The result is that Augustine's interpretive methods, while also involving the transformation of the individual reader, reinscribes the reading self into the larger community of the church, creation, and human history, as well as the not yet, the heavenly kingdom which is to come. The dialectical reading process moves back and forth between the individual life and what is known, and the larger entities of communal identity and the obscure unknown future for which one hopes. Crusoe, on the other hand, interprets himself and his scripture-reading on a literal level only. Any truths gained through reading pertain only to his immediate personal life story; he never sees himself as participating in the larger orders of the church, human history, or God's creation. The Bible, it seems, has been written just for him.

Conversion for Augustine is a dialectical transformation. In the conversion scene, Augustine describes himself as entering the garden with contradictory wills. He longs to give himself up to Christ yet he also wants to cling to his physical desires: "This was the controversy raging in my heart, a controversy about myself against myself" (158). Augustine describes the contradictory human will as a dialectical entity:

> The will is commanding itself to be a will—commanding itself, not some other. But it does not in its fullness give the command, so that what it commands is not done. For if the will were so in its fullness, it would not command itself to will, for it would already will. It is therefore no monstrousness, partly to will, partly not to will, but a sickness of the soul to be so weighted down by custom that it cannot wholly rise even with the support of truth. Thus there are two wills in us, because neither of them is entire: and what is lacking in one is present in the other. (155)

Augustine's contradictory wills are constitutionally dependent on each other yet antagonistic to each other. As Augustine reads the biblical text,

his contradictory wills are drawn up into God's love and made into something new. He sees himself clearly, recognizes his false and true selves, as
Christ enters his heart through the text and resolves the contradictions,
bringing wholeness. Christ is the fullness of time that brings the "not yet"
into the "now," the future into the present.

This process of submitting one's conflicting wills is essentially what
occurs over and over again for Augustine while reading the Bible, for the
self in its earthly form is not yet the perfected self of paradise and needs
continual reorientation toward the imitation of Christ. The self in historical time, even after one's initial conversion, is always in a state of contradiction, always between the now and not yet. The reader might occupy a
temporary identifiable state but is also always moving out of that identity, denying or refining that identity, moving toward Christlikeness and
a future but unknowable perfection and redemption. Dying to self to live
in Christ is a process of Becoming, as Nothingness moves more and more
toward Being, as the type is drawn closer to the antitype.

Intriguingly, Hegel recognized the dialectical nature of Christian conversion and Bible-reading. When discussing the reconciliation toward
which Greek tragedy leads in the *Lectures on the Philosophy of Religion,*
Hegel suggests that the Christian idea of conversion is a similar process.
Christian conversion occurs "in the inner life, whereby that which is
done can be rendered undone" (327). In Christianity, "the man who is
'converted' gives up his one-sidedness" by which his own will contradicts
itself. This one-sidedness is drawn up into the God who takes favor on
him and "calls" him to himself (327). Inner dialectical contradiction is
resolved into something new. Hegel's dialectical theory of world history
maintains the Augustinian and Puritan logic of Christian conversion and
typology. Yet instead of seeing his theory of history as merely secularizing
the Christian narrative form while inserting new secular content, I argue
that Hegel actually develops his own "religion."

Crusoe also converts through typological reading. Crusoe identifies
his life as moving from Old Testament type needing deliverance from
physical affliction to New Testament type needing deliverance from spiritual sin (90). Unlike Augustine, however, he never extends his literal
interpretation to the higher levels of allegorical, moral, or anagogical levels. There is no dialectical movement between self-knowledge and that
which is beyond the self; for Crusoe, the self is the object of all interpretation. He therefore does not interpret fully his own ontological position
within the narrative of God's history, God's creation, or the church, and
the identification of his true self does not extend beyond his particular
story.

For example, Crusoe describes his Bible-reading as invoking "very serious Thoughts about my present Condition" (171) and as allowing him to apply "all the Comforts of it to my present State" (105). He never reflects on God literally forming Israel as a people in the Old Testament or the church in the New Testament, and as a consequence, he never sees himself as part of God's larger people. He does reflect once on God the Creator right before his conversion (86), but he never sustains a constant reflection on himself as created by God, as Augustine does. In these ways, Crusoe's interpretation of scripture never has ramifications beyond his own needs and situations as his life progresses.

With this limited understanding of the self's place within the narrative, he reflects on his solitary state often and concludes that he actually prefers being alone instead of being back in the world. On his fourth anniversary of being on the island, Crusoe reflects on his comfortable solitary position:

> I look'd now upon the World as a Thing remote, which I had nothing to do with, no Expectation from, and indeed no Desires about: In a Word, I had nothing indeed to do with it, nor was ever like to have; so I thought it look'd as we may perhaps look upon it hereafter, *viz.* as a Place I had liv'd in, but was come out of it; and well might I say, as Father *Abraham* to *Dives,* Between me and thee is a great Gulph fix'd. (119)

Crusoe displays no desire here to carry out the mission of the church or to be reunited with society in order to participate in God's plan for human history. Crusoe likes being alone and believes that in spiritual matters this is sufficient, even preferable.

Although *Confessions* is also mostly the story of an individual life, Augustine establishes from the beginning a much different picture of the self. The constant theme of *Confessions* is the self's submission and resubmission of itself to God, recognizing itself as made not for itself, but rather for praise and love of God. The text opens with a reflection on the individual's created status and ends with a lengthy reflection on the Genesis creation account. This framework poetically links God's creation of the "true self" in the individual to His creation of the cosmos and places the individual life within anagogical reality. The individual life is never the final end or reason for interpreting scripture or even for converting. Reading scripture should teach that the self's identity extends beyond one's own story.

For Augustine, the act of narrating one's life story is confession. This involves not only confessing one's sins, but also constant and continued confessing of one's own inadequacy before God, recognizing God as Creator, the self as created, and one's literal position in creation and in history. The act of confessing is never over, however, and must be continually employed. In fact, confession is a necessary epistemological practice for Augustine—it is the central way one comes to know and recognize one's true self and one's false self, to know and relearn over and over again one's ontological position, for the self is in this life ultimately unknowable and must constantly confess its inadequacy to know itself: "I will confess therefore what I know of myself and what I do not know; for what I know of myself I know through the shining of Your light; and what I do not know of myself, I continue not to know until my darkness shall be made as noonday in Your countenance" (193). Poignantly, Augustine describes reading the Bible at one point as a "slaying of the self that I had been" (170). Augustine's method of interweaving continually his life story with direct biblical quotations literally performs and demonstrates the subsuming of the self's story into the biblical story.[9] Confession through Bible-reading is an essential dialectical practice as the contradictory wills are repeatedly drawn into God's presence in the Word and made new.

Every time Augustine narrates himself reading scripture, the self-knowledge gained is experiential, known intuitively by the heart and not necessarily by the reasoning mind. Self-knowledge involves both not knowing and knowing. The not knowing is a powerful experience beyond the self's rational capabilities. He describes the experience of reading the Apostle Paul at the end of book VII this way: "Marvellously these truths graved themselves in my heart when I read that least of your Apostles and looked upon Your works and trembled" (137). Bible-reading is also described as: "Wisdom striking the heart with terror and longing" (239); the text speaking "in the ear of my Spirit" (269,271); and as "hearing with the heart" (263). The end of reading for Augustine is not to gain certain knowledge of himself, but rather to become one with the text, both literally and spiritually. David Jeffrey describes Augustine's idea beautifully: "It is less the explication of texts that matters than the Text itself; the authentic reader is one in whom that text has entered to become a living Presence" (51). As Kort says of Calvin's theory of reading, the texts "inscribe themselves on the reader's body and soul" (190). In Watson's terms the reader becomes a "walking Bible." Crusoe's failure to become

---

9. For particularly beautiful examples of this method see *Confessions*, 5, 136–37, and 297.

such a "living Word" in the end is disturbing. Rather than leading him to sacrifice himself to God and to evoke a desire to serve the church and creation, his conversion and Bible-reading seem only to bolster his own earthly authority and independence while helping him gain the strength to survive.[10]

Both Augustine and Crusoe participate in their transformative Bible-reading while alone. The individual life matters to God, but only Augustine also emphasizes that the "true self" is literally one with the church. Post-conversion, Augustine does something Crusoe never does—he acknowledges himself to be a part of God's people who transcend time:

> I confess not only before You, with inward exultation yet trembling, with inward sorrow yet with hope as well; but also in the ears of the believing sons of men, companions of my joy and sharers of my mortality, my fellow citizens, fellow pilgrims: those who have gone before, and those who are to come after, and those who walk the way of life with me. These are Your servants, my brethren, whom You have chosen that they should be Your sons, my masters whom You have commanded me to serve if I am to live with You and in You. (192)

Because the self is always insufficient, Augustine absolutely needs the church to pray for him, to encourage him, and to hear his confession. As with Puritan "godly reading," the self is both an individual and a communal self, and the community serves to help the self recognize its own limitations. Such recognition involves a dialectical movement between rational knowing and aesthetic or ethical unknowing.

Crusoe's errant and limited focus on the literal self involves the belief that the individual reader has the epistemological authority to interpret the truths of scripture and gain rational knowledge about the self. Because for Puritans spiritual meaning was plainly available in literal scripture, this potentially meant that, with the aid of the Holy Spirit, each reader had the ability to interpret accurately the spiritual truths of the Bible. As Crusoe says after Friday converts, all that is needed is the reader, the text, and the Holy Spirit: "the Word of God, and the Spirit of God promis'd for the Guide and Sanctifier of his People, are the absolutely necessary Instructors of the Souls of Men, in the saving Knowledge of God, and the Means of Salvation" (202). Believing that he and Friday do not need to be

---

10. Perhaps in a state of extreme suffering, in which arguably Crusoe is for the first part of the novel, focusing on the self is more justified. Of course, he is alone on the island for most of the novel as well.

in England to access the truth, Crusoe also implies that no other authority is needed. The individual Bible-reader, no matter how uneducated or untrained, is sufficient. Crusoe also explicitly rejects the need to read and understand the more complicated and obscure sections of scripture.

Augustine sees the rejection of the more difficult parts of scripture as immature. On the "open" level of "plain instruction," Augustine and Crusoe (and Calvin) agree that what is needed for salvation is clearly stated. Augustine argues in *On Christian Doctrine* that "Among those things which are said openly in Scripture are . . . all those teachings which involve faith, the mores of living, and . . . hope and charity" (113). Here, Augustine implies that the goal of all scripture-reading, because it is plainly elucidated in the text, is to cultivate the virtues of faith, hope, and love, which provide an understanding of how to live. The virtues are never to be cultivated for the self alone, however, for the two great commands are to love God wholly and to love neighbors as ourselves (*Confessions* 280).

Augustine also says that "Hardly anything may be found in the obscure places which is not found plainly said elsewhere" (*Doctrine* 112). Those who want to grow in the faith, who need more intellectual assurance, or who want to deepen their faith, *should* turn to those obscure places:

> Having become familiar with the language of Divine Scriptures, we should turn to those obscure things which must be opened up and explained so that we may take examples of those things that are manifest to illuminate the things which are obscure, bringing principles which are certain to bear on our doubts concerning those things which are uncertain. (*Doctrine* 113)

A more mature faith for Augustine is actually in conversation with mystery, pitting uncertainties against certainties, the knowable against the unknowable. The mature Christian subject willingly places herself in the midst of a difficult text.

Exploring obscure passages may bring up disagreements, but it is necessary, for God teaches through obscurities as well as through what is plain. "Marvelous is their profundity," says Augustine. The scriptures invoke a sense of awe for God, and exploring them is an act of humility and confession, for one has to recognize one's own inadequacy before the text in a "shudder of love" (*Confessions* 268). After conversion, Christians should continue their dialectical reading, exploring the eternal mysteries of the scriptures, seeking an understanding that moves beyond their own stories while at the same time recognizing their own limits.

For Augustine the individual interpreter with the aid of the holy spirit is never sufficient, for the individual reader is trapped in sin and is always ontologically distant from perfect understanding. For this reason, and because mature Christians should not shy away from obscurity, Bible-reading should be done in the context of the church. When Augustine reflects in *Confessions* on trying to determine the "spirit" or intention of Moses in the creation account, he confesses his need to interpret within the church:

> May I be with those in You, Lord, and rejoice with them in you who are nourished by Your truth in the breadth of Your charity; and may they and I together approach the words of Your Book and in them seek Your meaning through the meaning of Your servant by whose pen You gave them to us. (278)

Truth is common property, and Christians become the "living Word" only by sharing in truth together:

> It belongs to all of us because publicly You call us to share it, warning us most terribly not to possess it as our private property, lest we be deprived of it. For whoever claims for himself what You have given for the enjoyment of all, and would have as his own what is meant for everyone, is driven forth from the wealth of all to his own poor wealth, that is from truth to a lie. (279)

The purpose of communal interpretation is not to celebrate diversity and plurality; the purpose is to draw closer to the truth together. Such communal "godly reading," as Cambers shows, was also practiced by the Puritans.

It is true that Augustine structures his conversion plot with imitation in mind; he wants readers to place themselves into the narrative by identifying with the types much as Crusoe does. In fact, such narratives are the final impulse in his own conversion as he hears and typologically identifies with the "Prodigal Son" conversion stories told by Simplicianus and Ponticianus.[11] His emphasis after conversion, however, is "living

---

11. The *Life of St. Antony* figures prominently in the second story Augustine is told in which some youth typologically identify with Antony's literal faith story and convert.

the Word" and interpreting scripture in community. In the final books of *Confessions* typology moves beyond the individual life and its reading for self-identification and into a wider literal interpretation of the self as part of the church (ecclesial allegory), the "Living Word" which seeks to imitate Christ (moral) in order to bring about God's Kingdom (eschatology/anagogy). This stage of maturity, in which one recognizes the limits of the self in the face of God, is one Crusoe never reaches. Crusoe's Bible-reading practices restrict the reading of scripture to its application to individual particular lives and assume the individual reader is sufficiently authoritative to gain spiritual truths that are considered to be rationally knowable. This sort of individualized modern novelistic typology continues to shape the British novel as a genre. In fact, this aspect of novelistic typology helps lead to the formation of the stereotype about Protestants and Puritans as sovereign, liberal individuals; as rational and narrow-mindedly moral; as authoritarian yet blind to their own limits; as concerned for their own status in another world as they are fearful in this one. Crusoe is all of these things. As the novel in modernity increasingly fictionalizes and ironizes this "Puritan" self, the "outer" Biblical narrative within which the self abides and in which it participates is also increasingly fictionalized. The Puritan self becomes the surface, fictional false self while the inner deep realm of desires, passions, and emotions are seen to be the natural, true self. While Augustine had to face the contradictions in his inner self and submit them to Christ's resolution, the novelistic modern self now faces the contradiction of her "true" inner, natural, passionate self with her "false" outer, typological, social-moral "Puritan" self. No longer does the contradictory inner self need to be drawn up and made into something new through God's grace. Instead, the modern novelistic self "converts" when the inner, natural, passionate self breaks away from and escapes the false self of social-moral categories in order to become its true self in freedom, accepting epistemological uncertainty. Yet the escaping self is only part of the dialectic, for the Puritan always remains. The modern novelistic dialectic, then, is one of necessity and freedom; fundamentalism and irony; belief and doubt; the moral and the ethical; the type and what is left out of the type. In Puritan reading, the true self finds freedom *in* necessity (Christ); this is biblical typology. In novels that ironize or dismantle Puritanism, the true self is found only in freedom *from* necessity. In modern novels, there is less and less a "religious" basis for necessity, less and less a need for a God who can save the self from its contradictions or a narrative beyond the novel by which interpretations make sense or have real purpose. Freedom becomes the otherworldly goal, the ideal beyond. It is achievable by the autonomous individual, if only he can see through the Puritan fictions that restrict him. This novelistic narrative, with its modes of typological interpretation, becomes a new grand narrative of modernity.

MODERNIST novelists go further than previous novelists in their questioning of the validity of the Crusoe-esque Puritan self. Ontologically, modernist writers question whether there is a deep self or inner soul or conscience in the human subject that contains the "true self" and reflects one's moral and spiritual state. Epistemologically, modernist writers question whether, how, and to what extent one's moral and spiritual state can be read, identified, and interpreted. Ethically, modernists question whether human beings can learn morality or be formed or transformed morally through experience. They also react to the idea of moral judgment and moral categories, especially in matters of sexuality. All of these questions are joined to larger questions regarding the assumed context within which Puritan typology is practiced and believed, including whether there is a moral order or grand narrative that shapes the universe and human history; and whether there is a God that directs history, creates human beings, has full knowledge, and grounds a universal moral order. In contrast to the Puritan self, the ethical self is immanent or present in the world, unified in body and soul, autonomously free, and creative, yet to some degree ambiguous and unknowable.

Early modernists move away from the concept of moral character, then, by attempting to dismantle various aspects of it. The resultant ethical self, however, is dialectically dependent upon the Puritan self for its own existence. The authors examined in this book are to varying degrees self-consciously aware within their novels of this dependent relationship. While I have argued the attempted escape from the Puritan self has always been part of the novel's dialectical ironizing form, the modernist dismantling of the Puritan self generally becomes more extreme and more complete in nature than in earlier texts, and hence has traditionally been seen as radical formal experimentation. While a novel like *Tristram Shandy* may have ironized the limits of the Puritan self, it did so in the service of an alternative version of morality within the Christian biblical view.[12] Or, while the novels of George Eliot question or deny the legiti-

---

12. As Carol Stewart notes, Sterne makes "skepticism the grounding principle of his novel and embrac[es] its liberating possibilities, whilst still maintaining Anglican values" including "orthodox positions and attitudes" (139, 131).

macy of the biblical narrative, they are still very interested in maintaining an alternative moral system and hence some variation of moral character and social-moral life. The modernist ethical self, in contrast, seeks to extract itself entirely from the realm of "morality," both its guilt culture (morality bound to religion) and its shame culture (morality bound to society) forms. The modernist ethical self sees itself as participating in a higher ethics, which is often associated with the "aesthetic" and with art. This higher ethical life is seen to be an escape from social morality, character typology, and the soul–body duality, while at the same time a restoration of the human subject to its immanent, bodily, and natural position of freedom.

The writers and characters studied here take various attitudes toward such an ethical self who is willingly exiled from society, religion, and morality. Some see this as entirely dangerous, others as necessary. Others fall somewhere in between. In any case, early modernist experimentation with characterization leads to an inversion and dismantling of Puritan hermeneutics that eventually becomes dominant and conventional in high modernism. Rather than seeing modernist experimentation as radically new, however, this study suggests something less dramatic. The weights of the typological balance simply shift in modernist novels from the previous tradition's emphasis on moral character to an emphasis on the ethical self. Despite the best efforts of many of the high modernists, however, the moral and the ethical are not separable. Puritan hermeneutics cannot entirely be escaped in the novel. This sort of dialectical dependency of the modernist novel on the previous tradition, of the ethical on the moral, is the kind of thing of which McEwan's *Atonement* reminds us as it foregrounds questions about modernism and the novel. This sort of dialectic does *not* seem to be recognized or given full due, however, within several strands of current criticism that tend to see both the novel and modernism as secular phenomena, entities that have escaped the religious Puritan narrative.

Marxist novel theory has historically promoted the idea that the novel, beginning with *Robinson Crusoe*, is a secular genre of modern individualism. Recently, in her 2005 book, *How Novels Think: The Limits of British Individualism from 1719–1900,* Nancy Armstrong argues that "the history of the novel and the history of the modern subject are, quite literally, one and the same" (3). To Armstrong, writers formulate in novels certain types of subjects and then reproduce in their readers these same kinds of subjects. For Armstrong, the individuals formed in novels and through novel-reading are not individuals run rampant, out of control, or irrational, as might be depicted in competing genres such as the gothic romance. Rather, they are self-enclosed, self-governing liberal individuals who nonetheless are willing to subject themselves to civil morality through the larger institutions of the family and society, choosing to abide by the Lockean social contract and the moralities it demands (51). The novel's perpetuation of the sovereign self and civil morality is for Armstrong generally a negative development (10).

Armstrong extends a discussion about the "origins" of the novel and modernity that began with Ian Watt's 1957 *The Rise of the Novel,* which linked the development of the modern novel to the rise of individualism and middle-class interests.[13] In this line of thought, the British novel is not only a genre *for* individuals who usually read while alone, but it is also *about* individuals, dramatizing and even glorifying the experience of individuals within society, and even more importantly for Armstrong, creating its readers to be similar sorts of individuals. In such an argument, novels matter because they shape how readers view themselves and their place in the world. Ironically, while one gets the sense that Armstrong is lamenting the influence of "Puritanism" in creating modern individualism, her view of the novel and its effects on readers is exactly how Puritans thought of the reading process. They, too, believed the goal of reading was the moral and spiritual formation of the reader so that he or she might live more fully into a narrative—the biblical narrative of salvation history. Significantly, Armstrong's book ends in the late nineteenth century, implying that something new emerges with modernism, that an escape from "modern subjectivity" becomes more possible at the turn of the nineteenth century into the twentieth.

This line of thought certainly is convincing in many ways, but it focuses on only one side of the Puritan dialectic of the novel. What is undertreated in Armstrong's critique of novelistic morality (and was similarly undertreated by Watt) is the relation of novel-reading to Puritan Bible-reading, a gap occurring because she identifies the genre as secular. To her, the novel relies on religious forms evacuated of their religious content in order to serve secular ends. A footnote elucidates how Armstrong sees the novel replacing the Puritan religious concept of "work" with secular content:

---

13. I am indebted for this point to Miriam Burstein's March 2006 post, "How Novels Think," *The Valve: A Literary Organ,* www.thevalve.org, accessed June 23, 2010.

> I accept Max Weber's claim that many of the elements of what he calls "the spirit of modern capitalism," commonly known as the Protestant work ethic, "are the same as the content of the Puritan worldly asceticism, only without the religious basis." But this similarity does not mean the secular ethic of industrial capitalist cultures "was born . . . from the spirit of Christian aestheticism." . . . On the contrary, I argue, fiction rhetorically appropriated certain elements of Christian asceticism—specifically, the "sanctification of work as a calling," which entails delayed gratification—for an entirely new purpose: the harnessing of desire to serve the material ends of an emergent middle class. . . . The secularization of morality, from this perspective, is not the mechanism or wish on the part of that class to exploit the labor of others so much as the symptom of a cultural hegemony inducing members of that class themselves to embrace that rhetoric as truth and live out its master narrative. (161n1)

In this view, the novel "works" to perpetuate a new secular master narrative by which readers are to identify and reform themselves in order to conform to the world and function in it appropriately. This secular master narrative and its variations produce the modern, sovereign individual— the "Puritan" self with its emphases on moral character and moral development. Armstrong longs for a new kind of subjectivity, a self beyond the Puritan, and modernism is implicitly set up to be the force that can finally escape the limits the Puritan imposes. This line of thought emerges from within the "novelistic narrative."

A second current branch of criticism termed "New Ethical Theory" also sees the "ethical self" as the unique contribution of modernism. Contemporary ethical critics of the novel might be placed generally into one of three camps: moral philosophy, "new humanism," and "new ethical theory." The first category consists of philosophers who have taken up novels as texts from which to derive and discuss moral philosophy. This group includes most famously thinkers as diverse as Martha Nussbaum and Richard Rorty, but many others as well. It is probably safe to say that most moral philosophers remain unaware of ethical studies performed within literary studies and vice versa, although clearly there would be points of connection, and some are now calling for more interdisciplinary overlap. The second group, new humanism, is considered to be more traditional in its approach to literature and moral values, adhering to what the new ethicists call the "liberal imagination" and the "prestructuralist sense of the liberal individual" (Hale, "Aesthetics" 897). These critics might practice something more akin to New Criticism, or they may take an Aristotelian approach to narrative and virtue. In short, they speak of the reader as a definable human subject and, as Charles Altieri describes, they focus on practical moral concepts such as sympathy, empathy, and judgment (34). Current critics in this group include Colin McGinn, Frank Palmer, S. L. Goldberg, and David Parker, among others. The third group, the new ethical theorists, derives its ideas about novels from postmodern Continental thinkers such as Derrida, Foucault, and Levinas, and stresses a "deconstructive concern for an ethics of letting be" (Altieri 34). This group includes scholars like Judith Butler, D. A. Miller, Gayatri Spivak, J. Hillis Miller, Andrew Gibson, and Adam Zachary Newton. Of course, not everyone falls neatly into these camps. Wayne C. Booth's lifelong work on novels and ethics, for example, along with all whom he has influenced, might constitute a Chicago School camp of its own. My theory of the novelistic narrative presents a general challenge to new ethical theory. Yet as Altieri argues, the new humanist position and the new ethical position are "mirror images" of each other (34), and so this book implicitly addresses both of these camps. In many ways, these "mirror images" of new humanism and new ethics are merely repetitions of the Puritan dialectic of the novel.

Dorothy J. Hale has recently argued that despite their variations, general tendencies tie together scholars in moral philosophy and new ethical theory. According to Hale, thinkers as diverse as Nussbaum, Butler, Spivak, J. Hillis Miller, and Booth, among others, all generally argue that the modernist novel brings the reader to encounter alterity—the "unknowability" of the Other—such that she is forced to recognize the limits of the self ("Aesthetics" 896). This reading experience of having one's categories of interpretation and capacities for knowledge confounded, it is argued, is emotional and in itself ethical, for it forces the reader to acknowledge the Other that exceeds her own epistemological framework and to recognize the ways in which she herself participates in placing binding limitations on others. In other words, it helps the reader to learn how she assumes knowledge about others because she assumes sovereignty over interpretation. To give one example, Butler sees the experience of "literary difficulty" one feels at the end of Henry James's *Washington Square,* in which neither character nor author provide an explanation for Catherine's behavior, as an "estrangement from normative judgments" (Hale, "Fiction" 197). The novel "hails" the reader "to occupy the position made for [him] through narrative" but then "ejects" the reader from that position (197). Hitting the "limits of translation" in this way creates "the possibility for ethics" (Butler 208–9).

What is most intriguing about new ethical theory is that its proponents are not interested in the novelistic tradition in its entirety but rather
only in texts of the modernist tradition and of twentieth-century novel
theory, both fields seen to be inaugurated by Henry James. As Hale says,
James is prominent in "theories of ethical value from Trilling to Booth
and from [J. Hillis] Miller to Butler" as well as in the moral philosophy
of Nussbaum ("Fiction" 201). Hale believes James is crucial for all these
theorists because he inaugurates an "aesthetics of the novel that emerges
from the ethical value of voluntary self-binding" (201). In other words,
James's novels self-consciously highlight the fact that the novelist is the
inventor of the novel's "laws of composition" and hence that the world
and characters depicted therein are necessarily bound by those laws (201).
In a James novel, the Puritan fear about fiction is self-reflexively highlighted—it is the human author who both creates and offers the means of
interpretation. Yet James forces readers to see how characters are limited
by the circumstances, situations, and perspectives created by the author,
to realize how knowledge and truth are always partial. With a James
novel, the reader has willingly to occupy a position of uncertainty because
this is the only type of position there is.[14]

In focusing only on texts from James onward, new ethicists imply that
the modernist novel initiates a shift in the novelistic tradition that leads
to a "better" formation of the reading self than earlier novels were able
to do. Generally, these theorists differentiate the "ethical self" formed
in modernist novel-reading from the "autonomous liberal subject" (or
Puritan self) they see constituted in and by earlier novels. They also view
earlier ethical critics of the novel such as Lionel Trilling as well as current "new humanists" as relying upon a similar notion of the "liberal
subject." For example, Trilling saw encounters with otherness and diversity in the novel as evoking the "free play of the moral imagination" and
the "identification" of reader with character through love or sympathy
(Hale, "Aesthetics" 897). For some new ethicists such an idea is a form
of "imperialism" because it assumes the reading subject can gain rational,
objective, and complete knowledge of the characterological other. To the
new ethical theorist, the typological process of identification maintains
the sovereign autonomy of the reading self and is solely a rational process. The "ethical subject," on the other hand, willingly engages in what
Hale deems "self-restriction." This means the reader is willing to read

14. For an interesting study linking James and Puritanism, see Lewis, "Christopher
Newman's Haircloth Shirt: Worldly Asceticism, Conversion, and *Auto-Machia* in *The American*," *Studies in the Novel* 37:3 (2005): 308–28.

difficult novels, to occupy the position such novels create for her, to experience thereby the "estrangement" from certain knowledge that they bring, and to live with both the restrictions on her subjectivity and the "unverifiability" of the alterity she faces. In such reading, the new ethicists and modernist novels "bestow upon epistemological uncertainty a positive ethical content" (Hale, "Fiction" 190).

In the willingness of the reading self to recognize her lack of knowledge and certitude, she therein understands what it means to open herself to the Other. Such an experience, it is assumed, is absolutely necessary if the horrific implementations of limits, stereotypes, and false categories are to be overcome: those limits that serve sexist, racist, bigoted ends, that support typecasting attitudes and close-mindedness, and that lead to real harm and violence to human beings. While such ethical experience may indeed be necessary in order for ingrained social and historical attitudes to be overcome, and while modernist novels may in part provide this experience, this book, along with some of the novels it analyzes, nonetheless challenges the new ethical theorist's tendency to glorify epistemological uncertainty as a final end. Without devaluing the experience of epistemological uncertainty, without devaluing the absolutely necessary work we must do to break open all detrimental forms of typecasting, I want to challenge and complicate the new ethical position regarding both the novelistic tradition and the modernist novel. While I do not deny the value of the ethical experience of difficult reading, then, the limitations of that experience must be taken into account. "Unknowability" cannot be all for which one wishes if human communities are to undergo real change for the better.

It is possible that earlier texts of the novelistic tradition more often than not emphasized modern and individualistic "moral" aspects of typology and thereby perpetuated the liberal subject. It may also be generally true that modernist texts from James onward emphasize the ethical escape from typological moral categories and the experience of epistemological uncertainty. Indeed, many modernist descriptions of the "aesthetic" experience sound "ethical" in Gibson's sense as they extract art entirely from the realm of life and morality and indeed, expose the weaknesses, dangers, and flaws of typological limits. Frank Kermode describes Sartre's struggle with the novel's form, for example, as a struggle between the belief that life is contingent and the reality that novels are the "destroyer of contingency" (137). Novels have "beginnings, ends, and potentiality, even if the world has not," and novels have to lie, embodying forms and patterns which are the "enemies of truth" (Kermode 138, 140).

Iris Murdoch spoke of something similar: "Literature must always represent a battle between real people and images" (qtd. in Kermode 130). A. S. Byatt suggests that even though Murdoch resigned herself, like Sartre, to the truth that novels must have form, this always filled her with "metaphysical regret" (Kermode 131).

In many senses, "morality" is the side of typology with its bases of identification, self-formation, positive knowledge, categories and principles. The "ethical" is what one gets when one dismantles Puritan hermeneutics, the remainder that is revealed and that exposes the limitations of typological reading. Yet even though some, like Gibson, acknowledge the dependent relation of the moral and the ethical, new ethical theory as a whole tends to emphasize the ethical to the detriment of the moral. It tends to see the modernist shift to the ethical as more radical and dramatic than the model I formulated earlier in which merely a shift in dialectical balance occurs.

By exaggerating the ethical shift in modernism, new ethical theory is problematic in at least two ways. First, it oversimplifies the history of the novel's tradition. In the typological hermeneutics of the novel, the moral and the ethical—the type and its dismantling—are dependent upon each other, despite the best efforts of some novelists to escape. The ethical self and the narratives that generate it always imply a moral position in the world of life, whether recognized or not. On the flip side, the assumed moral emphases and modes of typological reading that are seen to dominate the earlier novelistic tradition often also involve ethical experience and hence should not be broadly superseded. The "ethical" and the "moral" always exist in dialectical tension in the novel's tradition, and this is something new ethical theorists tend to ignore. As a consequence, they tend to promote problematic moral positions in their elevation of the "ethical," including social detachment and what I see as an even more extreme version of sovereign individualism. They also tend to ignore the ways in which some modernists themselves warned about such positions.

The second problem in new ethical theory is that it seems to continue the modernist project uncritically. As the New Critics and others in the following decades did, new ethical theorists glorify modernist novelistic form in a manner that grants much spiritual and ethical power to that form but that also, in some cases, oversimplifies it. Indeed, because of its unique perceived ability to form the "ethical subject," the modernist novel essentially becomes a Bible for some. Spivak calls the reader's encounter with alterity a "sacred" experience for a secular world (qtd. in Hale, "Fiction" 201). "Sacred," Hale delineates,

not just because of the act of gaining righteousness through the abdi-
cation of the self, but also because of the condition of this ethical revelation: the willingness to hold the belief that literary meaning can be
divined, that it broods, visibly invisible, not on Milton's vast abyss but in
the concrete particularity of texts. ("Fiction" 201)

In keeping with this "sacred text" rhetoric, whether consciously or not,
new ethicists evoke the rhetoric of Puritan hermeneutics. In many ways,
the new ethicist deconstruction of identification is at heart a deconstruction of novelistic (and biblical) typology and Puritan hermeneutics. In
the modernist novel, according to the new ethical theory, typological
identification is rendered impossible because the epistemological limits of
both reader and character are foregrounded and highlighted. The reader
experiences an "ethical" moment because she recognizes the unknowability of the Other and the self and the processes by which limits are
made. Not only do new ethical theorists laud this experience, however.
Similar ideas were perpetuated by the New Critics, who often identified such an experience as "aesthetic." This idea is also still promoted by
many critics in their descriptions of modernism. The elevation of "ethical" or "aesthetic" experience furthers the myth that escape or full freedom of the self is possible and that Puritanism and Christianity are the
root of all woes.

In many ways, new ethical theory, like the novel itself, is a remnant
of modern morality: a product of the breakdown of the biblical narrative
and its accompanying sense of universal order, a discourse whose terms
are constituted by the "novelistic narrative." In the end, I see recent new
ethical theory's relation to biblical hermeneutics in much the same way
that Suzy Anger sees twentieth-century literary theory in relation to Victorian hermeneutics. A main argument of Anger's book, *Victorian Interpretation,* is that "secular interpretation in both the Victorian age and today
is far more indebted to the strategies and conceptual models of sacred
hermeneutics than has been acknowledged. . . . Methods developed for
biblical exegesis have left their mark on *all* current theoretical approaches
to literature" (4). While Anger allows for contemporary literary theory
to be labeled "secular," I would say that new ethical theory is not "secular." Its attention to the "ethical" itself becomes the "religious," and its
concerns are remarkably similar to the Puritan biblical hermeneutics from
which it is descended.

Although their ideological bases are quite different, both Armstrong
and the new ethical theorists seem to long for a hermeneutics of the self
that is akin to Augustine's in the *Confessions* and to Puritan biblical

typology rather than to the hermeneutics of the self in novelistic typology. When Armstrong says she has never believed that human beings are really individuals, she echoes the Augustinian, biblical idea that the Christian subject is part of something outside of itself, part of a larger reality that extends through past, present, and future, both individual and communal. The new ethical theorists laud the state of "unknowability" that they believe modernist novels lead the reader to experience. They believe this experience forces the reader to recognize the limits of the self and its interpretive capabilities. In other words, it helps one to overcome one's false Puritan or Protestant self. This experience is "ethical" because it opens the self to the other and prepares one to think beyond or before the categories by which we judge and label the other, to recognize that the other exceeds our ability to know. Yet this too is Augustinian. He sees parts of the Bible as beyond human comprehension, and he encourages Christian subjects to dwell in the obscurity, ambiguity, and authority of God's Word. This experience serves as a constant reminder of the limitations of human knowledge and of the self's ontological position before God and within creation and history—it causes one to confess the limitations of the self. For Augustine, only in this experience of self-limitation can one truly learn to love as God loves, without prejudice or false judgment.

Just as the modernist novel, according to the new ethical theorists, leads the reader along with known categories of interpretation but then "ejects" the reader from that framework to face the unknowable Other and the limitations of the self, so Bible-reading leads the reader to insert himself into the position of a character in order to find a point of identification but then pulls that reader into the temporality of the "now and not yet," into the process of knowing and unknowing himself as he ponders and tries to imitate Christ more fully. Augustinian biblical typology involves a dialectical movement between inseparable processes of identification, moral commands, and living in the "now," and processes of self-restriction before God (Other), epistemological limitation, and ethical opening of the self to the unknowable "not yet." The "moral" evaluation of the self and character is dialectically related to the "ethical," then, as it properly reinscribes the reader within the larger order of the church, history, and creation, an order that extends beyond the self and is not yet fully discernable.

In both Augustinian typology and new ethical theory, the text holds authority over the reader. New ethicists suggest that the novel "hails" the reader, that the reader must "surrender" to the text and heed the text's "calling" If the reader "successfully occup[ies] the position made for

[him] through narrative," he undergoes both "avowal" and "disavowal" of his "social positionality" (Hale, "Aesthetics" 902). In other words, he acknowledges both the constructed limits of his identity and the ways in which he becomes blinded to those limits. Butler says this process of "conversion" has to occur repeatedly. Such rhetoric echoes Augustine, who sees Bible-reading as "confession," as the repeated practice of revealing one's own epistemological limits before God. For both Augustine and the new ethicists the encounter with alterity is an affective experience that exceeds rationality. Hale says modernist novel-reading gives "knowledge that is beyond reason, that is of the emotions, and that is so intuitive as to seem a bodily knowing. . . . Knowing is made possible by every felt failure to know and made new through every repetition" (Hale, "Aesthetics" 903). To echo Watson's line about Christians and the Bible, for the new ethical theorist, the reader becomes a walking modernist novel.

Yet despite their similar accounts of the effects of reading on the reader, Augustine and new ethicists contrast tremendously when it comes to the assumed context of reading. For Augustine, there is a grand narrative within which interpretation makes sense and which is assumed to be true, beautiful, and good. In Bible-reading the four traditional levels of interpretation seamlessly intersect with each other. Unlike the new ethicist, the Bible-reader goes on faith and hope that God as Other acts in the world and in history, and that the reading subject has partial or temporary access to God through both the Holy Spirit and the sacred text. The "now" and the "not yet" are not completely separable, then, despite the limited attainability and knowability of the "not yet" within the "now."

Interestingly, the new ethicists speak of the possibility that there is a "law" or moral order outside the self, but also argue that such a realm is entirely unverifiable, seemingly eternally "not yet." As Gibson says, postmodern ethics does not "emerge on the basis of a concept of a 'shared world.'" (85). Rather, it works "in the interests of a community to come whose values are still to be formulated, a solidarity that has yet to be created" (85). Augustinian Bible-reading subjects are ultimately made the same in their self-restriction before and within God's Otherness and the church (all are types who are becoming Christlike), but God also attends to the historical particularity of each subject, leading it to the "not yet" though the context of the "now." The "ethical subject," on the other hand, seems to be constituted by difference and contingency. Meaning can brood in the everyday and particular, but it is never universal as it is for the Bible-reader. There is no larger narrative by which to make sense of

individual reading experiences, no verifiable "law" that can shape morality in ways upon which people can agree. As Gibson boldly says, literary
theory has "stripped us of our faith in the constancy of moral structures," in the "novel's underpinning by those structures," and in the belief
that "ethics" involves a "totality" or "totalities" of value or perception
(6, 10). This book argues that this theory of dismantling yet hoping, is
also derived from within the novelistic narrative. Whereas Augustinian
typology involves a dialectic of moral identification and self-knowledge
and ethical self-restriction in the face of alterity (God), ethical theorists
emphasize the ethical not yet to the detriment of the moral now, the exact
inversion of what they perceive earlier novels to do.

This presents several more problems of which some modernist novelists are entirely aware. First, it seems the new ethicists do not admit
how the "ethical subject" can itself become a limiting identity, a type, a
normative category. The modernist novel may lead the reader to encounter Otherness, but when this becomes the norm for novels or elevated as
a more ideal telos, it becomes just as much a type as the types it works
to exceed. The ethical subject remains trapped in the novelistic narrative. Second, there tends to be no theory of how to translate ethical
experience into moral judgment and action. In repeatedly being opened
up to new possibilities, the reader may better himself somehow, but it
is unclear how such experience translates into real life. Even more significant, the ethical subject seems in the end just as autonomous as the
liberal subject. If ethical experience is to carry over into moral life, it is
not a matter of discerning truth, making decisions, and taking actions
in the corporate context of the church as it was for Augustine and the
Puritans, but instead is left solely up to the individual. J. Hillis Miller,
for example, as Hale outlines, says reading novels teaches the "meta-eth-
ical lesson" that "you are on your own making any decision" (81). To
Miller, ethical decisions are not verifiable by any outside source nor jus-
tifiable by rational explanation but are always "leaps in the dark" that
are made alone (qtd. in Hale, "Fiction" 83). As Hale shows, Butler seems
to discard moral judgment altogether, arguing the encounter with alterity causes us "to cease judging, paradoxically, in the name of ethics, to
cease judging in a way that assumes we already know in advance what
there is to be known" (208). The ethical subject, in the end, appears to be
Sartrean: free and open to the "not yet," but unconnected to any sense of
community or shared narrative and solely responsible for moral decisions
and actions. The individual remains the sole interpreter of her experience
and self. Isn't this an even more radical sovereign individualism than was

stereotyped as Puritanism? Without a larger narrative of truth and virtue, or any sense of shared values that might inspire action and change, even the recognition of the self's limits is still a focus on the self.

Perhaps on these problematic points we simply come up against the differences between the novel and the Bible. Without the Bible's ontological and teleological narrative (or any coherent narrative that adequately replaces it), maybe the novel can never truly shape any other type of subject than the sovereign one, whether on the moral or the ethical side of the dialectic. The new ethicists may be right that ethical experiences with alterity are necessary to any morality that is to overcome racism, sexism, hatred, oppression, and other negative limitations placed on humanity. In the end, however, if the new ethicist view of the modernist novel is our "prototype" for "ethical engagement" (Hale, "Fiction" 200), moral action in the "now" may not ever get undertaken. Escaping the typecasting identification processes involved in prejudice, violence, and oppression of others is one thing, absolutely necessary, but surely also there has to be some kind of moral vocabulary humans can use with each other to connect beyond the nebulous space of epistemological uncertainty. New ethical theory leaves us in a position of individuated tolerance and pluralism—a passive, static place. But this book asks a central question: Isn't there something better than tolerance?

The shift from typological identification to epistemological uncertainty, from the moral to the ethical, is the exact shift Briony Tallis undergoes in the scene discussed at the beginning of this book. It is the exact shift accorded to modernist novels within McEwan's *Atonement*. Briony experiences ethical moments when she recognizes she does not understand what she sees or who she is seeing at the fountain (as well as in the library and at the temple later that evening), and she supposedly comes to know something about the limits of her own self in the process. Yet McEwan's novel asks us, just as the editors at *Horizon* ask Briony, to consider quite seriously the moral value of reducing narrative to such epistemological uncertainty. In requesting that Briony engage with more traditional elements of storytelling, such as character and plot, the editors and *Atonement* itself suggest that novels may need to recover elements of the premodernist tradition in order to serve the reader well. Of course, delineating exactly what kind of "service" this ought to be is something *Atonement* does not answer clearly. Even though it is not easy to discern what McEwan himself might believe, *Atonement* implicitly criticizes the elevation of "ethical experience" over real, moral life. Its readers are forced to consider whether the glorification of the modernist novel as a conduit to recognizing one's own epistemological uncertainty really is a sacred avenue of moral (de)formation. Its readers are at least forced to consider whether that end is sufficient. The early modernist novelists analyzed in this book had something to say about the relation of the moral to the ethical. Like *Atonement,* their novels challenge the new ethicist position, even while confirming its valid contributions.

CHAPTER THREE

Historical Context

The Legacy of Puritanism in the Late Nineteenth Century

T O MANY early modernists, Puritanism had thoroughly infiltrated English society and culture and negatively shaped the historical trajectory of England as a nation. Their reaction to Puritanism in the novel is inextricably tied to their reaction to Puritanism in their own context. This chapter gives a historical-contextual snapshot of the legacy of Puritanism at the turn of the nineteenth century into the twentieth. Because outlining the extent to which Puritanism continued to shape English culture would take volumes, this chapter gives only a brief historical picture of Nonconformist Christianity in these decades. It spends some time on how Nonconformist Christianity was lived and on how it was stereotypically perceived. It also discusses Nonconformist Bible-reading practices and debates over reading. Finally, it examines the views of Puritanism held by two very influential nineteenth-century thinkers—John Henry Newman and Matthew Arnold.

According to the historian Dale A. Johnson, English Nonconformity was "transformed" over the course of the nineteenth century. With the label of "Dissent" at the beginning of the century, Nonconformity "bore the marks of exclusion from the established Church of England and the larger society through inherited disabilities and the accumulated scorn of most Anglicans" (4). By the end of the century, the disabilities in politics, education, and church obligations (having to be baptized, married, and buried in an Anglican church, for example) that Nonconformists "endured since the Restoration" had gradually been removed or were in the process of being removed (4). Nonconformists over the course of the century participated increasingly in economics and developed a stronghold in the middle class. Indeed, in the last quarter of the century, Nonconformity essentially dominated Britain's world ascendancy. Johnson argues that Nonconformist churches were reinvigorated by the Evangelical Revival of mid-century. This new energy led to: increased church attendance and allegiance; the formation of more voluntary church-based societies; more organized denominational bodies; and better training for ministers (4). By the end of the nineteenth century, the term "Dissent" had largely been replaced by the term "Free Church," which according to Johnson signaled Nonconformity's "altered consciousness" about its status and its desire to participate "at every level of national and religious life" (4). Early modernists certainly reacted to the prevalence of Nonconformist influence in all areas of Victorian life.

Contrary to a typical view of early modernism, however, that might see the 1900s and 1910s as largely an experimental and rebellious period, Christianity remained the "general ethos" in Great Britain, and the United Kingdom certainly considered itself to be a "Christian country" (Robbins 46, 23). Being attached to a particular denominational identity was simply a part of life in these decades for many people. Keith Robbins characterizes the period of 1900 to 1914 as a time when this ethos was "under pressure," however, from the challenges of modernity, including "class, gender, culture, war, nation, empire" (46–47). He discusses many trends and debates that shaped Christian churches at the turn of the century. In 1901, over 50 percent of non-Roman Catholics in England and Wales were Nonconformist (Munson 9). Nonconformist or "Free Church" denominations were seeking more unity from within, trying to inspire their various branches to join larger "unions" as well as seeking more unity ecumenically (Robbins 6). Robbins states that all Anglican archbishops were also preoccupied by the late nineteenth century with "keeping the church [of England] together" (13). Despite this, many new churches were being built, occupying "prominent physical space throughout the British Isles" (23). The term "church" usually referred to an Anglican building, while the term "chapel" referred either to a Protestant Nonconformist building or to a Catholic one. According to Robbins, Christianity in England was mostly middle class (49), and although not universally true, typically the working classes did not participate significantly in churches. How to reach the working classes and the poor was a constant concern for churches, however, and in these decades missions and settlements were cropping up in the cities to try to reach the poorer population (54). Free churches also started to become more institutional in that they developed larger buildings and expanded programming (55).

Denominations formed their own historical societies, and church historians began documenting denominational histories. This may have been in part because as historiography became more and more a prevalent and dominant discipline in the latter half of the nineteenth century, European history was increasingly portrayed as undergoing a process of secularization, beginning in the Renaissance and continuing throughout modernity. Such historiography and the resulting period formations of the Medieval, Renaissance, and Modern became a way to narrate modernity's breaking away from Christianity, Puritanism and the Reformation. Chapter 5 treats such historiography more thoroughly in its examination of E. M. Forster and *A Room with a View,* a novel that uses these historical periods as a structuring device for similar reasons—for escape.

At the turn of the century, despite Nonconformity's success in many areas, debates continued over the Establishment of the Anglican Church and its dominance in politics. Historically, Nonconformists believed that because the Establishment was in the majority and wealthy, it never needed to consider the validity of its principles (Munson 226). The Nonconformists took it upon themselves, therefore, to question the Establishment and fight for reform. Historically, however, Nonconformists had always felt belittled and abused, not only by the Establishment in legal ways but also by Roman Catholics. In the 1900s, therefore, Nonconformity continued its quest for legitimacy, especially in raising the status of its clergy and its educational institutions. As James Munson discusses, although the Nonconformist goal of achieving disestablishment constitutionally was unrealized in 1896, in effect "legislation had given *de facto* disestablishment" and had removed many grievances (222). By 1900 "church" and "chapel" were basically equally established in law (222), but not equally established culturally, intellectually, or socially.

Despite the legal advances, nonconformists continued to exert political pressure on the Establishment as they responded to several decades of Anglican attacks. As the Reverend J. Guinness Rogers put it 1892, Nonconformity is "something more than a mere objection to a particular church. It is an assertion of the right of the individual conscience, a protest against invidious class privilege and distinction, an emphatic testimony on behalf of liberty and progress" (qtd. in Munson 220). In the wake of the Parnell divorce case in the late 1880s and early 1890s, which is treated more fully in chapter 6 on James Joyce and *A Portrait of the*

Artist as a Young Man, Nonconformists increasingly put moral pressure on Parliament. They played a key role in trying to hold church, state, and public morality together when the legitimacy and necessity of their connections were increasingly being debated. Such debates, especially regarding the role of church and state in issues of divorce and marriage, integrally shaped Ford Madox Ford's novel, *The Good Soldier.* These topics are treated more completely in chapter 7. Nonconformist moral pressure in these years even led to the coining of the term "Nonconformist Conscience," which was the centralized point of attack for modernists. Other areas in which the "Nonconformist Conscience" exerted pressure in the 1900s were over the Boer War, Irish Home Rule, and especially the Education Act of 1902. This act would have made any spiritual instruction at public schools necessarily Anglican, while taxing everyone for it no matter their denomination. Nonconformist political pressure aided the Liberal Party's unprecedented victory in the 1906 elections, and in 1908, the first Nonconformist prime minister took office.

The spiritual or religious practices of Nonconformity were of course always intertwined with its political and moral public voice. Of most interest here are the Bible-reading practices of the Nonconformist denominations and the ways in which reading was seen to be a serious moral and spiritual endeavor. As with the early modern Puritans, Nonconformists at the end of the nineteenth century continued to have debates over the nature of fiction, reading, and character formation. In addition, the fundamental dialectic of the "Nonconformist Conscience" and its dismantling continued to shape novels, especially for those authors aware of the relation of the novel tradition to Puritanism.

In late-nineteenth- and early-twentieth-century England, the Bible remained a leading best-selling book.[1] As Timothy Larsen outlines in *A People of One Book,* from the Evangelical, Anglican, or Roman Catholic, to the agnostic or atheist, most Victorians were well-versed in and knowledgeable of the Bible—the "common cultural currency of the Victorians" (2). Victorians "tended to be educated and raised in a way that immersed them in the Scriptures" (295), and many still upheld the "expectation that one would read the Bible daily, with four times—private and household in both the morning and the evening—being the ideal" (296). Intellectual debates among Victorian academics assumed biblical knowledge on all

---

1. For more on religion and the Victorian age, see Julie Melnyk, *Victorian Religion: Faith and Life in Britain* (Westport: Praeger, 2008), and Sue Zemka, *Victorian Testaments: The Bible, Christology, and Literary Authority in Early-Nineteenth-Century British Culture* (Stanford: Stanford UP, 1997).

sides. Although the "higher" or scientific biblical criticism of the nineteenth century continues to receive the most scholarly attention today, certainly typological or Puritan devotional reading as outlined in chapter 2 remained a widespread practice.[2] As Larsen suggests, "There was a strong impulse to understand one's life or situation by recasting it within the experience of a specific biblical character or narrative" (296). This idea that as one identifies with the biblical types one comes to understand oneself more thoroughly continued to shape personal Bible-reading practices into the twentieth century. J. B. Greenhough, who served for a while as president of the Free Church Council of the British Isles, exemplifies this approach in his 1903 *Half Hours in God's Older Picture Gallery: A Course of Character Studies from the Old Testament*:

> There is a gulf four thousand years wide between them and ourselves, and an almost greater distance in matters of race, speech, dress, occupations, modes of thought and habits of life; yet human nature is the same, whether it belongs to hoary antiquity, or to our brand new civilization. And the men of the Bible are always intensely human. . . . They are men and women the like of which we can find at any moment by stripping off the modern surface from our own lives and the lives of our neighbors. These stories always come home to us with a personal application if we know how to read them. (14)

Such a Puritan sense of typological Bible-reading and identification was likely strongest among Evangelical and Old Dissenting or Nonconformist denominations (Baptist, Presbyterian, Congregationalist), but certainly was not limited to them. In fact, what separates the more Puritan-like groups from others is not the respective status, value, and centrality given to the Bible; indeed, all denominations in this time, even Unitarians, valued the Bible as central. Rather, what separates groups are doctrinal issues, including the question of interpretive authority. Just as in the early modern era, in the Victorian period Christians remained divided over whether or not the individual reader had the authority to interpret the truth of scripture. As E. B. Pusey put it an 1839 letter:

> The Ultra-Protestants . . . assert that to be truth which each individual himself derives from Holy Scripture . . . the Ultra-Protestant believes "the

---

2. See Larsen, *Contested Christianity*. Larsen argues that rather than an age of increasing unbelief and a waning of the faith due to higher criticism of the Bible, the Victorian age was rather one of "contested" versions of Christianity.

good man," the individual, to be infallibly "guided into all truth"; . . .
People can interpret Scripture as they please, in great measure, and therefore it costs them no submission. (Qtd. in Larsen, *People* 15)

Pusey, on the other hand, who wanted the Anglican Church to return
more fully to its Catholic roots, believed people should be guided in
their biblical interpretation by the collective tradition of the early church
fathers (Larsen 14). Nicholas Wiseman, the first Catholic archbishop of
Westminster, likewise believed the Protestant notion of "the right (indeed
duty) of private judgment" was in error, for it "places on ordinary people—every individual—the impossible burden of proving the entire faith
for themselves from scratch" (Larsen 51). The Protestant and Puritan are
critiqued for believing themselves epistemologically self-sufficient and for
being sovereign interpreters of the Bible as individuals, just as Crusoe
saw himself to be.

The most famous and dominant proponent of Nonconformist reading practices in the nineteenth century certainly had to be the famous
Baptist preacher, Charles H. Spurgeon (1834–1892). Deemed the *Ulti-
mus Puritanorum* or "the last of the Puritans" by many (a title he repu-
diated), Spurgeon was one of the most outspoken and prolific preachers
of the nineteenth century. He saw himself as helping "to train hundreds
of men who would continue the Puritanical succession after he was gone
from their midst" (*Autobiography* 296). He defended Calvinism, com-
piled a catechism for his church that he titled *A Puritan Catechism*, was
a leading voice in many public debates, and published many books, sermons, and Bible commentaries. Spurgeon grew up reading Puritan devotional books and sermons in his grandfather's library and avidly collected
Puritan volumes his entire life. He read voraciously and was extremely
well-learned. At his death he had 12,000 volumes in his library, 7,000 of
which were Puritan texts *(Autobiography* 287). On reading Puritan theology he said in 1872:

> We assert this day that, when we take down a volume of Puritan theol-
> ogy, we find in a solitary page more thinking and more learning, more
> Scripture, more real teaching, than in whole folios of the effusions of
> modern thought. The modern men would be rich if they possessed even
> the crumbs that fall from the table of the Puritans. (Qtd. in Bacon 121)

Of course reading early modern Puritan texts always took second place
to reading the Bible itself. Sounding like Watson or any number of early
modern Puritans, Spurgeon says this of Bible-reading:

> It is blessed to eat into the very soul of the Bible, until at last you come to
> talk in Scriptural language, and your spirit is flavoured with the words of
> the Lord, so that your blood is *Bibline,* and the very essence of the Bible
> flows from you. Hundreds of times have I surely felt that presence of God
> in the pages of Scripture. (Qtd. in Bacon 109)

Spurgeon's devotional texts continue to be published and read even today.

As others have shown, most notably George P. Landow in *Victorian Types, Victorian Shadows,* biblical typology continued to inform Victorian literature almost universally.[3] One could even codify the biblical allusions made by so-called atheist Victorian authors. The general idea of moral typologies was a common literary application. The moral natures of Shakespeare's characters, for example, were analyzed typologically in texts like James Bell's 1894 *Biblical and Shakespearean Characters Compared* and Mary Cowden Clarke's 1850 *The Girlhood of Shakespeare's Heroines.* One 1873 text, *Traits of Character and Notes of Incident in the Bible Story* by Francis Jacox, thoroughly intersperses biblical and literary references on the premise that the moral-spiritual types presented in the Bible are universal and that "novels and poetry confirm these characteristic traits and incidents" (2). The Bible was a source of foundational moral and spiritual types that then shaped literary characters and gave readers clues for interpreting them. This seemed to be a convention no matter what an author believed about the truth of the biblical narrative.

Despite this influence of the Bible on literature, a Puritan-like fear and distrust of fiction persisted for some throughout the nineteenth century and into the twentieth.[4] Many novelists continued to make fun of this fear and exploited it as they dismantled Puritan morality. As had happened ever since the Reformation and the emergence of the modern novel in England, Puritans in the late nineteenth century continued to voice concern over the attitudes portrayed in novels and the ways in which novels might negatively form their readers morally and spiritually, leading them away from a biblical view. Bound up in this central question of character formation was the question of the novel's relation to truth. An 1873 text, for example, titled *Youth and Its Duties: A Book for Young Gentlemen, Containing Useful Hints of the Formation of Character,* by Harvey Newcomb, suggests that novels can "fill corrupt minds"

---

3. See also Korshin.

4. Cunningham's *Everywhere Spoken Against* shows how this Puritan fear of fiction is itself an exaggerated stereotype. While certainly many Puritans felt novels were dangerous, others actually wrote novels and attempted thereby to combat the novels that falsely stereotyped dissent. Puritans took a wide range of positions on novel-reading.

with "false and dangerous principles" that are "more fascinating to the youthful heart than the example itself would be, because the mischief is artfully concealed behind the drapery of fine literary taste, and beautiful language" (183). The author goes on suggest that "It is better to read the Bible alone, than to spend time over a poor book," and that youth should avoid the "appetite for novel reading" which can lead to a habit of "moral intoxication" (185). A 1909 text, *Bible Miniatures: Character Sketches of One Hundred and Fifty Heroes and Heroines of Holy Writ* by Amos R. Wells, outlines as one example the character of Eve and suggests that her plot "has been the essential plot of many a modern novel, because it is the essential plot of many a modern life: a foolishly ambitious, insanely credulous, but divinely loving and gloriously daring woman, who decides that she can get through Satan for her beloved what she and he cannot get from God." The author goes on to suggest, however, that the biblical version of Eve's plot is superior: "If we read our Genesis better, we need not read, at so much greater length, our Thackeray." Clearly the novel continued to suffer a poor reputation among many Christians because unlike religious faith, fiction was not based on any sense of a shared morality or narrative.

Puritan fear of fiction may have been reinvigorated in the late nineteenth century by developments in theology. Johnson suggests that over the course of the nineteenth century, Nonconformist theology shifted over "the foundational question of religious authority" (124). At the beginning of the century there was consensus among Nonconformists that natural theology provided the objective grounds for certainty about biblical authority. In the wake of the scientific revolution, Darwinism, the higher criticism of the Bible, and increasing skepticism over the course of the century, that consensus gradually turned into a pluralism in which several theories of biblical authority were being put forth in Nonconformist circles and schools. One of these theories argued that religious experience was a ground for religious certainty, but this was often considered to be too subjective and liberal by many. While Nonconformists maintained "common commitment and purpose" in their faith, says Johnson, such a shift "must have contributed to the growing sense of unease and fragmentation" that was being expressed outside the church and slowly infiltrating it (124).

Yet while early-twentieth-century novels that portrayed this increasing religious skepticism strengthened Puritan fears about fiction for some, others saw the situation as ripe for Christian authors to step forward. For example, two papers in the 1908 volume, *Pan-Anglican Papers:*

Being Problems for Consideration at the Pan-Anglican Congress, published by the Society for Promoting Christian Knowledge, address recent literature's leaning toward "skeptical speculation" (3). One paper suggests that the church need not be afraid of such literature, for it genuinely interests readers, and "indifference is worse than irreverence" (7). The other paper acknowledges how thoroughly the popular literature of the day is "concerned with religious questions" (13) and that while the "public has little sympathy for the supernatural or for clergy, law or discipline, . . . they still wish to cloak their aspirations in the trappings of religion" (15). Both authors suggest that the current climate calls for the church and Christian writers to meet the public at the level of its questioning and to be the first to address various modes of thought instead of being the first to stifle and censor them (7).

One has to remember as well that certainly not all Nonconformists were afraid of novels. Additionally, some Nonconformists throughout the nineteenth century wrote novels that maintained the Puritan emphasis on character formation.[5] Even Spurgeon felt that novel-reading was appropriate to some degree. When asked "Should novel-reading be indulged in by ministers?," he is noted to have replied thus (even though he had read many novels himself): "That depends on what you mean by a novel." He cites *The Pilgrim's Progress* (a text he read over one hundred times), Sir Walter Scott, and some of Dickens as worthy of reading, though the last employed "gross caricatures" of the religious life of his times. "As for the general run of novels now being issued in shoals," he went on, "you will probably be wise to leave them alone; few of them would likely to do you any good, and many of them are morally *tainted, or worse*" (*Autobiography* 283).

Here Spurgeon participates in some of the general discourse on moral character, moral education, virtue, and character development that was prevalent throughout the nineteenth century and persisted into the twentieth.[6] Often discussed was whether novels were appropriate reading

---

5. See Cunningham, *Everywhere Spoken Against.*

6. A sampling of titles includes: J. H. Robinson, *Advice to the Young, on the Formation of their Character, and on Their Moral and Intellectual Improvement* (Manchester: John Harrison, 1843); Thomas Wyles, *The Duty of the Schoolmaster in Relation to the Formation of Character* (Edinburgh, 1865); Gustave Cohen, *The Formation of Character* (London: Cohen, 1884); Ernest R. Hull, *The Formation of Character* (London: Sands, 1909); Nathaniel Haycroft, *The Formation of Character* (London, 1849); Eber Carpenter, *Formation of Christian Character in Early Life* (Merrian and Cooke, 1842); James Bardsley, *The Formation of English Character* (London: YMCA, 1861); J. H. Friswell, *The Gentle Life: Essays in Aid of the Formation of Character* (Sampson, 1866); Charles Beatty,

for the formation of one's character. An 1851 text, *Religion in Earnest: Designed to Aid in Forming and Perfecting the Christian Character* by Silas Henn, ties virtue and biblical typology together: "You must be pious and virtuous in your own life, and must strive to promote piety and virtue in the lives of those around you" (9). While there may be disagreement among Christians on doctrinal issues, says Henn, the "possession of true religion" is marked by one who "orders his conduct . . . after the fashion of Jesus the carpenter; of Paul, the tent-maker; of Peter, the fisherman" (10). Henn goes on to argue against novel-reading, saying some prefer "obscene novel-reading to the reading of scriptures—the tales of the ungodly to the conversation of Christ and his disciples" (21). Trying to explain why the Bible may not be as popular among those who like novels, the author reveals his typological view of reading:

> People dislike the scriptures, because they see in them, as in a glass, their own odious character. . . . They hate the mirror in which they see themselves so plainly. . . . Read the scriptures, and they will assist you in learning your state and danger. They will show you clearly that you are transgressors. (24)

According to this author, Bible-reading reveals a true picture of the self, the state of its conscience, and its virtue (or lack thereof), while novels lead only to a false self-image. Because novels are fictional, they help lead the reader away from reality and true knowledge of themselves and God.

Lecture on the Formation of Female Character (Steubenville: Wilson and Harper, 1848); Ernest Barker, *National Character and the Factors of Its Formation* (London: Methuen, 1927); Mrs. Anne Hope, *On Self-Education with Formation of Character* (London, 1843); J. B. Greenhough, *Half Hours in God's Older Picture Gallery: A Course of Character Studies from the Old Testament* (London: Arthur Stockwell, 1904?); John Brinton, *Bible Character Sketches* (London: Siegle, 1905); Frederick J. Cross, *A Little Book of Effort, for the Strengthening of Character and the Record of Achievement* (London: Simpkin, Marshall, Hamilton, Kent: 1911?); William Brameld, *In Type and Shadow, Being Lesson Sketches on Certain Old Testament Types of Christ* (London: Skeffington, 1880); A. M. Tennant, *Earthen Vessels; or, Women of the Old Testament: Character Studies* (London: Mowbray, 1914); John Taylor, *Picture Truths: A Series of Practical Lessons on the Formation of Character, from Bible Emblems and Proverbs* (London: T. Woolmer, 1883); Anne Woodrooffe, *Shades of Character: or, Mental and Moral Delineations; Designed to Promote the Formation of the Female Character on the Basis of Christian Principles* (London: Hamilton, Adams, 1841); Charlotte Mason, *Some Studies in the Formation of Character* (London: Kegan Paul, 1906); Philip Bennett Power, *The Bible Gentleman: Containing Certain Infallible Receipts of Which the Poorest and Most Uneducated Man Can Become a True Gentleman* (London: Hamilton, Adams, & Co., n.d.).

Another question addressed more frequently at the turn of the century was whether religion or philosophy should be the foundation of moral character formation. At the heart of this question for Christians was the idea that morality and religion could not be seen as separate realms of knowledge. Truth and virtue are intimately linked. For example, in a 1908 lecture delivered to the ethological society titled "The Influence of Religion on Character," the archdeacon of London, the Venerable William Sinclair, argued that religion, not philosophy, was able to "supply the motive and the power to secure" virtue and the inner life (1). While recent thinkers such as Matthew Arnold "worship" the moral law and its authority outside of religion, only Christianity, says Sinclair, "enables men to see in the world outside them the working out of their own moral aspirations" (4). Edward Lyttelton describes his 1912 book, *Character and Religion,* as "a contribution to the question recently come into prominence, how far are we, ordinary people, justified in believing that character can be trained on moral principles alone." He suggests that "during the last forty years the gulf between religion and morality may be thought to have widened considerably," yet at the same time there is now also a widespread attention to religious questions (3). Lyttelton assesses that in his day, "the adult moralist is reduced to the humiliating position of having to base the teaching of his child in what he concedes to be the first thing in life, conduct, on something which to him is of quite secondary importance": religion (3). At the same time that moral philosophy and popular thought see morality as separable from religion, then, others argue that only in their connection will true virtue be established. As William Bruce put it in his 1902 *The Formation of Christian Character,* there are Christians who want to ignore the character or moral aspect of the faith, and there are others who "attend to character and ethics without Christianity" (7). According to these texts, then, MacIntyre's claim that modernity is constituted by the separation of religion and morality is generally descriptively true, yet Puritans and others in the church had always persisted in their arguments for the inseparability of the two realms.

In sum, Puritan or Nonconformist Bible-readers in the late nineteenth and early twentieth centuries continue to have the same concerns about the novel that early modern Puritans did. They share concern for the effects of novel-reading on the reader's personal moral and spiritual character. They believe narratives invite the reader to take a position in the story as he identifies with the character types. They believe such a process enables moral and spiritual insight regarding the reader's own soul or conscience and can lead to change or conversion in the self. They believe narratives can shape the reader's desires, emotions, and values, and they worry about how much a novel's fictional theory of history and life, as well as its questioning of religion, might draw a reader away from seeing the biblical narrative as truth. To these believers, the novel and the Bible require similar hermeneutics and have parallel moral and spiritual effects on their readers. For some, the novel is in competition with the Bible for winning souls. For some, the novelist competes with God.

Two of the most influential Victorian thinkers for the early modernists—John Henry Newman and Matthew Arnold—also see Bible-reading as analogous to novel-reading. They both critique the Puritan Bible-reading subject for being overly rational, for believing the self is sovereign epistemologically, for being too focused on the moral realm. Although Newman was a Roman Catholic writing primarily against the Protestant Anglican Establishment and Arnold was a skeptic specifically targeting Puritans, they shared many ideas. Their writings established views and theories of Protestantism and Puritanism that surely helped shape all subsequent views. Both Newman's argument in his 1851 "Lectures on the Present Position of Catholics in England" and Arnold's arguments in his 1869 *Culture and Anarchy* focus on critiquing Puritan hermeneutics and epistemology, the foundation of Protestant reading and interpreting. However, as they both argue against the supposed certainty of Protestant rationality and judgment as well as the stereotyping, limiting views they see being produced by Puritan interpretive practices, they both, like the novel, ironically stereotype the Puritan.

Newman's series of "Lectures on the Present Position of Catholics in England," which he considered to be among his best writings, were delivered once a week during the summer of 1851. Newman describes the purpose of the lectures thus:

> I am going to inquire why it is that, in this intelligent nation, and in this rational nineteenth century, we Catholics are so despised and hated by our own countrymen, with whom we have lived all our lives, that they are prompt to believe any story, however extravagant, that is told to our disadvantage; as if beyond a doubt we were, every one of us, either brutishly deluded or preternaturally hypocritical, and they themselves, on the contrary were in comparison of us absolute specimens of sagacity, wisdom, uprightness, manly virtue, and enlightened Christianity. (1)

At one point, Newman admits that "when I use the word Protestant, I do not mean thereby all who are not Catholics, but distinctly the disciples of the Elizabethan Tradition." He refers to the Anglican Establishment essentially founded by Elizabeth in the sixteenth century in conjunction with the forced exile of English Catholics (170). The lectures foundationally attack Protestantism on epistemological and moral grounds and carefully dissect what Newman calls Protestant anti-Catholic "Prejudice" and "Bigotry." Newman's characterization of English Protestants as too hardened into their typecasting attitudes and methods is a critique of the limits of Puritan hermeneutics.

To Newman, Protestants hold their negative views of Catholics merely based on what he calls the "Protestant Tradition" which has long been ingrained in the English identity. "Our received policy, as Englishmen, our traditionary view of things, [is] to paint up the Pope and Papists in a certain style," says Newman (10). Certain "facts" about Catholicism, which are actually falsities or fictions, are so ingrained in English Protestantism that they have become "first principles": assumptions never questioned for their adherence to truth. This "great Protestant Tradition" of "First Principles" is made up of "many rivulets": "the Tradition of the Court, the Tradition of the Law, the Tradition of the Legislature, the Tradition of the Establishment, the Tradition of Literature, the Tradition of Domestic Circles, the Tradition of the Populace" (120). Yet this tradition is not only of learned or professional men. It is a tradition of

> nursery stories, school stories, public-house stories, club-house stories, drawing-room stories, platform stories, pulpit stories—a tradition of newspapers, magazines, reviews, pamphlets, romances, novels, poems, and light literature of all kind, literature of the day—a tradition of selections from the English classics, bits of poetry, passages of history, sermons, chance essays, extracts from books of travel, anonymous anecdotes, lectures of prophecy, statements and arguments of polemical writers, made up into small octavos for class-books, and into pretty miniatures for presents—a tradition floating in the air; which we found in being when we first came to years of reason; which has been borne in upon us by all we saw, heard, or read, in high life, in parliament, in law courts, in general society; which our fathers told us had ever been in their day; a tradition, therefore, truly universal and immemorial, and good so far as a tradition can be good, but after all, no more than a tradition is worth: I mean, requiring some ultimate authority to make it trustworthy. (84)

The "Protestant Tradition" of anti-Catholic typecasting is an inescapable aspect of being English, according to Newman, yet it lacks a foundation of authoritative truth, and hence must be exposed as a mere cultural construct, a "waxwork," a "fiction," a "counterfeit" (9). Ironically, however, while Newman wants to dismantle the fictional typecasting of Catholics within Protestant discourse, he maintains his own negative stereotypical depictions of Protestants as if they were facts. I say this not to defend Protestants or Catholics, but to point out how difficult it is to dismantle a long-ingrained typological (novelistic) narrative when one is arguing from within that narrative and is therefore limited by its dialectical structure.

The main aspect of the "Protestant Tradition" that Newman attacks is its epistemology that assumes the autonomy of the individual mind. One of the most characteristic "marks or notes of a Protestant" for Newman is his "one-sidedness," his inability to view things from a different perspective: "He has always viewed things in one light, and he cannot adapt himself to any other; he cannot throw himself into the ideas of other men, fix upon the principles on which those ideas depend, and then set himself to ascertain how those principles differ, or whether they differ at all, from those which he acts upon himself" (170). Protestants not only refuse to try to understand Catholicism or to see it in a new light, but they also refuse to be questioned themselves and to take criticism. They thereby always act out of hardened fear and remain unaware of their own limitations, according to Newman.

Most intriguingly, Newman feels that fiction has the ability to reveal knowledge about human identity which Protestants fail to see. Fiction often reveals that different people have different views of the very same things, he says:

> The interest in which such an exhibition creates in the reader . . . is that each of the persons in question is living in his own world, and cannot enter the world of another, and therefore paints that other in his own way, and presents us with a caricature instead of a likeness, though he does not intend it. (6)

Fiction, in other words, exposes the processes of typecasting and helps readers to open their perspectives on people who are different from themselves. Fiction can reveal to readers their own tendencies to stereotype. Fiction thus can lead the reader to understand the limits of the self in a way that Protestants seem unable to accomplish. How like new ethical theory this sounds!

According to Newman, Protestant epistemology and hermeneutics make the individual the authority of interpretive judgment, an assumption he sees as the foundation of "Prejudice": "that narrow, ungenerous spirit which energizes and operates so widely and so unweariedly in the Protestant community" (227). For Newman, "the Prejudiced man takes it for granted, or feels an undoubted persuasion—not only that he himself is in possession of divine truth, for this is a matter of opinion, and he has a right to his own—but that we, who differ from him, are universally imposters, tyrants, hypocrites, cowards, and slaves" (227). The "Prejudiced man," or "Protestant Scripture Reader," as Newman also calls him, is self-sufficient to make judgments about truth and reality because the "Protestant Tradition" has naturally ingrained in him the idea that he is "the measure of everything" (227). To Newman, this is unethical and "Bigoted" and is the root of Protestantism as a "persecuting power" (209). He defines "Bigotry" as "the imposition of private reason—that is, of our own views and theories of our own First Principles, as if they were the absolute truth, and the standard of all argument, investigation, and judgment" on others, and then "treating others with scorn or hatred for not accepting them" (278). For Newman, English Protestantism's "First Principles" are lauded "as oracles and standards of all truth," but they are generated from the "private factory of man," not "from the Author of our being" (279). The "Protestant Tradition" is hence flawed at its very foundation. To Newman, the sovereign Protestant self in England becomes his own source of truth, his own God.

Paradoxically, Newman's critique of Protestantism simultaneously creates and furthers the stereotype of the "Ultra-Protestant" or "Puritan" as autonomous liberal individual. In his account, Protestantism is associated with individualism; self-sufficient rationality, judgment, and epistemology; cultural instantiation of false first principles; and social and political power, all of which need to be critiqued and dismantled. While in other writings Newman is not so harsh, these lectures create a negative view of Protestantism that influences many. George Eliot, for example, is known to have attended some of Newman's lectures and to have been pleasantly surprised with his level of wit and sarcasm about Protestants. Like the new ethical theorist, Newman finds dramatized in fiction the Puritan processes of typecasting by epistemologically limited characters. In the process of reading, he suggests, fiction becomes the means by which one can experience something beyond the limits of the self. He seems to wish that English society, especially Protestants, could take on a more novelistic mode of reading and interpreting others, such that they could understand better the limits of their views and of themselves and move past their bigotry.

In *Culture and Anarchy* Matthew Arnold promotes "Culture," not the Catholic Church, as the institution by which to advance England's development, and thereby has quite different ends than Newman. Despite this, his critique of Puritanism and its effects on national life correspond to Newman's views. In fact, Arnold makes it clear that he is continuing what Newman had begun. Arnold suggests that Newman and the Oxford Movement primarily fought against "middle-class liberalism" or the Establishment, which had for the "cardinal points of its belief":

> The Reform Bill of 1832, and local self-government, in politics; in the social sphere, free trade, unrestricted competition, and the making of large industrial fortunes; in the religious sphere, the Dissidence of Dissent and the Protestantism of the Protestant Religion. (73)

Yet Arnold suggests that this power no longer has dominance:

> Who will estimate how much the currents of feeling created by Dr. Newman's movement, the keen desire for beauty and sweetness which it nourished, the deep aversion it manifested to the hardness and vulgarity of middle-class liberalism, the strong light it turned on the hideous and grotesque illusions of middle-class Protestantism—who will estimate how much all these contributed to swell the tide of dissatisfaction which has mined the ground under the self-confident liberalism of the last thirty years, and has prepared the way for its sudden collapse and supersession? (74)

Arnold is most concerned to attack Puritanism specifically. He believes Puritanism developed historically in England as a counter to the "Renascence." It was "originally the reaction in the seventeenth century of the conscience and moral sense of our race, against the moral indifference and lax rule of conduct" that the Renascence introduced in the sixteenth century (136). In Arnold's famous terms, it was a reaction of "Hebraism against Hellenism" (136). For Arnold, the natural movement of history was leading to the Renascence and its return to and recovery of the ancients. When Puritanism countered this movement, a "contravention of the natural order" occurred in England, the full effects and disorder of which Arnold sees as only beginning to be identified in his current day (137). The rise of early modern Puritanism is nothing like the rise of primitive Christianity. To Arnold, Christianity's emergence and domination over Hellenism in antiquity was also the natural course of history, for "the way of mankind's progress lay through [Christianity's] full development" (137). When Puritanism emerged, in contrast, it was a mere "side stream" trying to overcome the natural flow of history, yet it confused itself as the "main stream of man's advance" (137). Thus at the beginning of the seventeenth century, through this unnatural development, the English middle class "entered the prison of Puritanism, and had the key turned there upon its spirit for two hundred years" (Arnold, "Equality" 229).

Arnold sees his call for a return to Hellenism and to culture as a correction to the dominance of middle-class liberalism and Puritanism in England, especially with its incomplete ideas about man's perfection. Echoing Newman's sentiments, Arnold argues that

> the Puritan's great danger is that he imagines himself in possession of a rule telling him the *unum necessarium,* or the one thing needful, and that he remains very satisfied with a very crude conception of what this rule really is and what it tells him, thinks he has now knowledge and henceforth needs only to act, and, in this dangerous state of assurance and self-satisfaction, proceeds to give full swing to a number of the instincts of his ordinary self. (142)

Some of these instincts (e.g., man's "animality") the Puritan has successfully conquered, and for this the Puritan deserves some admiration, "but others which he has not conquered by this help he is so far from perceiving to need subjugation, and to be instincts of an inferior self, that he even fancies it to be his right and duty, in virtue of having conquered a limited part of himself, to give unchecked swing to the remainder" (142). He is, in other words, "a victim of Hebraism" who has cultivated a "strictness of conscience" while leaving undeveloped his "spontaneity of consciousness" (142). What the Puritan lacks for Arnold is a "larger conception of human nature" that extends beyond the moral sphere (142). The real *unum necessarium,* says Arnold, is that humans strive to "come to our best at all points," not merely on moral ones (142). The result of Puritanism's one-sided emphasis is that it justifies "vulgarity, hideousness, ignorance, violence," instead of attending to the "full and harmonious development of ourselves" (143). Morality and religion for the Puritan become mere "machinery"—"mechanical, absolute law" (147).

In another essay, "Equality," Arnold extends this description of the Puritan type:

> Those who offer us the Puritan type of life offer us a religion not true,
> the claims of intellect and knowledge not satisfied, the claim of beauty
> not satisfied, the claim of manners not satisfied. In its strong sense for
> conduct that life touches truth; but its other imperfections hinder it from
> employing even this sense aright. The type mastered our nation for a
> time. Then came the reaction. . . . The type retired into our middle class,
> and fortified itself there. It seeks to endure, to emerge, to deny its own
> imperfections, to impose itself again—impossible! If we continue to live,
> we must outgrow it. The very class in which it is rooted, our middle class,
> will have to acknowledge the type's inadequacy, will have to acknowl-
> edge the hideousness, the immense ennui of the life which this type has
> created, will have to transform itself thoroughly. (232)

Arnold calls for an escape from the dominant Puritan type, an escape
from the categories and narratives he sees dominating English culture. His
project relies on a narrative of confinement and escape.

In the end, England's religious institutions and "the Dissidence of
Dissent and the Protestantism of the Protestant religion will never bring
humanity to its true goal," which for Arnold is "a human nature complete on all sides," morally, intellectually, aesthetically, and otherwise
("Culture" 70). It is important to note that Arnold does not condemn
outright all attention to morality; indeed, he says "morality is indispens-
able," and men of culture who ignore it are "punished" for that inatten-
tion. While he does not promote an amoral "culture" of aesthetics only,
then, he calls for a moral sensibility tempered by intellect and beauty, a
more complicated view of morality than what he sees Puritanism providing. Like Newman, Arnold sees Protestant England as engendering a view
of the human subject that is too one-sided, too rational, too certain, too
incomplete a picture of humanity's potential. Arnold performs a critique
or dismantling of the Puritan type and calls for a new order, but he does
not outline specifically how moral-social life should be reconfigured.

Very intriguingly, Arnold spends time in *Culture and Anarchy* critiquing Puritan Bible-reading. Newman had seen novel-reading as potentially
providing to the reader a wider perspective of the human self and truth
than Protestants were able to achieve. In parallel, Arnold sees Protestant
interpretation of the Bible as too narrow-minded and limited. Arnold suggests that:

> Nothing is more striking than to observe in how many ways a limited
> conception of human nature, the notion of a one thing needful, a one

side in us to be made uppermost, the disregard of a full and harmonious development of ourselves, tells injuriously on our thinking and acting. (142–43)

He goes on to suggest that "the dealings of Puritanism with the writings of St. Paul provide a noteworthy illustration of this" (143). Arnold argues that nowhere else has Puritanism found its "canons of truth" and a sense of the "one thing needful" than in Paul's Epistle to the Romans (143). Yet the Puritans distort and oversimplify Paul's complex thought, the mystery of that which he treats:

> And who . . . must not feel how terms which St. Paul employs, in trying to follow with his analysis of such profound power and originality some of the most delicate, intricate, obscure, and contradictory workings and states of the human spirit, are detached and employed by Puritanism, not in the connected and fluid way in which St. Paul employs them, and for which alone words are really meant, but in an isolated, fixed, mechanical way, as if they were talismans; and how all trace and sense of St. Paul's true movement of ideas, and sustained masterly analysis, is thus lost? Who, I say, that has watched Puritanism—the force which so strongly Hebraises, which so strongly takes St. Paul's writings as something absolute and final, containing the one thing needful—handle such terms as *grace, faith, election, righteousness*, but must feel, not only that these terms have for the mind of Puritanism a sense false and misleading, but also that this sense is the most monstrous and grotesque caricature of the sense of St. Paul, and that his true meaning is by these worshippers of his words altogether lost? (143–44)

Here, Arnold critiques Puritanism's hermeneutics of rational certitude, epistemological narrowness, and moral simplicity. Instead, to Arnold, the Bible is obscure, intricate, mysterious, and despite the Puritan claim that the Bible (or St. Paul) gives the "one thing needful," the man of culture knows that "No man, who knows nothing else, knows even his Bible" (144). The Bible, Arnold implies, is infinitely more complex and uncertain in meaning than the Puritans admit; full knowledge of the text is always beyond the reader's understanding. This very sense of obscurity, incompleteness, and mystery—the incomprehensibility and beauty of the Bible— is what has been lost for so long in English culture. In this sense, the Bible for Arnold is like Newman's novel, a literary text, for it can potentially show the reader who opens the self the epistemological limits of the self.

For both Newman and Arnold, reading has the potential to help one overcome one's "Puritan self." Ironically, however, Newman and Arnold at the same time create and further the stereotype of what Puritanism is. They both seek to dismantle Puritanism in order to find something new—a new social attitude toward Catholics for Newman, a new cultural "best self" to which the English might aspire for Arnold—but they remain dialectically tied to that which they mean to escape. They become the sovereign interpreters and identifiers of English Protestantism even as they critique English Protestantism's modes of sovereign interpretation. They are thinking from within the dialectic of the novelistic narrative—the dialectic of confinement and escape—a narrative placing a circle of limits on them they are unable to see because it is further out and encompasses more than the limits they are critiquing. In pointing this out, I do not want to belittle the fact that Catholics in England faced horrible oppression for centuries. Obviously, Newman was heroic to speak out against and try to dismantle the ingrained anti-Catholic prejudices. But there has to be some better way to meet the Others who estrange than to estrange and Other them right back.

Obviously, the reality of Puritanism and Protestantism in the Victorian era was far more complex and rich than these stereotypes and theories ever allow, just as were those of the original early modern Puritan cultures. Yet these stereotypes and theories, including ironically the stereotype that the tendency to stereotype is Puritan, persist, not only shaping how modernist writers and artists thought but continuing to shape how we view literary history today.

PART TWO

Puritanism in Four
Early Modernist Novels

CHAPTER FOUR

Reading and Hegelian Tragedy in
Oscar Wilde's *The Picture of Dorian Gray*

$\mathbb{W}$ RITING IN one of his autobiographies about what he called the "tragic generation" of the 1880s and 1890s, W. B. Yeats asks: "Why are these strange souls born everywhere today, with hearts that Christianity, as shaped by history, cannot satisfy?"[1] Yeats identifies a tendency to despair among the young artists and writers of the late nineteenth century—including Oscar Wilde—that he sees fueled by the failure of historical Christianity to meet their theological, existential yearnings. This failure of historical Christianity's institutions, practices, and teachings to satisfy the soul is certainly a central theme of Wilde's novel, *The Picture of Dorian Gray*. Yet after an era of criticism and biography that tended either to ignore or to dismiss Wilde's longstanding interest in Christianity, religion is only now emerging as a serious concern in Wilde studies.[2] Most recent research explores Wilde's interest in Roman Cathol-

---

1. Ronald Schuchard's essay first alerted me to Yeats's comments on the "tragic generation." See Yeats's autobiography, *The Trembling of the Veil*. London: T. Werner Laurie, 1922.

2. Richard Ellmann's biography, *Oscar Wilde* (New York: Knopf, 1988), is most often cited as turning Wilde scholarship away from Wilde's interests in Christianity. Ellmann called Christianity an "attractive fiction" of Wilde's early life (297). As Jarlath Killeen suggests: "Ellmann unambiguously maintains throughout the biography that Wilde's interest in the Church was aesthetic rather than spiritual, and that even this aesthetic interest had largely deserted him by the time he came to write his most important texts" (17). Jonathan Dollimore, in *Sexual Dissidence: Augustine to Wilde, Freud to Foucault* (New York: Oxford UP, 1991), sees Wilde's interest in Christianity as incompatible with his sexuality and hence similarly dismisses Wilde's religious interests.

icism and attempts to delineate the specific Catholic influences in his writings as well as the extent and legitimacy of his personal religious commitments. Some focus on Wilde's biographical life, even going so far as to label Wilde an "orthodox Catholic" whose long conversion followed the *via negativa*.[3] Others delineate specific cultural expressions of Catholicism that shaped Wilde's writings. These include the Oxford Catholicism of John Henry Newman, the folk Irish Catholicism of Wilde's Ireland in which his parents took such great interest, and perhaps most significantly, the "decadent Catholicism" of nineteenth-century French aesthetes who influenced so many of those connected to British aestheticism.[4] Yet having been born and raised in an Irish Protestant home, Wilde was certainly shaped by Protestantism and Puritanism as well, and these influences also deserve more treatment

This chapter examines Wilde's engagement in *The Picture of Dorian Gray* with late-nineteenth-century ideas about character formation and Puritan hermeneutics. Following in the wake of Matthew Arnold, Wilde often stereotypically condemned Puritanism for causing England's cultural stagnation. In an 1882 interview during his visit to the United States, for example, Wilde said: "And then came the Puritan movement and destroyed all the artistic impulse. We are just beginning to recover from Puritanism in England" (qtd. in Hofer 43). Yet despite his ironic aphorisms and quips about morality, Wilde understood Puritan Bible-reading and interpretation at a deep level, and he gave Puritanism much more respect than many in his day did. In *Dorian Gray*, Wilde pits Puritanism against aestheticist discourse through the use of Hegelian tragedy.[5] Analyzing this conflict in light of Puritan hermeneutics and Wilde's engagement of Hegelian tragedy provides a new reading of the text, especially

---

3. See Schuchard; Joseph Pearce, *The Unmasking of Oscar Wilde* (London: HarperCollins, 2000); Andrew McCracken, "The Long Conversion of Oscar Wilde," *Catholic Education* (April 2003); and John Allen Quintus, "Christ, Christianity, and Oscar Wilde," *Texas Studies in Literature and Language* 33:4 (1991): 514–27.

4. Frederick Roden links Wilde to the Oxford Catholics in *Same-Sex Desire in Victorian Religious Culture* (New York: Palgrave Macmillan, 2002). For studies of Wilde and French decadent Catholicism, see Schuchard; O'Malley; and also Ellis Hanson, *Decadence and Catholicism* (Cambridge, MA: Harvard UP, 1997). Killeen acknowledges the influence of the Oxford Catholics but writes his book on Irish folk Catholicism.

5. For a study that argues Wilde juxtaposes Puritanism and aestheticism in his play, *A Woman of No Importance*, see Margaret Wright, "Wilde's 'Puritanism': Hester Worsley and the American Dream," *The Wildean: Journal of the Oscar Wilde Society* 35 (2009): 52–61. Wright's argument that Wilde is not completely condemnatory of Puritanism but actually values some of its ideals while critiquing "dandyism" correlates with my own argument about *The Picture of Dorian Gray*.

revising interpretations of the novel's stance on morality and religion.[6] After first outlining some of Wilde's ideas about reading and readers, this chapter offers a close analysis of the novel, ending with a Hegelian reading of the novel's climactic scene.

It makes sense that both Hegelian tragedy and Puritanism influence the structure of *Dorian Gray*, for as Alison Hennegan outlines, the "two literary sources which did most to shape [Wilde] were the pagan writings of Ancient Greece and the Authorized Version of the Bible, the translation commanded by King James VI" (216–17). Wilde was always interested in the "apparent conflict between pagan Greek and Christian values" (Hennegan 217), as well as in the "various models of tragedy" (230). Wilde is also concerned for the effects of reading in all of his writings. *A Picture of Dorian Gray* is fundamentally interested in the same things as Puritan hermeneutics is: the moral formation that might occur while reading, the aesthetic (or spiritual or "ethical") experience of reading, and the relation between the two. In fact, I believe Wilde's only novel is in essence an exploration of Puritan hermeneutical principles. The text is centrally concerned with the legacy of Puritan "guilt culture," its idea of an inner conscience and truth, and its theory of typological reading. It is also concerned with how, in late-nineteenth-century England, these elements of "guilt culture" have fragmented to become the shambles of a "shame culture." In the juxtaposition of the two Dorians—the picture of Dorian and the living Dorian—the novel pits Puritanism against its aestheticist dismantling. This framework of opposing the "Puritan" to the "dandy" is one Wilde also uses in his comedic plays.[7] In *Dorian Gray*, this juxtaposition allows readers to explore the proper relation of the moral to the aesthetic. Because Wilde consciously places this juxtaposition in a tragic form in the novel, he implies, as did the Hegelian theory of Greek tragedy on which he relied, that both his society and the novel were facing a moral and spiritual crisis point.

Like the majority of educated Victorians, Wilde studied the Bible early in his education. At his first boarding school, Portora Royal, an English Protestant school about one hundred miles from Dublin, students were expected to know the King James Version of the Bible "almost by

---

6. To my knowledge no one has linked the novel to Hegel's theory of tragedy.

7. See Rodney Shewan, *Oscar Wilde: Art and Egoism* (London: Macmillan, 1977). Shewan connects Wilde's interest in what he vaguely calls Hegel's "system of contraries" to such juxtapositions of the dandy and the Puritan in the plays, concluding that Wilde's position is an "all-inclusive" pluralism. This chapter's more detailed reading of *Dorian Gray* in light of Hegel's theory of tragedy argues against a pluralist reading of the novel.

heart." Wilde won a prize for scripture studies (Wright 47). This biblical knowledge clearly stayed with him throughout his life and informed all of his writing. As Patrick O'Malley puts it, in *The Picture of Dorian Gray,* as with "all the genres that Wilde produced," there is a "recurrent—and overt—obsession with the fundamental questions of theology and scriptural representation" (168). Wright concurs, reminding readers that Wilde's writings are "saturated with stories, themes, and phrases from the King James Bible" (47). Because Wilde is fundamentally concerned for the relation between art and life in many of his writings, it seems he must have been exposed to the late-nineteenth-century Nonconformist discussions about novel-reading, Bible-reading, and moral character formation outlined in the previous chapter. Yet one can also imagine that these debates irked him at some level. Wilde was not raised with much parental concern for character formation, which was considered to be an English tendency, not an Irish one. His parents were both of the well-educated, English-speaking, Protestant Anglo-Irish elite, which meant their families had originally settled in Ireland generations earlier and had played a dominant role in Ireland ever since. Despite this, Wilde's parents were both staunch Irish nationalists and tried to distance themselves from English culture. They studied Ireland's native oral traditions and were fascinated by Irish folk Catholicism. Wilde's mother even had him baptized twice, once Protestant and once Catholic. The family constantly had groups of intellectuals in their house and were not afraid to discuss ideas from the Continent, especially from France and Germany. Although he was loosely raised Protestant, Wilde was allowed to read all kinds of things as a boy, and according to Wright, was "spared the religious fare that formed the staple diet of many English children" (43). Despite this, however, Wilde was also familiar with the typical moral handbooks and stories that Puritan parents would have given their children; later on he even had some of these on his shelves for his own children as well as many "quintessentially Victorian volumes" (Wright 137).

Even though he plays with and ironizes the effects of Puritan reading, Wilde views the process of reading in much the same way Puritans did. Throughout his life, Wilde was a passionate reader of all kinds of texts, and as Wright outlines, he had almost every book imaginable in his library. Wright argues that Wilde "did not so much discover as create himself through his reading: he was a man who built himself out of books," letting books change the type of character he was at different stages of his life (5). Wilde's passion for problematizing and playing with the relation of life and art is at root an exploration of Puritan reading and the relationship of text and reader, and it informs all of his writing. In "The Decay of Lying," for example, Vivian argues that: "life imitates art far more than art imitates life. . . . Life holds the mirror up to art, and either reproduces some strange type imagined by a painter or sculptor, or realizes in fact what has been dreamed of in fiction" (666). In *De Profundis* Wilde suggests that "at every single moment of one's life one is what one is going to be no less than what one has been. Art is a symbol, because man is a symbol" (64). In this text, Wilde elevates Christ as an "artist" who can negotiate the moral and the ethical: Christ "felt that life was changeful, fluid, active, and that to allow it to be stereotyped into any form was death" (87). For Wilde, human life is a process of developing types, images, and identities that form themselves fluidly in the negotiations between readers and texts and that move and change as life moves in a narrative.

This idea of a fluid self instead of a fixed self is not contrary to Puritan reading, for the whole point of reading the Bible for the Puritans is to move and change as one draws closer to God and to imitating Christ, living in the now while at the same time aiming for the not yet. Significantly, many critics also discuss Wilde's writings as spiritually and morally formative for readers even if they neglect to make connections to historical Bible-reading practices. For example, Frederick S. Roden says he will not apologize for "suggesting such a moral Wilde" and for seeing Wilde's texts as having spiritual purposes for the reader. He sees *De Profundis,* for example, as "invit[ing] the reader to experience death and potential resurrection for her- or himself" ("Introduction" 1). Allison Pease argues that Wilde's texts lead readers to "self-realization" and, as Wilde saw Jesus doing, helping others to develop their personalities (108). John Albert even urges readers to consider Wilde's writings as "material for the monastic exercise of *lectio* that leads to meditation, prayer, and contemplation" (241).

Experimenting with Puritan hermeneutics, the spiritual and moral relation of reader to text, life to art, is foundational in Wilde's thought.[8] He is not afraid to question typology, however, or to test the basic ideas upon which it rests. *Dorian Gray* puts into tension two dominant strains of thought in Wilde's day: Puritan social morality and reading practices, which are seen to emphasize moral character formation; and decadence or aestheticism, which stresses a sort of aesthetic experience that is

---

8. Individual Bible-reading became extremely important to Wilde during his days in prison. According to Killeen, "Wilde fell back on sole consumption of the King James Bible. This dependence on *sola scriptura* faith led him further along the road toward liberal Protestant thought than he had ever ventured before" (162).

presumably detached from the concerns of morality. In many ways, these ideologies shape Dorian's contradictory wills and his spiritual and moral trajectory.

Fundamentally, *The Picture of Dorian Gray* plays with the conversion plot of false to true self, type to antitype. In this plot, however, God does not create and reveal Dorian Gray's "true self"; rather, two human creators, Basil Hallward and Lord Henry Wotten, create not one true self but two "true selves" of Dorian Gray. The novel is about Dorian's struggle to know which is "the real Dorian" (45). Basil Hallward claims to capture the "real Dorian" in his portrait of him, and in fact, tells Dorian and Lord Henry that the painting is more real than the version of Dorian that Henry is creating (45). Henry also believes the living Dorian he creates is the "real Dorian Gray" (43).

Both Basil and Lord Henry acknowledge their roles as creators, and ironically, both see themselves infusing their own souls into Dorian. Basil retains moral concerns about this process: he will not sell or display the painting because he is worried he has revealed too much of his own soul therein, and later in the novel, he confesses to what he calls his "idolatry" of Dorian, seeking remission of sorts for his adoration of him.[9] Henry, on the other hand, believes that to "influence" or create a person is immoral, but he does it anyway. Henry argues that "to influence a person is to give him one's own soul" such that all of that person's sins, passions, virtues, and thoughts become borrowed and are not his own (34). Despite this stance, Henry directs Dorian's plot, even vowing "to dominate him" (52). He openly admits that "to a large extent the lad was his own creation" (72), and that he essentially uses him to perform an "experiment" (73). Dorian's two true selves, then, are made in the image of his two creators.

Dorian feels Henry more than Basil identifies most powerfully his true self. His first encounter with Henry is narrated in dramatic terms of self-discovery: Dorian wonders "why it had been left to a stranger to reveal him to himself" (38), and Henry states that "the moment I met you I saw that you were quite unconscious of what you really are" (39). Aristotelian-like, Henry believes "the aim of life is self-development. To realize one's nature perfectly," so he consciously makes efforts to "influence" and guide Dorian into developing into his true self. Dorian to Henry is a

---

9. The 1890 first edition of the story contained much more explicit homoerotic suggestions regarding Basil's relationship with Dorian during the painting of the portrait. Wilde removed these for the 1891 edition. For more on the differences between the two texts, see Joseph Bristow's introduction to third volume of the Oxford University Press's *The Complete Works of Oscar Wilde* (2005).

"marvelous type," or "could be fashioned into a marvelous type, at any rate" (52). Henry's words about youthfulness and beauty strike Dorian's soul to the core in what is described as a dramatic conversion moment: "the full reality of the description flashed across him" (41), and "a sharp pang of pain struck through him like a knife and made each delicate fiber of his nature quiver" (42). At this point, Dorian prays his body will remain forever young and that the painting instead will show the effects of time. This prayer, which seems to come true, is much like the pact Christopher Marlowe's Faustus makes with Mephistopheles and links the novel to the Faustian tragic tradition as well.

Both Basil and Henry refer to the "soul" and see their creation of Dorian as a new type of human being united in materiality and spirit. Basil feels Dorian has inspired in him a new modality of art, one that recovers the "harmony of soul and body" in an age where "in our madness we have separated the two, and have invented a realism that is vulgar, an ideality that is void" (28). Henry also believes the Dorian he creates will unite matter and spirit: "Nothing can cure the soul but the senses, just as nothing can cure the senses but the soul" (37). While both use the term "soul," Basil and Henry have different views of the "conscience." Basil's idea of the "soul" retains the Puritan idea of an inner truth or moral conscience, while Henry's reunion of body and soul produces a uniform, singular entity that is not separable nor gradated by depth.

This quest to reunite matter and spirit is a common one for many late-Victorian aesthetes and early modernists, and it arises as a response to the sort of moral judgment that is seen to dominate late-nineteenth-century British culture, to separate body and soul, and is often labeled "Puritan." This tension is narrated often in terms of "asceticism" and "aestheticism," which are also terms Henry and Dorian use. In late-nineteenth-century discourse, both words are generalized into vague umbrella concepts. The "ascetic" is associated with the moral and with anything that restricts the body such that human fulfillment is thought to be hindered or repressed and drawn into an empty realm of abstraction. The "aesthetic" transcends both moral consequences and the consequent hindering of bodily life. However, despite the notion that the "aesthetic" transcends the "ascetic," aesthetic experience is narrated as involving a return of the soul to the body in order that a fuller presence or immanence in the world is possible. The "aesthetic," in other words, provides a rich spiritual experience in which one comes to embody one's self more authentically, more freely, more naturally, and in a more unified way than the disciplinary effects of asceticism could ever allow. Wilde's use of the terms is part of a wider discourse in the late nineteenth century, and many across Europe speak in these same terms of the ascetic and the aesthetic. Wilde was particularly enthralled with and shaped by Walter Pater's *The Renaissance,* perhaps the quintessential English aestheticist text, and he often publically proclaimed his allegiance to aestheticism. His novel shows, however, that aestheticism and asceticism are much more complicated than merely being two mutually exclusive options.

Both Lord Henry and Dorian tie the ascetic to Puritanism. For example, Dorian thinks of his self-development as "a new Hedonism, that was to recreate life and to save it from that harsh, uncomely Puritanism that is having . . . a curious revival" (143). He views the philosophy of "experience itself" as having nothing to do with that "asceticism" that "deadens the senses" (143). Dorian and Henry see their aestheticist theory, in contrast, as promoting a "new spirituality" for the modern age (143). Aesthetic experience in their sense, then, is "spiritual," and being "aesthetic" is the way in which Henry and Dorian practice a "religion."[10] Their use of the word "aesthetic" is akin to the term "ethical" in this book, although not equivalent entirely. I argue that the aesthetes were generally not interested in a formal theory of beauty or philosophical aesthetics, but rather in a certain type of experience. This experience of aesthetic discernment and unity was also often thought to embody a higher "ethics." Several have argued that this is what Wilde promoted: an aestheticist higher ethics. Pease, for example, argues that even though Wilde maintains often that art and morality are distinct, in actuality ethics for Wilde are "bound up in the idea of individual becoming, a process that is dependent on aesthetic consciousness. To be aesthetically conscious, to contemplate, is to act ethically" (112).[11] This sounds quite similar to how the New Ethical critics see the ethical. To them, the experience of interpretive difficulty, of unknowability, involves some sort of aesthetic contemplation. Unlike the New Ethical theorists, however, Lord Henry never maintains a concern for others or for the limits of his own understanding and knowledge. The aestheticist higher ethics for Henry is non-communal and solipsistic.

This novel is a good example of how the terms "aesthetic" and "ethical" might overlap in meaning and connotation. While Henry's aestheticism has some elements of the "ethical" (in the terms of this book) in that

---

10. Pericles Lewis argues in *Religious Experience and the Modernist Novel* that modernist novelists develop a form of spirituality he calls the "secular sacred."

11. For a similar argument about the ethical and the aesthetic in Wilde, see Benjamin Smith, "The Ethics of Man under Aestheticism," *Irish Studies Review* 13:3 (2005): 317–23.

he purports to exist outside the norms of social morality, generally the "aesthetic" for Henry and Dorian is not about trying to understand or accept others or to recognize the self's limits. As this chapter shows, Wilde judges and rejects this failure of aestheticism. Because Henry's term "aesthetic" is not entirely equivalent to what this book calls the "ethical," I will continue to use "aesthetic" to refer to Lord Henry's theories and to the experiences of his "Dorian," keeping in mind the similarities in the two formulations. The novel contrasts Henry's aestheticized Dorian with Basil's moral Dorian, producing a dialectic parallel to the larger novelistic narrative's dialectic of the ethical and the moral.

In the two "true" Dorians Wilde pits a painting against a living reality, but Wilde ironically reverses the functions one might normally attribute to painting and to narrative. Paintings in the late 1800s are beginning to be discussed in terms of the "significant form" they capture, the "aesthetic emotion" they invoke in the viewer, and the sense of presence they achieve, capturing a spiritual realm in material form in a manner that is normally not accessible to the inhabitant of modernity.[12] Paintings are still, an image not bound to the movement of time. In Wilde's novel, however, Basil's painting takes on a function normally attributable to the novel and to narrative; instead of capturing eternally an unchanging image of Dorian, the painting develops and changes as time passes. It does what narratives do in capturing the moral and social trajectory of a person. In this sense, the painting is like the typological reader of a novel, with the novel being Dorian's life. Embodying the moral conscience of its creator, Basil, the painting identifies with Dorian's "true moral self" and transforms itself accordingly. In turn, Dorian in his real life, at least for a while, becomes like a painting and does not change over time or develop. He remains the same outwardly, young and beautiful, a captured image in which others fail to detect signs of change. Dorian supposedly achieves the experience of living without any typical moral concerns and this "true aesthetic self" reflects Henry's aestheticist stance. In this reversal, the painting, which is more like the reader of a narrative, imitates the living Dorian, who is more like a painting, and art imitates life such that it is difficult to tell which is more real. So why does Wilde reverse the normal functions associated with painting and with narrative? Why have the painting reveal a moral self that changes over time and the living Dorian a static aesthetic self?

---

12. See the writings of Walter Pater, Bernard Berenson, and Roger Fry for examples of English and American art historians who develop similar ideas in this period.

What is at stake in Wilde's pairing of the two Dorians is the epistemological, ontological, and ethical nature of the self upon which Puritan reading is based. Basil and the painting retain something like the Puritan function of art by which the self can see his own inner nature revealed in the narrative, although it reverses the positions of subject and object. Dorian's social body, on the other hand, reflects Henry's aesthetics, which are founded merely upon a dismantling of Puritan hermeneutics. In pitting Puritanism against that which escapes it but exchanging the functions of narrative and painting, Wilde is not just presenting a playful game, although it always does seem to be that in part. Rather, the contrasts and reversals highlight the hermeneutical concepts Wilde examines and cause the reader to engage actively and rationally with those concepts. Does art shape the reader or viewer morally and spiritually (ethically)? How? What is the efficacy of Puritan hermeneutics (Basil) and of its aestheticist dismantling (Henry)? Although the novel might seem at first to be a harsh attack on Puritanism or Christianity, in the end, neither the Puritan nor the aestheticist view is able to encompass Dorian's "true self" on its own. Before arguing that idea, however, and looking at the climactic scenes of the novel, I first examine in more detail the nature of Dorian's two selves—the aesthetic self and the moral self.

Dorian's aesthetic self at first seems to embody his creator's (Henry's) ideas. Significantly, Henry sees England governed by two forces which he sees as hopelessly intertwined but about which he can speak separately: "the terror of society, which is the basis of morals, the terror of God, which is the secret of religion" (35). To use Benedict's terms, Henry sees England governed by a mix of "shame culture" (social morality) and "guilt culture" (religion). Unlike the Puritan ideal in which social morality and Christian spirituality are perfectly confluent, in Henry's late-Victorian England, morality and religion are seen as influencing each other but as discursively separable from one another. Henry labels these moral and religious forces at various times "Puritan," "modern" (29), "medieval" (35, 93), and "middle class" (123). Henry speaks often of the separability of social-moral categories from "reality," and in fact, he does not see value in any categories. All concepts of virtue, faith, and morality are not real to him because they are merely theoretical: "It is in the brain, and in the brain only, that the great sins of the world take place" (35). In a very Nietzschean-like statement, with whom Wilde may have been familiar through his mother's studies, the concept of sin for Henry causes humanity to become sick, for any impulse having to be "strangled" simply "broods in the mind and poisons us," hindering humans from a fulfilled life (35).[13] Henry sees all classes preaching the importance of virtue but seeing no necessity for it in their own lives (30). In these statements and others, Henry reacts against the ways in which both morality and religion abstract life into an empty realm of concepts, ideas, and spirit, which then regulate the body such that its freedom is contained and its desires disciplined. Such extraction and regulation, both in religion and in social morality, are associated by Henry with Puritanism.[14]

Henry's views, however exaggerated or inaccurate, reflect a wider dissatisfaction present in Wilde's era. What once seemed a coherent view of the world for early modern Puritans by the late nineteenth century seems fragmented at best, to some inefficacious, inauthentic, even dangerous. Following in the wake of Newman and Arnold, aestheticist and modernist responses in art and literature that highlight aesthetic-ethical experience over moral judgment often express deep discontent with modern social morality and its shallow typecasting practices. Wilde's novel seems unique, however, because it is entirely self-conscious of the tension between Puritan hermeneutics and its ironic dismantling, and it presents a plot in which Dorian's two selves embody and dramatize this tension, highlighting the idea that both modern morality and the novel are at a crisis point.

The inauthenticity and emptiness of the modern social-moral discourse that "Puritans" uphold is in part what Wilde's character, Henry, is reacting against when he says things like: "Modern morality consists in accepting the standards of one's age. I consider that for any man of culture to accept the standard of his age is a form of the grossest immorality" (92). Through Henry, Wilde's novel exposes the ways in which the social-moral discourse has become abstracted from the idea of a real inner moral conscience ("guilt culture") to become merely a hypocritical social and moral typecasting ("shame culture"). Of course, Henry rejects *both* the ideas of Puritan guilt culture (conscience, sin, moral absolutes) *and* the practices of his society's shame culture. It is important to remember that Henry's is only one possible response (and not Wilde's) to the state of modern morality as he rejects all things moral *and* religious in favor of the aesthetic.

---

13. Wright suggests that Wilde's mother, Speranza, read many continental philosophers in their original languages and thus was probably familiar with Nietzsche (96). See also Thomas Mann, "Wilde and Nietzsche," in *Oscar Wilde: A Collection of Critical Essays,* ed. Richard Ellmann (Englewood Cliffs: Prentice Hall, 1969).

14. Wilde is influenced by both John Ruskin and Walter Pater, and in many ways, one could trace the ideas of both teachers on Wilde's thought.

Another way in which Henry dismantles Puritanism is in his refusal to believe in the idea of "character formation" upon which it is based. The human soul needs no refining or transformation through conversion. Life's experiences, to Henry, "have no ethical value":

> Experience was merely the name men gave to their mistakes. Moralists, had, as a rule, regarded it as a mode of warning, had claimed for it a certain ethical efficacy in the formation of character, had praised it as something that taught us what to follow and showed us what to avoid. But there was no motive power in experience. It was as little of an active cause as conscience itself. (73)

These remnants of Puritan guilt culture that Henry links to English social morality—virtue, sin, character formation, the conscience, learning through experience and reading, and moral lessons—are also the typical concerns of the English novel tradition which Wilde consciously enters but has his character, Henry, attack almost outrageously. At several points, Henry bashes the tradition for its moral concerns, saying for example: "Of all the people of the world the English have the least sense of the beauty of literature" (58). English novels adhere to "medieval emotions" (93) as they explore concepts of virtue and vice through their "vulgar realism" (206). Reading an English novel is like going out on the town at too early an hour (70). In these statements Henry echoes many of Wilde's thoughts about English fiction, which he felt was poorly written, too moralistic, too middle class, and an embarrassment. Yet while Henry's life seems to be formed only by its rebellion against and supposed escape from English social morality and Puritan religion, we should not necessarily believe he reflects Wilde's position. Henry is an extreme sovereign subject who wills his views onto others and who believes an escape from the Puritan influences in society is entirely possible.

Henry also consciously inverts the ontology and epistemology of typological moral judgment. In biblical typology, as one reads the narrative and in turn allows the reading process to read the self, surface clues reveal deep truths about the characters one is reading about as well as about the self—one's true nature lies deep within, but the surface provides evidence as to this nature. To Henry, in contrast, people who attempt to "look deeply" are really quite "shallow," for to him there is no mysterious inner moral and spiritual reality to be discerned (39). Instead, Henry calls for aesthetic judgment of the surface: "It is only shallow people who do not judge by appearances. The true mystery of the world is the visible, not the invisible" (39). For Henry there is no need in society for moral judgment. "One's own life, that is the important thing. As for the lives of one's neighbors, if one wishes to be a prig or Puritan, one can flaunt one's moral views about them, but they are not one's concern. Besides, individualism really has the higher aim" (92). The only judgments that should be made are of surface beauty, which reflects soul and body in unison. Any identification that assumes there is a separate deep reality or conscience that can be discerned based on surface clues automatically limits human potential because according to Henry "to define is to limit" (207).

Henry cites both "Nature" and the "Hellenic ideal" (35) as the foundation for his approach to life, reflecting the influence of Walter Pater and others involved in Victorian Hellenism. The "aesthetic self" involves a perfect union of senses and spirit, body and soul; an immanent presence in the world; a "harmony with one's self" that is authentic (92); an individualistic fulfillment of the self without regard to one's neighbors. This aesthetic state is for Henry and Dorian a spiritual state of human flourishing. In an argument with Basil, Henry claims that pleasure and beauty are the highest goods: "When we are happy, we are always good, but when we are good, we are not always happy" (92). Living aesthetically opens up the limits of Puritan morality in both its "guilt" and "shame" culture forms, and this opening of the categories to achieve immanence is itself seen to be a superior ethical and spiritual position because it restores man to his natural state and to his fullest possibilities. Henry strives after the same sort of experience outside categories and limits that the new ethical theorist does, but without the latter's concern for the "Other" or for his own limitations. To Henry, the individual self is the measure of all things, the sole interpreter of self and truth, the sovereign.

To summarize so far, Henry's "aesthetic self" emerges in the dismantling of the Puritan idea of the self. Ontologically, Henry denies that there is a deep and essential true self that struggles to emerge from false senses of self. Instead, he sees no separation of body and soul, materiality and spirituality, surface and depth. As Dorian reflects later: "those who conceive the ego in man as a thing simple, permanent, reliable, and of one essence" demonstrate only a "shallow psychology" (155). Instead, following Pater, "man was a being with myriad lives and myriad sensations, a complex multiform creature that bore within itself strange legacies of thought and passion, and whose very flesh was tainted with the monstrous maladies of the dead" (155). Historical traditions and legacies of thought bear themselves out in the flesh, shaping man and limiting his body and hence his soul in a myriad of ways. The goal for Henry is to be free of such limitations, to recover one's natural and essential presence in the world in which body and soul are unified, never allowing any one narrative, theory, or set of categories (limits) regarding human identity to regulate that union. Epistemologically, Puritan typology relies on physical or outer signs to identify the nature or status of the soul, to read the depths of the true self. People have "characters" that can be identified and known, at least in part, but ultimately only fully by God. Henry, in contrast, believes there is only surface, no depth, and hence only aesthetic judgment can be performed. Morally, in Puritan typology the human soul needs constant refining over time, and hence reading and experience, with God's help and with proper self-reflection, can aid in the development of one's character or true self. Henry, in contrast, does not believe in the ideas of "character" and "character formation" and hence simply seeks experience for itself, not for some other end.

Despite his outspokenness, Henry's position is ironically subverted within the text. Dorian the beautiful painting who walks the streets of London himself becomes a type, and the aestheticist stance that dismantles Puritan typology and stresses the aesthetic to the detriment of the moral is revealed to be the very process that creates types and the limits Lord Henry is so desperate to escape. Dorian becomes more his "true self" through typological reading of a sacred text, the famous "yellow book," and Henry's aestheticizing process is depicted as itself an asceticism learned through typological identification. As Dorian reads the book and lets the book read him, as his real life gradually imitates the life of the main character in the yellow book, one could say Wilde is again merely playing around with one of his favorite themes, the fluid relation between art and life. But more than just play is going on. Wilde is showing us that the fluid relation between art and life—the experience of identification and transformation of the self that occurs in the interaction of reader and text and that in turn shapes our artistic expressions—not only is unavoidable, but also is the same relationship of text and reader involved in Puritan Bible-reading.

It is well-established that Wilde's inspiration for the yellow book is a text by which he himself was fascinated from the French aestheticist and Catholic decadent movement: J. K. Huysmans' 1884 *À Rebours*.[15] Dorian's reading of it begins immediately after he flings away the newspaper report of Sibyl Vane's suicide ("how horribly real ugliness made things!" [137]). Just as Marlowe's Faustus has the deadly sins paraded before him, Dorian

---

15. For more on this text see Guy and Small, and also Schuchard.

finds in the book "the sins of the world" laid out before him (138). The book is described as

> a novel without a plot and with only one character, being, indeed, simply a psychological study of a certain young Parisian who spent his life trying to realize in the nineteenth century all the passions and modes of thought that belonged to every century but his own, . . . [loving equally] those renunciations that men have unwisely called virtue, as much as those natural rebellions that wise men still call sin. (138)

The book draws Dorian into an experience of reverie, simultaneously mystical and lurid, such that "one hardly knew at times whether one was reading the spiritual ecstasies of some medieval saint or the morbid confessions of a modern sinner" (138). It is exactly one of those novels from which some Puritans tried to keep their youth (and it sounds a bit like Briony Tallis's novella in *Atonement*). Moral judgments are impossible to make while reading this book because the typological limitations demarcating sin and mystical ecstasy, virtue and vice, are blurred. On one level, then, Wilde presents Dorian's experience of reading the novel as an ethical experience he has for its own sake—authentic, outside morality and the limits of the self, achieving immanence, restoring spirit to body, a simple "letting be."

Yet Dorian also seems self-consciously aware of the nature of typology, and he reads both the yellow book and history this way intentionally, rationally understanding his transformation into the ultimate antitype. The narrator tells us that for years, Dorian does not free himself from the influence of this book. He buys nine copies of the first edition in Paris and has each bound in a different color, "so that they might suit his various moods and changing fancies" (139). He reads the main character typologically: "The hero, the wonderful Parisian in whom the romantic and scientific temperaments were so strangely blended, became to him a kind of prefiguring type of himself. And, indeed, the whole book seemed to him to contain the story of his own life, written before he had lived it" (139). Despite Henry's rejection of Puritanism, and later his claim that art and books can never actually influence action, Wilde still has his hero "develop" through typological reading. Although his outward appearance does not change, Dorian reforms himself based on his identification with the aesthete character he is reading about. This implies that Henry's view of the self is just as much a type as the Puritan-like types Henry critiques. Ironically, then, aestheticism is merely another form of asceticism:

the aesthetic self is formed or constructed through discourse and practices that also imply boundaries and limitations, and this self, too, although it thinks of itself as amoral, nevertheless implies a moral position. Just as Puritans felt Bible-reading was simultaneously morally and spiritually instructive, so Wilde, despite his playful claims to the contrary in the preface, portrays novel-reading as simultaneously morally and spiritually formative.

Through the influence of the book, Dorian self-consciously reads himself as the antitype or fulfillment of history, both in his own family line and in literature. He loves to walk the halls of portraits in his home, imagining the ancestors depicted there and wondering if "his own actions were merely the dreams that the dead man had not dared to realize?" (155). Dorian also feels he has ancestors in literary history, who are "nearer perhaps in type and temperament" to him than those of his own family (156). Dorian imagines that all of literary history has led to himself, that "in some mysterious way their lives had been his own" (156). The hero of the yellow book also feels this way, and Dorian reads repeatedly those chapters in which the hero identifies with ancient heroes of the past and reflects on all the seemingly "amoral" types of the Renaissance, developing a "horrible fascination" with them all (157–58). The yellow book itself, then, outlines the trajectory of the amoral aesthete as social type and historical category, and although he is aesthetically and imaginatively drawn to the character, Dorian also rationally sees himself becoming its antitype within his present English society. He relishes in maintaining his surface beauty while the painting hidden away in the attic reflects the moral self, such that many in society look to him as "the true realization of a type" of which they themselves had only dreamed (142). He sees himself becoming a model that represents a new "spirituality" for society that would find in the spiritualizing of the senses and the instinct for beauty its "highest realization" (143).

Dorian's typological identification of self with the character in the yellow book is an aesthetic experience because the reading experience allows Dorian to rethink himself as somehow above or outside both guilt culture and shame culture—it is through reading the yellow book that Dorian is able to forget his moral failings in the Sibyl Vane case and even to forget the dead body of Basil in the attic. He becomes the sole interpreter of text and self. Surely Wilde wants his readers to react to this. However much one may be drawn to the sort of experience, freedom, and fulfillment of desire that Dorian supposedly achieves, one also has to judge his escape from morality: murder, causing and then not caring about the suicide of the once-beloved Sibyl, surely these are reprehensible.[16] The novel shows readers that Henry's Dorian is an inefficacious theory of self because it utterly fails to take moral responsibility for its actions in the world. It believes itself to be ethically superior but fails to recognize its own inadequate moral position. In explicitly highlighting the reading process and its effects, Wilde's story suggests that all narratives have an implied morality, no matter how much they attempt to escape it, and all reading, however aesthetic, ethical, or spiritual, implies a moral position and potentially shapes the reader.

On the other hand, Basil and the true self of Dorian in the painting retain their moral functions in Dorian's life. Readers may respond negatively at times to their asceticizing effects on Dorian or to the lack of agency Basil and the painting exhibit, but they should also be relieved there are some forces in the novel that still judge and seek accountability for moral and social behavior. The painting performs a narrative typological function—it marks the life and time of Dorian, increasing in its horrors with the weight of events and revealing what experience does to Dorian's moral and spiritual nature. Basil, too, although initially overcome by Dorian's beauty, is and remains a moral agent. When Henry spouts that pleasure is the highest good, Basil raises questions about moral consequences that Henry then labels medieval: "But surely, if one lives merely for one's self, Harry, one pays a terrible price for doing so?" (92). Basil goes on to discuss things such as remorse, suffering, and the "consciousness of degradation" which might accompany the narcissistic pursuit of pleasure (93). Unlike Henry, Basil approves of Dorian's love interest in Sibyl Vane, and later, after she commits suicide, Basil challenges Dorian on moral grounds for his role in the affair. Basil also confesses his "idolatry" of Dorian that had occurred during the painting of the portrait. Yet in the end Basil's Dorian is also an inefficacious theory of the self because it is unable to take action in the world: even though it retains

---

16. The reader perhaps notes by now the conspicuous absence of any discussion of sexuality or sexual desire in this chapter. Clearly this was one of the moral issues with which Wilde played in the novel, which generated controversy about the novel, and which has recently been a dominant topic in Wilde scholarship. Surely part of Wilde's concern *is* the moral judgment made on same-sex desire by his "Puritan" society, yet at the same time, the aestheticized sexuality alluded to in the novel is bound up with Dorian's other immoral actions, making it difficult to determine what, if anything, Wilde was implying. My intent here is not to draw a conclusion about Wilde and this topic. Those who wish for more can perhaps work further with the general conclusions drawn at the end of the essay regarding typological hermeneutics. In any case, the murder of Basil, the suicide of Sibyl, and Dorian's general lack of care for others seem to me to be the events of the novel that Wilde sets up to evoke universal moral condemnation when judging Dorian's "aesthetic self."

a moral function, the painting remains passive and alone in the attic, unavailable to others for viewing, judgment, or interaction. It acts like the reader of a narrative, but it cannot escape its position as a stationary piece of art.

The climactic chapters of the novel pit the two selves of Dorian against each other over the exact issues of Puritan moral judgment and epistemology. Gradually, fears infiltrate Dorian's existence, such that his modes of "forgetfulness" allow "the great fear that seemed to him at times almost too great to be borne" to seep in (152). When Dorian's secret life has reached its darkest depths, Basil stops in to confront Dorian over the rumors he has heard and to express his disappointment in the course Dorian's life has taken. At first, Basil can not believe the rumors because he does not detect anything in Dorian's appearance: "I can't believe them when I see you. Sin is a thing that writes itself across a man's face. It cannot be concealed. People talk sometimes of secret vices. There are no such things" (158). Basil believes one can read people's faces and bodies and identify clues as to a person's inner moral and spiritual state, and that this is crucial in identifying and formulating moral judgments: "If a wretched man has a vice, it shows itself in the lines of his mouth, the droop of his eyelids, the moulding of his hands, even" (158). He admits, however, that he does not know Dorian fully: "I wonder do I know you? Before I could answer that I should have to see your soul" (164). Immediately he adds, but "only God can do that" (164). When Dorian shows him the painting, Basil receives information he thought reserved for God, and his theory is shown to be true—one's moral state is revealed in the body. Basil believes that "the foulness and horror [of the painting] had come from within" and not from the paint he had applied (170). The painting has a deep spiritual self that reveals itself in the surface, and the surface provides evidence of the inner self's state. After this revelation, Basil judges Dorian on moral grounds, but he also offers redemption, pleading with Dorian to pray, to confess, to seek cleansing (170). Dorian, however, believes it is too late, does not believe the words of scripture, and in a fitful rage, murders Basil.

The painting, which reveals Dorian's moral self, acts like a narrative, the genre by which Puritan hermeneutics operates. There is a narrative according to which Basil makes his moral judgments and by which they are viewed as the truth, yet this narrative allows for movement in time. In this sense of biblical narrative, one is never locked into a type for one can always convert or turn, with God's help, from one's previous self. Based on a communal tradition and narrative larger than the self, one can always imagine new possibilities for one's own story with the help of the Holy Spirit and the sacred text. Dorian thinks of himself as a type, however, and this prevents him from undergoing any change, despite Basil's encouragement that it is possible. Henry's aestheticism locks Dorian into one theory of how the self may be fulfilled and allows no room for alteration. In this way, the painting, which reflects the moral self that many in the nineteenth century link to the stiffening, deadening effects of Puritanism, actually retains the narrative context within which Puritan typology was ideally originally practiced, a context allowing for judgment but also for change, seeing the human subject both in the "now and the not yet." The living Dorian is like an unchanging painting and is associated with aesthetic experience and ethical freedom. This "true self" is ironically revealed to be the product of that process which creates the types and limitations from which escape is supposedly needed. Ironically, aestheticism is a narrow vision that thinks it has the "one thing needful," to echo Arnold, yet it fails to perceive its own limitations. It even seems to be more "Protestant" in Newman's sense than Puritanism is.

After the murder of Basil, the struggle among Dorian's two selves intensifies. The canvas "sweats blood" and becomes more horrifying, giving Dorian a longing to convert to what he calls his "good self" (220). Dorian challenges Henry on some of his ideological positions, and in a moment of desperation Dorian confesses to Basil's murder. Henry, however, who has rejected all forms of Puritan ontology and epistemology, does not know how to read Dorian's moral character at all: "I would say, dear fellow, that you were posing for a character that doesn't suit you" (223). He does not believe that someone as beautiful as Dorian could commit a crime (224). Henry thinks Dorian has remained "the same" and continues to be the "the perfect type": "you are the type of what the age is searching for, and what it is afraid it has found. I am so glad you have never done anything, never carved a statue, or painted a picture, or produced anything outside yourself! Life has been your art. You have set yourself to music. Your days are your sonnets" (227). Dorian believes the yellow book poisoned him, and he begs Henry never to give it to anyone else, but Henry denies the power of any book to do such a thing: "Art has no influence upon action. It annihilates the desire to act. . . . The books that the world calls immoral are the books that show the world its own shame" (228). Henry's inability or unwillingness to participate in any moral judgment makes him culpable in evil: his influence helps lead to the deaths of three people and the demise of countless others whom Dorian has influenced. Because he fails to see how his creation of Dorian as an aesthetic self is itself a limiting typological identity, Henry is unable to discern Dorian's true moral and spiritual nature as murderer. The aesthetic type implies a moral stance in the world of life, whether Henry sees it or not. The aesthetic type believes it is has achieved a higher ethical freedom, but that freedom is a fiction.

Henry also seems to remain oblivious to the manner in which his dismantling of Puritan hermeneutics reinforces the very processes he reacts against. The aesthetic experience he wants Dorian to embody involves the creation of the self into the antitype of the new spirituality and is the very process that creates limits and lasting images of a person. It isn't the Puritan moral conscience that does this; it is the moral deformation that occurs in aesthetic experience that does this, a process that is not simply an imaginative experience of letting be but also involves rational judgment. In Henry's Dorian, the novel highlights the inseparability of the aesthetic (or ethical) from the moral and the inseparability of aesthetic experience from rational activity. In Basil's Dorian, the novel exposes as false the perception that Puritan guilt culture is the source of all limits: Puritan morality instead works within a narrative that allows for change and openness. The aestheticist inversion of that view, ironically, is exposed as the process that creates lasting images and identities. Yet neither position alone is satisfying, for the painting retains its moral function while unable to act in the world, and the aesthetic subject experiences beauty and pleasure only at the cost of social and moral irresponsibility and criminal activity. Guilt culture is not enough. Shame culture is not enough. And Henry's aestheticist individualism is also not enough. Wilde's novel critiques equally Victorian aestheticism and Puritan social morality, revealing both to be limiting forms of asceticism.

These tensions reach their climax in the ending: an incredible tragic scene. Dorian stabs the painting, but the knife ends up killing his body, which turns old and decrepit, while the painting recovers his youthful beauty. The ending has generated several main lines of interpretation. Some argue the story is a "moral tale" and the dead Dorian whose body now reflects the passing of time and the moral effects of his actions is the real Dorian.[17] Others posit that the story is predominantly aestheticist and hedonist and the young and beautiful Dorian in the painting is the real Dorian, captured eternally in art, the final fulfillment of his desire and potential. Alternatively, others have argued that both are equally

---

17. See Philip K. Cohen, *The Moral Vision of Oscar Wilde* (London: Associated University P, 1978).

valid interpretations left juxtaposed to represent a pluralistic view.[18] As Josephine Guy and Ian Small put it: the novel "integrates" decadent themes into a "conventional morality tale while simultaneously leaving the values of both intact" (173). As they see it, Christian piety opposes aestheticist decadence but in the end does not supersede it (176). Both responses are "simultaneously available to readers" as the novel leaves us in a "morally ambiguous" situation of "moral pluralism" (177). At one level, this line of interpretation seems right: both Dorians do remain juxtaposed in the imagination at novel's end and afterwards. Dorian is both the dead body and the image in the portrait. He is both the static type and that which the type failed to capture, and the mind goes back and forth dialectically between the two, shaping and at the same time disrupting the memory of who he is and was. This dialectical movement to which the reader is led, however, does not leave us in the passive position of accepting or tolerating pluralism. Rather, the ending dramatizes the typological reading process, an active movement: we detect surface clues and try to make rational sense of it all by placing those clues into conceptual categories or types, but with the difficulty of doing this, we also at some level have imaginatively to let the paradox of who Dorian ultimately is, his "unknowability," simply "be." At this ending point of the novel, readers are forced to go back and forth between rational moral judgment that derives from what they currently know and believe, and intuitive "ethical" experience that forces them to recognize their interpretive and epistemological limits.

Examining Wilde's use of Hegelian tragic form helps delineate this dialectical movement of the reader and to challenge Guy and Small's idea of "interpretive plurality." Hennegan argues that for his entire life Wilde was concerned both with Greek and Christian tragedy. We know from Wilde's notebooks how thoroughly he engaged in reading and thinking specifically about the Greek tragic tradition, both its primary texts (e.g., Aeschylus, Sophocles) and its history of interpreters (e.g., Hegel, Schopenhauer). As Smith and Helfand have shown, the notebooks and other writings also reveal Wilde's profound engagement with and reworking of Hegel's thought, especially his philosophy of history and art. Hegel's theory of tragedy, which appears scattered throughout his writings but is seen especially in *The Philosophy of Fine Art,* integrally informs the structure of Wilde's novel.

---

18. Critics who argue for the moral pluralism and hence moral ambiguity of the novel include: Guy and Small; Gillespie ("Ethics"); and also O'Malley.

Mark Roche describes the core structure of Hegel's tragedy as involving the "collision" of "two substantive positions, each of which is justified, yet each of which is wrong to the extent that it fails either to recognize the validity of the other position or to grant it its moment of truth" (12). In Hegel's words, while each opposed side has its "justification," at the same time, each "tends to carry into effect the true and positive content of their end and specific characterization merely as the negation and violation of the other equally legitimate power," and as a consequence, both are condemned (48). In other words, "each stance is constituted through its [negative] relation to the other" (Roche 17). For Hegel, both stances have "their own validity, but a validity which is equalized. It is only the one-sidedness in their claims which justice comes forward to oppose" (325).

Certainly one can see these ideas in the two Dorians Wilde juxtaposes and collides. The Puritan moral self and its aestheticist dismantling in the novel are dialectically dependent on each other, defined against each other. Yet because both positions hold what MacIntyre calls "truth claims," neither one can dominate. This unresolvable collision of two partially valid yet constitutionally related positions can only result in the fall of the hero. Hegel argues that when the two one-sided moral powers "divest themselves of the one-sidedness attaching to the assertion of independent validity, . . . this discarding of the one-sidedness reveals itself outwardly in the fact that the individuals who have aimed at the realization in themselves of a single separate moral power, perish" (Hegel 324–25). Dorian cannot withstand the collision and contradiction of the two one-sided truth claims in himself. Both Dorians are incomplete and thus are false selves.

Yet for Hegel, while "the human result [of tragedy] is death, . . . the absolute end is the reestablishment of ethical substance" (Roche 17). At the end of a Greek tragedy, the conflict is drawn up into the process of history, the spirit of the Absolute. As MacIntyre might put this (MacIntyre's analysis of Sophoclean tragedy in *After Virtue* is essentially Hegelian), in tragedy, particular historical expressions of an objective moral order are such that epistemologically humans cannot access the full reality of that moral order. Instead, different partial narratives "appear as making rival and incompatible claims on us" (143). The only universal moral order considered in this text within which moral truth claims could make sense is the biblical narrative, but as Wilde perceives it in his particular nineteenth-century context, neither the rival claims of aestheticism nor of late-Victorian social morality completely harmonize with or embody fully this narrative. The tragic hero cannot overcome the conflict of two partially true formative narratives to achieve wholeness in himself.

The challenge, then, is left to the reader. The pluralist argument seems like the new ethical theorist's argument. Rather than acknowledging one's incapacity to reconcile rival truths and deeming it impossible to find a rational way to bring the two together, opting instead to simply "let the ending be" in passive appreciation of pluralism and ethical experience, however, the tragic ending calls for the reader to work harder to engage the competing moral truths. Such a reading is consistent with how both Hegel and Wilde thought of catharsis. For Hegel, the catharsis of tragedy takes place in the "consciousness of the audience" as it "recognizes the supremacy of the whole of ethical life and sees it purged of one-sidedness" (Roche 17). Within the experience of tragic drama for Hegel there is a reconciliation in which "definite ends and individuals unite in harmonious action without mutual violation and contradiction" (Hegel 49). Through catharsis or the "annulment of contradictions," the audience gains a sense of the greater moral order and historical process that can draw the collisions of one-sided truth claims into itself (Hegel 71). To Wilde, catharsis is a "spiritualizing" experience, an awakening of the soul to new knowledge (Smith and Helfand 72). The Hegelian tragic form Wilde uses, then, urges the reader to engage dialectically the rival moral claims, to seek reconciliation of what is rightfully authoritative in each set of claims with the guiding hope that an objective order of moral truth exists. The tragic ending thus might be seen as "lyrical" in Charles Altieri's sense, a powerful moment in the text that evokes the *will* of the reader to seek reconciliation and a wider truth, to act upon its new awakening (51).

What MacIntyre calls a "Sophoclean insight" seems also to be a "Wildean insight": "it is through conflict and sometimes only through conflict that we learn what our ends and purposes are" (164). The tragic structure of *Dorian Gray* suggests that in order to recover a valid morality for society, one has to have a narrative by which moral judgments are agreed upon to be true, and Wilde's novel, as so many novels do, still regards the biblical narrative, however fragmented, as the most valid historical possibility. At the same time, the fullness and truth of that narrative and its moral and spiritual order needs to be recovered and revitalized so that it is more viable, open, living, effective, accessible, and responsible in the historical, moral world of action. The Hegelian tragic conflict of the novel reveals that while both late-Victorian Puritan social morality and its aestheticist dismantling are inadequate in and of themselves, each must be granted its "moment of truth" in light of the other. Yet on this point, while Michael Gillespie's claim that the novel calls for an "intellectualism based on a receptiveness to numerous systems of values" seems right, the novel does not simply promote "inclusiveness" or "pluralistic interpretive patterns" (*Poetics* 56, 48). Instead, the dialectical structure rests on the idea that a universal order of truth does exist, and for Wilde and the novel genre, whether ironized or not, this order is grounded in the biblical narrative of history. Truth is thus not endlessly deferred, but must be actively pursued, taking into account the partial truths offered in various historical narratives while pursuing the ultimate truth of the not yet.

While many have interpreted Wilde's own life as an enactment of Dorian's tragedy, implying that he did not achieve a sense of reconciliation in his own soul, his novel implies that the key to reconciling the moral and spiritual truth claims of these colliding views (as well as others) is that the tendency or desire to divide and then oppose the moral to the aesthetic (and to the higher ethics associated with the aesthetic), has to be overcome, for it is a tragic collision. According to this novel, in fact, moral and aesthetic discernment cannot be separated. They do not use different human faculties (both use rationality and imagination), nor do they access separable kinds of knowledge. They work together dialectically in the typological reading of novels, the self, and art, in the inescapable fluid exchanges that shape the self and its views of reality and truth.

The tragic form of Wilde's novel suggests that true moral and spiritual knowledge is something for which humans strive from within the trappings of the historical world, and by which they seek access to a larger process or narrative of moral and spiritual order. The novel also implies that true moral and spiritual knowledge is gained only through some sort of dialectic between 1) moral judgments based upon the interpretation of surface evidence and the placement of that evidence into conceptual categories or types that are agreed upon to be true and thought to be known, and 2) the ability to step away from that process, recognizing one's knowledge as always incomplete, merely to experience the beauty of one's presence, face to face with others, in a world much bigger than the self. In this sense, the moral and the aesthetic/ethical, rationality and imagination, constantly need to be dialectically harmonized. To see them as separate entities or as irreconcilable—as Henry (and much of modernity) did—is very dangerous indeed. To choose one over the other is tragic, but to see the self as passively existing among the two is equally tragic. The fate of the novel and the fate of society, *The Picture of Dorian Gray* implies, both depend on the wills of readers to reconcile actively the ethical (aesthetic) and the moral as they read, experience, and interpret the texts that are art, the texts that are living people, the texts that are themselves, all the while maintaining hope that there exists a moral and spiritual order to the universe.

Wilde's Hegelian ending brings the reader to a point of unknowability but with a hope that a higher order exists and even more importantly, with an imperative that unknowability does not condone passivity in the moral, historical world. This structure is parallel to what typological Bible-reading ideally also does as it engages a self that is both "now and not yet." Puritan Bible-reading was not merely a moral, rational reading of the self, as by the late nineteenth century it was stereotypically identified, but also involved aesthetic faculties and sensibilities.[19] One goal of Bible-reading was intimate and personal spiritual and moral growth and insight, a process that could not occur solely in a rational way, a process always in process, never finished. Ideally, typological Bible-reading involves a dialectical movement between an ethical or spiritual "letting be" as one reads, and a rational consciousness of one's reading experience and self. Identifying with a character, seeing points of contact and surface clues in the text and also in the self involves imagination and intellect, emotional connection and rational judgment, an opening of the self to text that may be unconscious at first but can lead to conscious transformation. The self's dialectical contradictions are repeatedly drawn up into the truth of Christ. To reduce reading to only the moral or only the aesthetic-ethical, especially in stereotypical and exaggerated ways, is to limit the human soul and society's potential. For Puritans, there is a moral and spiritual order to the universe, and Bible-reading reminds the reader of his proper place within this order. Wilde's use of Hegelian tragic form problematizes what is seen to be human knowledge regarding a universal moral and spiritual order within which the reader might place herself; nevertheless, it does not try to escape completely the Christian view. Wilde seems to know that the Puritan narrative is the narrative upon which the novel is built and against which it has always reacted. Yet his novel suggests that the novelistic dialectic of Puritanism and its disman-

---

19. Recent criticism on Wilde tends to oppose Protestantism as a whole to various strands of Catholicism, reducing Protestantism either to a "rationalism" that opposes Catholic decadence, imagination, and aesthetics, or to a "realism" that opposes a Catholic-influenced sense of the fantastic, the ritualistic, the folkloric, the romantic, the Irish. Killeen, for example, tends to overgeneralize Protestantism as emphasizing the "empirical and the rational" in order to contrast it with Catholicism (168). Such oppositions are too narrow, or at best reflect Protestantism's straying in modernity from the fullest senses of Puritan reading practices.

tling, confinement and escape, which assumes the moral and the aesthetic-ethical are mutually exclusive modes of life, is itself a limiting narrative. His novel leaves us at the point of wondering how and whether society and the novel—and even historical Christianity—might become something new.

sance to identify Lucy's movement from her false, Puritan, outer self to her true passionate, natural, inner self.

As a young lady, Lucy is thoroughly formed by the Puritanism of her day, which is narrated as conflicting with her true self. Her sense of reality is often described as muddled and her deep self as obscure: "like most of us, she only faced the situation that encompassed her. She never gazed inwards" (138). A few other characters can detect something of Lucy's true self. Mr. Beebe, the newly appointed local rector for Lucy's parish, glimpses this deep self when Lucy plays Beethoven on the piano in Italy and tells her: "If Miss Honeychurch ever takes to live as she plays, it will be very exciting—both for us and for her" (30). In the diary he keeps while in Italy, Mr. Beebe draws two drawings, one of Lucy as a kite held down by her traveling chaperon and elderly spinster cousin, Charlotte Bartlett; the other of the kite (Lucy) set free. For Mr. Beebe, Lucy's true self can only be found in complete freedom from the reins of others, especially her puritanical cousin. For Mr. Beebe himself, finding freedom has meant celibacy. In contrast, when Mr. Emerson begs Lucy in Santa Croce early in the novel to forge a friendship with his son, George, he feels both will find something of their true selves in their relation with each other:

> You are inclined to get muddled, if I may judge from last night. Let yourself go. Pull out from the depths those thoughts that you do not understand, and spread them out in the sunlight and know the meaning of them. By understanding George you may learn to understand yourself. It will be good for both of you. (25)

It is Mr. Emerson's idea of freedom and selfhood found in union with another, rather than Mr. Beebe's seemingly religious solitude, toward which the novel's plot moves.

For most of the novel Lucy, like Augustine and Crusoe, runs from the true deep self that the narrator constantly hints exists. Four of the last chapter titles begin with the word "Lying" to indicate how much Lucy hides from herself. In one of these chapters the narrator describes Lucy this way:

> She gave up trying to understand herself, and joined the armies of the benighted, who follow neither the heart nor the brain, and march to their destiny by catch-words. The armies are full of pleasant and pious folk. But they have yielded to the only enemy that matters—the enemy within.

They have sinned against passion and truth, and vain will be their strife after virtue. As the years pass, they are censured. Their pleasantry and piety show cracks, their wit becomes cynicism, their unselfishness hypocrisy; they feel and produce discomfort wherever they go. . . . Lucy entered this army when she pretended to George that she did not love him, and pretended to Cecil that she loved no one. The night received her, as it had received Miss Bartlett thirty years before. (170)

Similar to the ways in which Wilde's Lord Henry spoke, although not nearly as harshly, the narrative identifies Charlotte Bartlett as thoroughly imbued with Puritan social morality. Such a person strives after an outer discourse of virtue and piety, while working against her inner self. This "army," found all over England, goes to great lengths to preserve its ideals, hardening into cynical, hypocritical, and difficult people in the process.

In this novel, the typological narrative that will read Lucy's true self and allow her to escape the "night" is no longer founded upon a biblical narrative assumed to be historically true. Rather, it is based on a periodized historical narrative in which the Renaissance, which is seen as historically true, is the prefiguration of the present day. In Forster's text, there is no Bible to pick up and randomly open through which God points out one's true deep self in the reading process. Nonetheless, ironically there *is* a central text by which and through which Lucy reads herself: the romance novel. Like Wilde's *Dorian Gray, A Room with a View* self-referentially plays with the idea of the novel as sacred text, as the means by which Lucy's true self is accessed, read, and formed. The novel relies on the typological structure of the conversion narrative while inverting and even satirizing its ontological basis. The result is that Lucy's conversion leads to a very different sort of true self. Rather than aiming for a truth that is only partially present in the now and is ultimately beyond this world in the not yet, the true self finds its highest and fullest spirituality in the present, material world. Rather than a never-ending and often thwarted quest for moral perfection, the true self in Forster's novel lives ethically in egalitarianism and the body. And rather than aiming for an otherworldly paradise, Forster's true self has a new historical telos that involves an earthly escape from social-moral and religious norms. Forster through Mr. Emerson attempts to create a more acceptable and communal version of the ethical self. His vision is more playful and humorous about Puritanism than Wilde's Lord Henry is. It also maintains concern for others.

A Room with a View was published at the height of an era deemed by some "the cult of the Renaissance." In the wake of Jacob Burckhardt's 1860 *The Civilization of the Renaissance in Italy* and John Addington Symonds's seven-volume *The Renaissance in Italy,* published from 1875 to 1886, many modernist writers began to see themselves as ushering in a new Renaissance and found inspiration in historiography of the Italian Renaissance.[5] The number of texts and historical novels in the late nineteenth century and early twentieth that take up the Renaissance as a topic of inquiry is staggering. The idea of one historical period superseding another inspired the modernists. They often perceived themselves to be escaping from and superseding the Victorian era, much as the Renaissance was narrated as a break from the Middle Ages. In both narratives, from medieval to Renaissance and from Victorian to modern, entire spans of time are assumed to be similar as they are created into historical periods. In both narratives, an old social and moral order shaped by Christianity is assumed to be left behind and surpassed. Yet this idea that an entire age and culture can "secularize," replacing the Christian past, is the great myth of Renaissance historiography. In such narratives, "religion" is not necessarily abandoned, but Christian theology is. Symonds, for example, much like Lord Henry, saw a new modern "spirituality" emerging that would be based on individualism and reason rather than on a sense of Puritan conscience, social morality, and religion. Ethical experience—like the amoral Renaissance types in Dorian's yellow book—becomes the new "religion" or spirituality.

Forster uses typology in his novel not simply because this is how novels are written, nor simply because he inherits and works within a tradition deeply shaped by Puritan hermeneutics and the satirization thereof, both of which he is certainly aware. He also dismantles and makes fun of the Puritan worldview because he wants to see its mode of judging moral character replaced in his own society with a new sense of equality (egalitarianism), tolerance, and sexual ethics.

The structure of the Renaissance myth of secularization—that Christianity or Puritanism can simply be replaced—is typological. Much as the New Testament is seen to be the fulfillment of Old Testament types, the Renaissance is constructed as the period that recovers, fulfills, and perfects the types of antiquity. Similarly, in the early twentieth century the present was commonly narrated as the fulfillment or antitype of the Renaissance type. Ezra Pound admitted to adhering to such supersessionary historiog-

---

5. See Hinojosa.

raphy most blatantly when he proclaimed in 1922: "The Christian era is over, and the Pound era has begun." In the process of typologically relating two separate periods of history, the entire Middle Ages and subsequently the Victorian Age are dismissed as the "dark ages," a threshold that has been passed. In such a historical scheme, the ancient, the medieval, the Renaissance, the Victorian, all become types that can be seen as spiritually fulfilled in people and in places in Forster's novel. Instead of a movement from Old Testament type to a new self found in Christ, Lucy's movement is from the medieval to the Renaissance, from Victorian to modern, and the novel provides coded clues to its readers for interpreting characters and events according to this framework.

The novel associates Italy with the Renaissance and England with the Middle Ages. In the first part of the novel, Lucy begins to gain some insight into her true self while vacationing in Italy with her cousin, Charlotte, but the visit is cut short in order to avoid a scandal over Lucy's kiss with the young George Emerson. When Lucy returns to England, where the second half of the novel takes place, and becomes engaged to Cecil Vyse in a chapter titled "Medieval," the reader knows she is regressing into her false self. Seeing that the last chapter of the novel is titled "The End of the Middle Ages," a reader can predict something of the movement Lucy's story will take. Just as the reader of *Robinson Crusoe* could decode biblical types embedded within the narrative and thereby predict the plot to come, so readers of Forster's novel, who were steeped in the historical narrative of medieval and Renaissance and deeply fascinated with Italy, could detect the narrative clues and make predictions regarding character types and plot.

Lucy's movement from the Middle Ages to the Renaissance and from England to Italy involves a movement from a Puritan ontology and epistemology of judging character to a new ethical egalitarianism and tolerance. Yet while the novel pokes fun at the dominance of social-moral typecasting in English culture, it can not escape the method itself. As the names of his characters humorously reflect—Lucy Honeychurch, Cecil Vyse, Mr. Eager, Mr. Emerson—Forster seems aware that completely escaping such modes of categorization is impossible. Nevertheless, the narration attaches Puritan character typology to England, the Middle Ages, the Victorian era, and Christianity, while it connects the "Renaissance"—the escape from morality—to Italy and the Emersons.

The British propensity to typecast people is highlighted throughout the first half of the novel, which focuses on a number of British tourists who have all by chance taken up temporary residence in the same *pensione* in Florence. In judging and interpreting each other, the British characters rely on multiple typing systems that they perceive on the surface and by which they assume knowledge about who a person is: social class, nationality, gender, political party, religion. For example, when Mr. Emerson offers to give Lucy and Charlotte his rooms that have a view, Charlotte can tell that he is "ill-bred, even before she glanced at him" (4). Even Miss Lavish, the novelist who prides herself on her "originality," typecasts others at times as "commercial travelers," "early Victorians," or British tourists ("The true Italy is only to be found by patient observation," she instructs Lucy) (34). Yet Miss Lavish is herself a type that the novel playfully mocks: the "student of human nature" who seeks to depict the "true Italy" in her novel is herself entirely conventional, never missing a chance to stand up for "Bohemianism" and "adventure."[6] While the British characters typecast the Italians often, the Italians seem to live in a society that does not rely on typecasting.

In many conversations in the first chapters the British characters try to assess Mr. Emerson's character: Is he nice? Is he deplorable or just disagreeable? Is he a socialist? (8). The elderly Miss Alans believe he lacks delicacy but that he does beautiful things, but in the end, the British at the pension do not accept Mr. Emerson because they do not have a framework for understanding him. He seems to resist typological interpretation as he alone "speaks the truth" (8). Most of the British characters are depicted as failing to see the true selves of other people; they may detect vague hints, but they tend to make hasty character judgments and value rankings based on surface codes of behavior, appearance, and language. In this novel, character typology or Puritan social morality is of the "false self," a hermeneutics of the surface. The "true self" is something deeper, more essential, than any typology can capture. Such a view dismantles Puritan ontology and epistemology.

Such typecasting and value judgments are associated with the medieval. Curiously, even though he tries to be a sort of modern aesthete or dandy, Cecil Vyse is coded as medieval:

> Like a Gothic statue. Tall and refined, . . . he resembled those fastidious saints who guard the portals of a French cathedral. Well educated, well endowed, and not deficient physically, he remained in the grip of a

---

6. In the last decades of the nineteenth century and the first of the twentieth, historical fiction and romance novels such as Miss Lavish writes were extremely popular. Many of these were set in Italy and were written by female authors. Forster is in part poking fun at this trend.

certain devil whom the modern world knows as self-consciousness, and whom the medieval, with dimmer vision, worshipped as asceticism. A Gothic statue implies celibacy, just as a Greek statue implies fruition. (85)

Cecil is medieval and ascetic because he seems removed from his own body and because he fervently tries to forge himself to be a certain type of person, thereby submitting himself to a limited definition of what a human can be. He fancies himself an "Inglese Italianato," a self-proclaimed aesthete who defies the conventions of British society, especially Lucy's family and the surrounding country gentility. Yet in his quest to be a certain type, Cecil constantly makes negative judgments and insolent comments about and to others, judging them by their furniture, music, or hobbies, by the types of gatherings they hold, or by how they pronounce the names of Italian painters. He tries "to affect a cosmopolitan naughtiness which he was far from possessing," and which even Lucy sees as silly when applied to one who has spent the winter vacationing with his mother. Cecil constantly fashions himself, but he is of the surface only, and he completely lacks the inner freedom and physicality of the Renaissance type he strives to be. Instead of embodying new Renaissance values and amoral experience, then, he utterly fails to live a life of the body. His botched attempt to kiss Lucy passionately in the woods is a hilarious foil to the kissing George is able to perform, and Lucy admits that she always thinks of Cecil in a room rather than outdoors. Instead of living out his true, natural self, the self who acknowledges his desires, Cecil self-consciously tries to create himself to be a certain type, and this is medieval and ascetic.

Just as Cecil is uncharitable in his interpretations of others, Cecil also is unable to read Lucy's true self. He thinks of her as a "woman of Leonardo da Vinci's, whom we love not so much for herself as for the things that she will not tell us" (87). Lucy takes on light and shadow, shades of beauty (one chapter is titled "Lucy as a Work of Art"), but Cecil never penetrates her inner reality, and the narrator leads the reader to detect this conflict right away. The only relationship Cecil enacts with Lucy and with other people is "feudal: that of protected and protector" (149). Through Cecil's character, the novel is not portraying as its ideal a self who has the authority to fashion itself into whatever type it wants; rather, the novel promotes the self's authority to transcend spiritually the need for all such typecasting and limiting moral narratives.

Charlotte Bartlett is also attached to the medieval, especially because of her view of women. As she explains to Lucy:

It was not that ladies were inferior to men; it was that they were different. Their mission was to inspire others to achievement rather than to
achieve themselves. Indirectly, by means of tact and a spotless name, a
lady could accomplish much. But if she rushed into the fray herself she
would be first censured, then despised, and finally ignored. Poems had
been written to illustrate this point. (38)

The narrator goes on to label this description one of an immortal "medieval lady": "The dragons have gone, and so have the knights, but still she
lingers in our midst. She reigned in many an early Victorian castle, and
was Queen of much early Victorian song" (39).

For much of the novel, Charlotte seems to hold ascetic power over
Lucy, and at the end the narrator makes it clear that this disciplinary
influence is immoral. After the kiss with George in Italy, Lucy imagines
that she and Charlotte will have a debriefing session in which "together
in divine confidence they would disentangle and interpret" her "sensations, her spasms of courage, her moments of unreasonable joy, her mysterious discontent" (71). Instead, Charlotte cuts off such talk and is much
more worried about stifling the moral and social scandal that she believes
potentially could ensue. The narrator calls this "the most grievous wrong
this world has yet discovered," that Charlotte ignores Lucy's sincerity and
"craving for sympathy and love." Instead of being able to discuss Lucy's
truest passions and desires, Charlotte presents to her

the complete picture of a cheerless, loveless world in which the young
rush to destruction until they learn better—a shamefaced world of pre-
cautions and barriers which may avert evil, but which do not seem to
bring good, if we may judge from those who have used them most. (76)

Through Lucy's interactions with the medieval Charlotte and Cecil, the
novel links the supersession of Puritan social morality by egalitarianism
specifically to feminism. The boundaries placed on women are but one
example of the immoral "fencing in" of human life that Forster sees
resulting from Puritan-like character typology. Echoing Arnold, Puritanism may be successful at averting evil, the narrator says, but it does not
bring about the highest goods.

Mr. Emerson and his son George represent the "new age" or "renaissance" toward which the reader wants Lucy to move. Mr. Emerson's philosophy of life is clearly juxtaposed to Puritan Christianity and its types
and is revealed in the novel through his encounters with church figures,

especially with Mr. Eager, the British rector in Florence. In this novel the church's authority to read and form the deep self is replaced with a philosophy that seems to reject any foundational narrative or moral system, just as the Renaissance and the modern supersede the medieval and the Victorian. According to the narrator, all such moral systems take the human out of the body and into the surface world of types and restrictive moral judgments, possibly protecting from evil but not seeking the good. A "renaissance" in Mr. Emerson's terms involves a return to the body, a simple being or presence in the world outside of any typological interpretation, and the fullest living of the body in a life of love among other humans. For him, each human should be equally capable of living this way in freedom.

Influenced by modern philosophy and literature (Mr. Emerson's personal book shelves are filled with Nietzsche, Schopenhauer, A. E. Housman, and Samuel Butler, among other authors), Mr. Emerson promotes a personal philosophy of love and kindness. George describes him to Lucy as "kind to people because he loves them," not like most of us, who think "it improves our characters" to be nice (23). Mr. Emerson is capable of loving people for their true selves, and he does so without concern for the status of his own virtue. For Mr. Emerson the true self can only be experienced if the body is free. When the Italian cab driver brings his girlfriend along on the excursion to Fiesole, Mr. Eager disapproves, but Mr. Emerson defends them saying: "Do we find happiness so often that we should turn it off the box when it happens to sit there? To be driven by lovers— A king might envy us, and if we part them it's more like sacrilege than anything I know. . . . We have no rights over his soul" (61–62). Interestingly, Mr. Emerson later tells Lucy that he does believe in the "soul," but that he hates to use the term because "superstition has wrapped it round" (197). Rather than viewing the soul as separate from the body, Mr. Emerson sees the soul and the body as inseparably conjoined.

While he acknowledges no God or biblical narrative that guides history and morality, Emerson still sees an end toward which he hopes humanity is moving, and he casts that end in reverse Christian typological terms. When discussing the equality of women with men, he tells Mr. Beebe: "The Garden of Eden . . . which you place in the past, is really yet to come. We shall enter it when we no longer despise our bodies. . . . In this—not in other things—we men are ahead. We despise the body less than women do. But not until we are comrades shall we enter the garden" (123). Such an Eden in which the soul is returned to the body in ethical freedom is the telos of *A Room with a View*. In the closing scene,

Lucy and George are in one another's arms, back at the *pensione* in Florence. Breaking away from England and Puritan social morality, they have recovered freedom and a life of the body. They are autonomous morally and spiritually, finding their true selves in love of each other.

In opposing Mr. Emerson's philosophy to the dominant Puritan social morality of British society, associating the Renaissance with the former and the medieval with the latter, Forster is influenced by Victorian Hellenism and the differing ideas of Walter Pater and John Ruskin. Mr. Emerson's "spirituality" in which life is lived in the body, reuniting what was once separate while not conforming to any outside, transcendent moral system, seems directly shaped by Pater's idea of "renaissance." For Pater, a "renaissance" is not simply a historical period term but also an aesthetic (ethical) experience potentially available to all in which all human sensibilities—the imagination, the rational mind, the emotions, the sensations—are unified in a moment of wholeness. In such an experience, one "absorb[s] the past and future in an intense consciousness of the present," such that one simply lives in all possible fullness (Pater 118). A "renaissance" recovers what Pater and others called the Hellenic ideal: the idea that the Greek man was at unity with himself and that no divisions existed between form and content, body and soul, flesh and spirit. In a sense, then, Pater narrates the Renaissance as a recovery of humanity's true self, and it is this kind of experience of unashamed wholeness in the body which Mr. Emerson promotes. While at Cambridge, Forster was deeply immersed in discourses of Hellenism emerging from the ideas of Pater and other Victorian thinkers such as John Addington Symonds, Samuel Butler, and G. Lowes Dickinson, but as Ann Ardis notes, Forster was always highly critical of Hellenism if it separated the intellect from sensual and emotional experience (65). This quest to reunite emotion and rationality, mind and body, certainly dominates *A Room with a View*, and as Ardis argues, Italy in all of Forster's novels seems to be the setting to which English characters must go to recover their emotional, sensual, bodily nature (66).

Reading Mr. Emerson's philosophy by way of the Paterian notion of "renaissance" provides insight into Forster's novelistic characterizations, which many readers have felt link his novels more to the nineteenth century than to modernism. Mr. Emerson's natural inclination is not to typecast people or make moral judgments. For him, the acquisition and judgment of moral character are of the false self; such surface narratives always crack under the pressure of reality, according to the narrator. Instead of typological interpretation, the body (materiality),

passion, true kindness, love, tolerance, and egalitarianism are of humanity's true self. Such ethical presence in the world somehow both allows
one to reject abstract moral codes and to live out a life of real love that
allows all people to be equal. In *Aspects of the Novel,* Forster titles his
two lectures on characterization "People," not "Characters." Forster
sees the novel telling the story of people as simply real people who live
real lives, not as "characters" to whom specific moral judgments need be
applied in a Puritan-like way or who need to be reshaped and converted
by such principles. As Langland notes, Forster's dropping of the word
"character" does not imply that he was not concerned about morality,
however (94). In *A Room with a View,* Forster ridicules and makes fun
of Puritan morality while providing a new view in which a "renaissance"
or reuniting of one's true self in ethical experience somehow naturally
(yet vaguely) leads to a moral life of egalitarianism and love. To achieve
this, all conventional and idealistic (Puritan) notions of character and
morality have to be discarded—the limits of the Puritan self have to be
acknowledged. In this way, although Forster does not explore the consciousness and inner workings of his characters' psyches as his modernist
contemporaries did, his reworking and inversion of the ontology, epistemology, and morality of Puritanism points to a very modernist view of
the individual, ethical self.

Forster clearly depicts Mr. Emerson's new mode of ethical spirituality as typologically superseding the church, which Emerson feels has only
taught men "to hate one another in the name of God" (25). His anti-
church stance arises early in the novel, when Lucy finds herself touring
Santa Croce at the same time as the Emersons. Leading a tour group, Mr.
Eager provides Ruskinian interpretations of Giotto's frescoes based on
"standards of the spirit": "Remember . . . the facts about this church of
Santa Croce; how it was built by faith in the full fervour of medievalism,
before any taint of the Renaissance had appeared" (22). Mr. Emerson
loudly rejects this interpretation and provides a materialist one instead:
"'Remember nothing of the sort! Built by faith indeed! That simply means
the workmen weren't paid properly. And as for the frescoes, I see no truth
in them. Look at that fat man in blue! He must weigh as much as I do,
and he is shooting into the sky like an air-balloon" (22).

The Santa Croce scene enacts the reaction so prevalent among modernists in the early twentieth century against the Ruskinian union of
aesthetic judgment and Christian morality. Forster's and Mr. Emerson's
"Renaissance values" are obvious narrative clues to those readers familiar with discourses that pitted Pater against Ruskin, Renaissance against

medieval. Indeed, Ruskin came to represent a Puritan mindset to the modernists, for Ruskin hated the Renaissance and lauded the Gothic (or medieval) because he felt that Gothic artists were perfectly attuned to God as creator and exegete of nature while Renaissance artists shifted the focus to themselves as creators of representative art. Ruskin even labeled Renaissance artists "evil" for focusing on their own ability to achieve perfection, aristocratic ideals, scientific conventions, and surface beauty instead of being concerned for conveying God's truth. For Ruskin, a work of art could only be judged aesthetically beautiful if it also embodied a proper view of Christian morality, spirituality, and truth.[7] Forster and Mr. Emerson reject such a view, seeing such Puritan-like worldviews as only leading to the corrupted and harmful "muddle" of English society.

While not directly labeled "medieval," the clergymen in this novel are presented as ineffective authorities in the process of character formation and moral judgment, and they are unable to provide a narrative of the "good life" that can compete with the Emersonian one. In fact, they are even bad representatives of Ruskinian thought. Mr. Beebe is depicted as the most likeable clergyman in the novel because he tries hard not to fulfill his character type. "No one would take him for a clergyman," says Lucy (9), and "Who would have supposed that tolerance, sympathy, and a sense of humour would inhabit that militant form?" think the Miss Alans (32). Mr. Beebe does not like to hear that people enjoyed his sermons; instead, he wants to coordinate social events and "provide people with happy memories" (36). He still attempts to maintain some authority over people's souls, but he never makes moral judgments as a Puritan interpreter would be perceived to do. He takes great interest in Lucy, for example, and makes arrangements with Charlotte for Lucy's trip to Greece after she cuts off her engagement to Cecil, but the reader is made to see his mission as repressed and somewhat askew. He is glad Lucy will not marry, but his intention for her to remain celibate is "to help not only Lucy, but religion also" (182).

Mr. Eager also fails as a moral and spiritual authority. He is a "parson of the cultured type" (97) whose parishioners carry a Bible in one hand and a Baedeker in the other. Seeing himself as a superior reader of Italy's culture (49), he is portrayed as morally rigid and judgmental. He swats at an Italian bookseller for no good reason, and he will not sway from his

---

7. See Ruskin's *Stones of Venice*. For more on Ruskin, Pater, and the Renaissance concept, see Hinojosa.

moral condemnation of Mr. Emerson who had, he tells Lucy, "murdered his wife in the sight of God" (53).

The facts of this "murder," mentioned so briefly by Mr. Eager early in the novel, are revealed to Lucy at the end by Mr. Emerson himself in what we could call Lucy's final conversion scene. Narrative clues in this scene make the typological succession of Christianity (medievalism) by Mr. Emerson's philosophy (Renaissance) obvious to the reader. Because the material details described in this chapter are of spiritual import as Lucy finally reads her true self, the whole scene is worth detailing here. Lucy meets Mr. Emerson by chance in Mr. Beebe's study. Mr. Beebe is absent, off at evening services, preaching to a congregation of only three: Lucy's mother, Charlotte Bartlett, and his own aged mother. While Mr. Emerson sits in Beebe's place, a new "priest," the church on the hill is described as receding in spiritual significance: "Built upon the slope of the hill so artfully, with its beautiful raised transept and its spire of silvery shingle—even their church had lost its charm; and the thing one never talked about—religion—was fading like all the other things" (191). Suffering greatly from rheumatism, Mr. Emerson is mourning his son's having "gone under" into seeming depression (192). When he asks Lucy if she remembers Italy, she picks up a volume of Old Testament commentaries, almost as a shield or as a symbolic last clutching to the old biblical narrative, and says: "I have no wish to discuss Italy or any subject connected with your son" (192). After he tells the story of George's mother, however, Lucy begins to soften. Mr. Emerson reveals that he and his wife had refused to have George baptized and that in the end, this had caused her death:

> "She agreed that baptism was nothing, but he caught that fever when he was twelve and she turned round. She thought it a judgment." He shuddered. "Oh, horrible, when we had given up that sort of thing and broken away from her parents. Oh, horrible—worst of all—worse than death, when you have made a little clearing in the wilderness, planted your little garden, let in your sunlight, and then the weeds creep in again! A judgment! And our boy had typhoid because no clergyman had dropped water on him in church! Is it possible, Miss Honeychurch? Shall we slip back into the darkness forever?" (193)

Mr. Emerson goes on to reveal that it was none other than Mr. Eager who came to visit Mrs. Emerson regularly during this time and who "made her think about sin, and she went under thinking about it" (193). This is how Mr. Emerson had "murdered his wife in the sight of God" (193). Even though Mr. and Mrs. Emerson had escaped the Puritanism of their parents, they could not escape the full ramifications of Puritanism in their society. Mr. Eager still existed.

Seemingly, although Mr. Emerson never blames him, Mr. Eager's typological reading of God working in human events (George's illness as punishment) caused a horrible tragedy. Like Dorian Gray, Mrs. Emerson could not handle the conflict between her Puritan sense of conscience and her modern sense of freedom. At this moment of the conversation, when Lucy does not know what to do, she "looked at the books again—black, brown, and that acrid theological blue. They surrounded the visitors on every side; they were piled on tables, they pressed against the very ceiling" (195). She feels physical pressure from these books of biblical interpretation, and she feels sorry for Mr. Emerson at having to find "sanctum" in this place (195). Here, the narrator intrudes to remind the reader that Mr. Emerson is also "profoundly religious," although Lucy can not see it (195). Next, Mr. Emerson does what no clergyman can do; he interprets Lucy's true self: "You love George!" (197). As he rambles on, Lucy doesn't understand his words, but gradually, the veils of darkness withdraw "and she [sees] to the bottom of her soul" (198). Mr. Emerson "had shown her the holiness of direct desire," not desire mediated and reordered by a sacred text or by social morality but the supposed "direct desire" of the body, and she resolves to go to George. Most significantly, in a scene in which the central act that demarcates one's conversion to the Christian faith—baptism—is narrated as having no real spiritual significance, Puritan hermeneutics and morality are replaced. The reordering of the desires and transformation of the false self into the true enabled by the Holy Spirit is inverted. Now, the individual self autonomously denies the false self of Puritan moral imprisonment and returns to the desires of the body and has ethical experience in freedom.

Mr. Eager interpreted George's illness as a twelve-year-old typologically, as having spiritual significance, and he used his authority to get Mrs. Emerson to see it in the same way. Despite Forster's humor, this event highlights the grave moral consequences he sees resulting from Puritan-like typological interpretation. *A Room with a View* is structured by other key typological events as well: amazing coincidental occurrences in the material world which have spiritual significance, but only if the characters can see it. Unlike Puritan texts in which Providence is clearly the cause of miraculous coincidences, the causes of events in this novel are intentionally left unclear. The narrator plays with various interpretations—whether human events occur by coincidence, by fate, or by providence—yet never provides a conclusive answer. The murder witnessed in the Piazza, the kiss at Fiesole, the novel-reading scene—all are potential conversion moments for Lucy, but like Crusoe, it takes a while for her to see and acknowledge her true self.

One of the most significant events occurs early, in the simply titled "Fourth Chapter," in which Lucy witnesses the murder of a man in the Piazza Signoria. By coincidence, George is also there. The narrative sets up the scene using typological clues. As Lucy enters the Piazza, statues of Neptune and satyrs are described as "unsubstantial" in the twilight, "half god, half ghost" (39). The imagery is of an archetypal entrance to an underworld, by which the knowing reader would expect a character to gain life-transforming knowledge: "The Loggia showed as the triple entrance of a cave, wherein dwelt many a deity, shadowy, but immortal, looking forth upon the arrivals and departures of mankind. It was the hour of unreality—the hour, that is, when unfamiliar things are real" (40). Later, the narrator describes the Piazza as a place where "experience" brings "immortality": "Here, not only in the solitude of Nature, might a hero meet a goddess, or a heroine a god" (55). In this scene, by which the narrator makes it clear that material events carry spiritual significance that could change one's life forever, the divine intervention is not performed by the Christian God, but rather by the Hellenic gods of antiquity who watch over the Piazza in Renaissance statuary.

George admits the significance of witnessing the murder almost immediately, and he senses a conversion of sorts within himself: "Something tremendous has happened; I must face it without getting muddled. It isn't exactly that a man has died" (42). As they overlook the River Arno afterwards, Lucy feels as if "she had crossed some spiritual boundary," but she retreats to her false self, concerned for the moral judgment of others and for George's ability to keep the events of the day secret (41). George, on the other hand, will not "return to the old life," as Lucy suggests they should do, but states that now, "I shall probably want to live" (43).

The next day, as Lucy ventures out with Charlotte in order to avoid George, things are different: she tries people "by some new test, and they were found wanting" (51). She attempts to "formulate the questions rioting in her brain," and she feels the "well-known world had broken up" (54). Ironically, however, Charlotte leads her right back to the scene of the previous day's event, where Lucy is forced to hear how others interpret the event before she can interpret it herself. Coincidentally, Miss Lavish is there, sitting on the exact spot of the murder, doing a "few calculations in realism" and "collecting material" for her novel (47). She interprets the murder scene scientifically and reduces its spiritual significance, wanting to "raise the tone of the tragedy, and at the same time furnish an excellent plot" (47). Also present in the square, Mr. Eager detects tones of evil in the event but seems more concerned for the degradation of culture than anything else: "To one who loves the Florence of Dante and Savonarola there is something portentous in such desecration—portentous and humiliating" (49).

There are also hints of divine intervention in the episode in which Lucy and George kiss in the field of violets at Fiesole. This time, however, divinity takes specific human form. The Italian cab driver is described as an ancient type, Phaethon, "a youth all irresponsibility and fire" whom "neither the Ages of Faith nor the Age of Doubt had touched" (57). When Lucy asks him to lead her to Mr. Beebe, she feels that "in the company of this common man the world was beautiful and direct. For the first time, she felt the influence of Spring" (65). He leads her not to the clergyman, but to George: "She fell out of the wood. Light and beauty enveloped her" (66). Surprised, George contemplates her, then kisses her passionately. The driver is described by the narrator as a seer: "He alone had divined what things were, and what he wished them to be. He alone had interpreted the message that Lucy had received five days before from the lips of a dying man" (68). This ancient type is able to work the plot according to the signs that had been planted: he reads the need for a "renaissance" and ensures its fulfillment.

On the drive home from Fiesole, a huge lightning storm occurs, and the narration plays with the Puritan idea that natural events bear spiritual significance. Mr. Emerson is petrified of the storm because he is worried about George, who has decided to walk back to Florence. Mr. Eager says the storm is a test of one's "courage and faith," but is neither a real threat from God nor a mystery: "If I might say so, there is something almost blasphemous in this horror of the elements. Are we seriously to suppose that all these clouds, all this immense electrical display, is simply called into existence to extinguish you or me?" (68). He provides a rational explanation and does not read nature typologically: "the chances against our being struck are enormous" (68). In a comic inversion of the earlier narrative comment that the pious always crack when faced with "reality," Mr. Eager goes on to judge Mr. Emerson's fear: "Typical behaviour. . . . In the presence of reality that kind of person invariably breaks down" (69). Yet despite Mr. Eager's authoritative interpretation of the storm, as they disembark the carriage, an explosion occurs up ahead and a tramline support crashes down. "If they had not stopped perhaps they might have been hurt. They chose to regard it as a miraculous preservation," and the group embraces each other (69). Interestingly, in the aftermath of the near miss, the older people recover quickly. Miss Lavish calculates realistically that they would not have been hit should they have continued on. Mr. Eager gives a "temperate prayer," and the drivers "poured their souls to the dryads and saints" (70). If there is divine intervention in the Italian events of this novel, it is something ancient yet prevalent everywhere to those who can see: to those who are truly of the Renaissance spirit.

In contrast, when in England the British characters debate rationally whether there is a force directing human events. Interestingly, Mr. Beebe, who should be instructive about God's providence, speaks of coincidence, telling George that he always meant to write a "History of Coincidence," although he believes "coincidences are much rarer than we suppose" (125). "For example," he tells George, "it isn't purely coincidentally that you are here now, when one comes to reflect," for we all have had Italy and an interest in "things Italian" in common, and it is no wonder that our paths have crossed. Cecil Vyse met the Emersons in the Italian rooms at the National Gallery, for example, because they both were fascinated with Italy, and he then convinced them to move to Summer Street. George, on the other hand, prefers to speak of Fate: "Everything is Fate. We are flung together by Fate, drawn apart by Fate—flung together, drawn apart. The twelve winds blow us—we settle nothing—" (125). At this, Mr. Beebe cautions him not to attribute anything to fate because he believes that humans are the cause of all actions; these causes work out to look like coincidences, but they can be rationally explained.

Ultimately the novel self-referentially inverts the Puritan view of God working in history by structuring its plot around key events that the narrator hints carry spiritual significance, yet any sense of the Christian God intervening in the lives of humans has dissipated. The great coincidences of the plot *may* be attributable to some ancient, pagan deity or Fate, or they *may* be rationally explained by dissecting human agency and motivation. Only one thing is clear: the novelist is now the creator and exegete of the human plot. In their differing interpretative modes regarding the spiritual significance of real events, the Italians and the English are portrayed as having differing ontological statuses. The Italian is of the true self: at one with the world, unified in passions, mind, and heart, living in the materiality of the body with ease. The Englishman is of the false self: applying a narrative or superstructure to the world, straying from the lower desires and the body while abiding safely in transcendence and abstraction.

For Lucy, it is not Bible-reading but rather typological reading of romance novels which reorders her desires and brings her closer to her Italian true self. Like so many other novels, this one self-reflexively plays with Puritan hermeneutics by portraying novel-reading as spiritually and morally formative of the main character's life. The influence of romance novels is first seen when Lucy confesses to Charlotte after the kiss with George: "But this time I'm not to blame. I want you to believe that. I simply slipped into those violets. No, I want to be really truthful. I am a little to blame. I had silly thoughts. The sky, you know, was gold, and the ground all blue, and for a moment he looked like some one in a book" (70). Lucy's desires and actions and way of seeing the world in moments of true self-knowledge align with those of the romance narrative. Later, when back in England, Lucy again remembers the scene of the kiss and unwittingly reveals her true self: "I fell into all those violets, and he was silly and surprised. I don't think we ought to blame him very much. It makes such a difference when you see a person with beautiful things behind him unexpectedly" (143). The narrator points out that there was "an unfortunate slip" in Lucy's "rather" good speech (note carefully the pronouns), but "whether Miss Bartlett detected the slip one cannot say" (143). In any case, the slip reveals to the reader that there is a disconnect between Lucy's surface behavior and her inner true self.

This self-referential play continues when Forster humorously sets up the romance novel as a sacred book lying in a garden in the chapter titled "The Disaster Within." One can not but see the comic parallel to Augustine's and Crusoe's conversion scenes. As Miss Bartlett, Mrs. Honeychurch, and Lucy all get ready to go to church, "the garden of Windy Corner was deserted except for a red book, which lay sunning itself upon the gravel path" (144). As the sun rises "higher on its journey, guided, not by Phaethon, this time, but by Apollo, competent, unswerving, divine," its rays are described as falling on all of the characters in their various settings, in their movements casting shadows. "But this book lies motionless, to be caressed all morning by the sun and to raise its covers slightly, as though acknowledging the caress" (144–45). The book is pure, in union with the true light of the sun, void of any shadow.

Of course the reader finds out later that afternoon as Lucy, Freddie, and George play tennis and Cecil strolls through the garden reading the book aloud occasionally when it is "so bad," that the novel has come from the lending library, is titled *Under a Loggia,* and is authored by none other than Joseph Emery Prank, the penname of Miss Lavish.[8] Gradually Lucy recognizes the book as the one Miss Lavish was writing while they were in Florence, and that it is about her and George. There is a murder scene in the Piazza, and when Cecil tries to find an "absurd" account of a view that he remembers in the novel, Lucy randomly finds and Cecil reads aloud the account of the kiss at Fiesole: "Miss Lavish knew, somehow, and had printed the past in draggled prose, for Cecil to read and for George to hear" (155). George also recognizes the scene, and a few moments later, when no one can see, George grabs Lucy and kisses her again. Later, he admits "the book made me do that." Hilariously, the semi-random coincidental reading of the "sacred" romance novel in the garden reveals to both characters their deep selves as they typologically identify with *themselves* as portrayed in the novel.

There are various ways to interpret this hermeneutical circle in which art imitates life and then life imitates art. The novel pokes fun at popular romance novels and authors who indeed were flourishing in Forster's day (or perhaps it pokes fun at the British propensity to typecast and morally judge such novels), yet at the same time, such novels are depicted as having the power to reveal and shape the reader's inner self. Additionally, Forster's novel itself participates fully in the genre, evoking similar desires in the reader. In making the romance novel a sacred text, the vehicle of truth for its readers, Forster satirizes the Puritan theology of fiction even while proving it correct: Puritans worried that fiction might reorder the reader's desires away from God and toward lower pursuits, and this is exactly what Forster's novel performs. At the same time, in its self-referential play, the idea also arises that the body's freedom and passion are also narratively constructed, shaped and cultivated in the typological reading of the romance. In this view, what Mr. Emerson hopes for—the absolute Renaissance or autonomy of the body and pure ethical experience of others—is an impossibility and is itself a narrative that orders the desires and limits the self, potentially becoming another form of asceticism.

This ironic playfulness is even more pronounced when the reader begins to notice how it is not just Miss Lavish's novel, but perhaps Charlotte Bartlett who is the real "author" and "exegete" of Lucy's plot. Instead of the Christian God coordinating spectacular coincidences and events as in *Robinson Crusoe,* intervening in time and space, now it might be an aging spinster who has the power to direct history, planting prefigurative clues all along the way. The reader is made to question the

---

8. The title of Miss Lavish's novel is also a chapter title in George Eliot's *Romola.*

legitimacy of coincidences just enough to wonder if this is the case. Miss Bartlett just happens to lead Lucy back to the scene of the murder where Miss Lavish is dissecting it for her novel. Charlotte and Miss Lavish discuss the characters of her novel, taking secret joy together, for example, when they find out that Mr. Emerson's work was on the "Railway" and what this might mean for his character in the novel. Charlotte just happens to see George kissing Lucy at Fiesole, and she later just happens to tell Miss Lavish all about it, despite her vows to secrecy. Miss Lavish just happens to bicycle through Summer Street where she just happens to meet the Emersons again, and then Charlotte just happens to write Lucy a letter that conjures up her memories of George as it discusses the coincidence of Miss Lavish meeting him. Hints that Charlotte is a providential agent are dropped more and more in the last chapters: "Miss Bartlett's sudden transitions were too uncanny. It sometimes seemed as if she planned every word she spoke or caused to be spoken; as if all this worry about cabs and change had been a ruse to surprise the soul" (141). When Charlotte and Lucy argue after Lucy's second kiss with George has occurred in the garden, Lucy finally resolves to talk to George herself, but then "realized that this was what her cousin had intended all along" (160).

In the last chapter, when George and Lucy are back in Italy, they discuss the events that led to their telos of freedom and passion. George considers the forces of Fate that "had swept him into this contentment": "all the people who had not meant to help—the Miss Lavishes, the Cecils, the Miss Bartletts!" (201). Then they realize together that Charlotte had arranged Lucy's last meeting with Mr. Emerson in Mr. Beebe's study on purpose: "She knew he was there, and yet she went to church" (203). George wonders about Charlotte aloud:

> That your cousin has always hoped. That from that very first moment we met, she hoped, far down in her mind, that we should be like this— of course, very far down. That she fought us on the surface, and yet she hoped. . . . The sight of us haunted her—or she couldn't have described us as she did to her friend. There are details—it burnt. I read the book afterwards. She is not frozen, Lucy, she is not withered up all through. . . . I do believe that, far down in her heart, far below all speech and behavior, she is glad. (204)

In this moment, readers are forced, just as George and Lucy are forced, to rid themselves of their tendency to interpret Charlotte typologically. Even Charlotte Bartlett has a deep, passionate self.

Lucy's plot in *A Room with a View* parallels the Christian conversion plot, yet it dismantles the ontological, epistemological, and moral basis on which the typology of such a plot is founded. Lucy converts to her true self by reuniting her body and soul, emotion and reason, and in the process, the narrative replaces the Christian conversion story with a new sort of Emersonian conversion. Instead of a giving up of one's false sinful self through the workings of the inner conscience and God's grace in order to find the freedom of the true self with God, in the Emersonian conversion, the restrictions of false social-moral judgments are escaped autonomously in order to recover the true material spirituality of the body in freedom, equality, and ethical experience. In the process, a modernist or "Renaissance" ethical spirituality replaces an outdated Christian, "medieval," Victorian ascetic spirituality. Additionally, the novel self-reflectively ironizes the idea that the typological reading of a sacred text leads one to convert to one's true self. Yet as the romance novel replaces the Bible as authoritative in reading Lucy's true self, the novel also points to the idea that any definition of the true self is necessarily constructed. In fact, the novel seems self-reflexively to know that the dichotomy of inner and outer self, and the dialectic of Puritan morality and its dismantling, is itself an entirely conventional narrative, given to us by novels themselves.

This engagement of the novel with the Puritan self is not only thematic. On a formal level the novel self-consciously plays with many Puritan hermeneutical ideas, including ideas about who directs history (or plot) and the events characters experience; who interprets those events and how; how moral judgments about character are made; and the relation of such judgments to the "truth" about who a person is. In these ways, the novel interrogates, ironizes, and inverts the Puritanism that still shapes English novelistic and social-moral traditions in Forster's day. As a result, we can see Forster's novel as pointing to more modernist treatments of novelistic characterization, ethical experience, plot, and the body, even if it never approaches the explorations of consciousness and language we might often label modernist.

Despite all its playful irony, the novel clearly elevates Mr. Emerson because he is able to achieve a new philosophy of life by breaking away from the Puritanism of earlier generations. He seems simply to be able to live in the present, to love others, to desire equality for all, and to find humor and joy in life. Certainly these are not ignoble goals. His ability to refrain from limiting people by typecasting them, his ability simply to "let be" and to let others "be," to not assume authoritative modes of judgment and knowledge, seems akin to the new ethical position. Mr. Emerson is open to the "Other" and lives comfortably within his own limitations.

Yet this new mode of spirituality does not seem equally achievable by all. Mrs. Emerson, for example, who on the question of her son's baptism faces the direct conflict of her new modern mode of life with the Puritan narrative from which she has escaped, "goes under" from the pressure. For a while, also, there is some question of whether the young George finds it a satisfying narrative of life. The Emersonian philosophy still has to cope with the remnants of Puritanism in society; it has to exist in dialectical relation to that from which it escapes, and negotiating this may be a very difficult task. Significantly, Lucy and George achieve their "Renaissance" only by escaping from England and returning to Italy, yet we never see them after this moment. We do not know if they are able to return to their family and society, to manage the dialectic in a satisfactory way. We also do not know whether outright rejection and rebellion is the only way to achieve this new spirituality. We do not know if complete freedom as a telos is sustainable, even if we as readers gain some satisfaction from seeing them in this final moment and imagining they are free. We are left to think that presumably Lucy and George will now live as Mr. Emerson does. Perhaps they are of the elect few who can supersede the falsities of social-moral conventions and the Puritan ontology and epistemology of the self to live out their true selves, but we do not know this for certain. While Mr. Emerson, Lucy, and George are able to access their true inner selves, then, they do so only by rebelling, rejecting, and thinking they have escaped the Puritan view of the self. This rebellion and idea of freedom may be another form of asceticism. Through its playfulness and self-ironizing, the novel leaves open the question of whether one can ever truly have a "renaissance" and fully and sustainably escape a particular narrative and its social-moral ideology.

Nevertheless, Forster is more hopeful about the consequences of such a dismantling than Wilde seems to be. For Dorian Gray, the idea of sheer "escape" becomes solipsistic, inefficacious, and ultimately tragic, bringing into question the whole value of escape and pointing to a dialectical approach instead. For Mr. Emerson, solidarity, friendship, personal relations, love, tolerance, and equality might best be produced and enabled by an escape from Puritan morality, although it can become tricky to negotiate with the remnants of that from which the escape is made. In the end, we are not given a picture of how this would transform society, and the escape seems possible only for a select few on an individualized basis.

What we see in *A Room with a View* and Mr. Emerson is in accord with much of what Forster says in his much later essay of the 1950s, "What I Believe." Here, he decries the power of modern institutions, especially Christianity, to offer redemption for the human race. He claims not to believe in "Belief" (with a capital "B"), but only in personal relationships (67). (He does mention a few other things he believes in: the press, Parliament, and the "holiness of the heart's affections" [74]) For Forster, the individual and his ability to love and be loyal to other individuals—to cultivate personal friendships—is humanity's only hope. Forster describes the virtues of personal relationships as "tolerance, good temper, and sympathy" (67). These are "what matters really," and "if the human race is not to collapse . . . must come to the front before long" (67). Forster also attributes to personal relationships the virtues of love, loyalty, reliability, "natural warmth," sensitivity, and creativity (68). Forster admits that his is a liberal and individualist position. He gives democracy "two cheers," and not three, because it allows individuals to flourish, and hence, friendships between individuals to form (70). Only among individuals and personal friendships does the potential lie for what Forster deems "civilization," which he identifies as the absence of force (70). Only personal relationships are "something comparatively solid in a world full of violence and cruelty" (70).

Forster contrasts his philosophy of personal relationships, what he calls his "creed," with Christianity and other forms of "Faith" and "Belief." To him, Christianity participates in the world of force, violence, and cruelty. It is an inadequate "civilizer" because it does not bring peace to the world. In parallel, it does not bring integrity to the individual, only inner conflict, and hence is not conducive to cultivating true friendships (71). Like other "Faiths," Christianity to Forster is "mental starch" and a "stiffening process" as it makes social morality a priority (67). Christianity also fails because it cannot fix the tragedy that in modernity private virtues remain private; Christianity cannot make the private virtues of personal relationships public in order to bring about real social change. It is not a narrative by whose terms everyone is willing to abide.

Forster longs for a "technique" and a "Saviour" that would make the admired qualities of personal relationships—"good will and good temper"—public such that human society would be transformed (75). But he is not hopeful that such a technique will be found, and so his hope lies only in the personal, in individual relationships. These will carry forward the best of humanity for the future. For Forster, then, individuals who can let other individuals "be" without judgment and with love, is the only valid ethical stance to take, and Mr. Emerson seems to represent just such a person.

Mr. Emerson's ideas bear much in common with the ideas of Nietzsche, who also sees only a select few as able to live truly, fully, and ethically, embodying humanity's utmost potential. Unlike Mr. Emerson, however, Nietzsche in his moral philosophy shows little if any concern for the concepts of love, equality, tolerance, democracy, or "good will." In fact, for Nietzsche, such limiting concepts are products of the Protestant tradition he so disdains. Forster in many senses is a product of modernity, Puritan hermeneutics, and the novelistic narrative and admits to being so, still lauding certain aspects of individual morality, equality, and freedom, for example. In contrast, Nietzsche takes the rebellion against Puritanism to a new level by seeing it to be the root of *all* the legacies of modernity that he hates, including liberal individualism and the concept of morality itself.

CHAPTER SIX

The Metaethical Self

Nietzsche and Joyce

THE RECEPTION of Friedrich Nietzsche's texts and ideas in England is a fascinating history that centers on questions of religion and morality.[1] Suffice it to say, Nietzsche abhorred England, and many Englishmen abhorred Nietzsche. He hated English culture and its lack of great music. He despised English philosophy and believed it was the origins of "the plebeianism of the modern spirit" (*Genealogy* 28). He did not understand why England held on to Christianity for "moral guidance" long after intellectually rejecting it (Thatcher 20). Later, the primary translator of Nietzsche's works into English, Oscar Levy, declared that English Protestantism was the primary object of Nietzsche's attack. When Nietzsche wrote to the Swedish playwright, August Strindberg, on the topic of finding an English translator, Strindberg wrote back: "With regard to England I have really nothing to say, for there we have to deal with a puritanical land, delivered into the hands of women—. . . English morality—you know what that means, my dear sir!" (qtd. in Thatcher 19). In many ways, Nietzsche saw England as the primary cause and source of the moral systems he wanted to dismantle. Indeed, the first essay in his 1887 *On the Genealogy of Morals,* the text upon which this chapter focuses, begins by briefly considering the shortcomings of English moral philosophy, history, psychology, and religion.

---

1. For studies of Nietzsche in England see Thatcher, Bridgewater, and also Foster.

Following the lead of Max Nordau, who spent sixty pages denouncing Nietzsche in his 1893 *Degeneration* (translated 1895), English reviewers initially despised Nietzsche (Thatcher 27). He was considered an "Egoist" who was decadent, unstable, heretical, overblown, and evil. The translation of Nietzsche's works into English thus was a long, slow process. Although some texts were translated by the late 1890s, the translations were not complete until 1913, having passed among several publishers and translators. David S. Thatcher credits A. R. Orage and his journal, *The New Age,* for expediting the process beginning in 1907.

There is no direct evidence in Joyce's *A Portrait of the Artist as a Young Man,* and little evidence in the body of his work, that Nietzsche's thought was integral to his projects. Richard Ellmann, one of Joyce's first biographers, says Joyce was familiar with Nietzsche from about 1903 or 1904. He read *Thus Spake Zarathustra* in German, but probably nothing else (Thatcher 135). Nonetheless, this text may have influenced his life as well as his unpublished novel, *Stephen Hero,* which was composed from 1903 to 1905. Thatcher argues that Joyce "went through a period of temporary infatuation with Nietzsche which left no mark of any consequence on his creative work," and points out that the references to Nietzsche in *Stephen Hero* and in *Ulysses* are scant in number and flippant in tone (136). Patrick Bridgewater agrees, calling Nietzsche a "passing whim" of Joyce's early years and reminding us that Joyce's fundamental, lasting influence was instead Thomas Aquinas (142). Any influence on Joyce in this early period would have involved then a limited knowledge of Nietzsche's texts and a generalized and perhaps exaggerated account of his ideas, especially of the *Übermensch* or "Superman" concept. Additionally, we know that Joyce admired Ibsen greatly, who was highly influenced by Nietzschean thought, and that Irish contemporaries of Joyce such as George Bernard Shaw, George Moore, William Butler Yeats, and Arthur Symons were greatly shaped by their study of Nietzsche.

Certainly interested readers in England could have accessed more than just *Zarathustra.* In addition to the German texts, several English translations were available by the time Joyce wrote *Stephen Hero.* These included: *The Case of Wagner* (1895), *The Twilight of the Idols* (1896), *Nietzsche con Wagner* (1896), *The Antichrist* (1896), and *The Genealogy of Morals* (1899). Perhaps their knowledge was oversimplified or not reflective of Nietzsche's full, developed thought, but many readers in England would have spent time discussing Nietzsche's philosophy at the turn of the century. Thatcher suggests that Nietzsche initially made an impact more in English artistic circles than in academic ones. Only from 1909 or so did English philosophical journals begin to discuss his ideas. By the time Joyce finished revising *Stephen Hero* into *Portrait* and published it in 1915, the translations were complete, and knowledge of Nietzsche's ideas would have been more widespread among English speakers.

In this chapter, then, the connections between the larger context being analyzed, Nietzsche's moral philosophy, and the primary text, Joyce's *A Portrait of the Artist as a Young Man,* are not explicit as they have been in earlier chapters.[2] Despite this, Stephen Dedalus's trajectory in the novel leads to the formation of a certain type of self that bears similarity to Nietzsche's "higher man" in *The Genealogy of Morals* and other texts. In many ways, Nietzsche and Joyce and Stephen react similarly to Englishness and Protestantism as they seek a different mode of being and a different sense of the ethical and the self. Comparing them not only helps elucidate each writer's ideas, but also provides an excellent description of the modernist "ethical self" and further means by which to assess its potential limitations. This chapter first delineates the type of self produced in Nietzsche's *Genealogy,* and then does the same with Joyce's *Portrait.*

Brian Leiter has described Nietzsche's moral philosophy as "primarily critical in orientation" (1). Quite simply, Nietzsche attacks "morality" itself: Kantian, European, English, German, Christian, utilitarian (1). All modern moralities are rooted in Christian morality, however, for to Nietzsche, Kantian and utilitarian moralities both derive from and are similar to it.[3] Nietzsche never critiques or provides a conventional "philosophical ethics" in the sense the discipline might have today. Rather, as Leiter suggests, his project is predominantly a critique of culture, most often of German and English Protestantism, which is equated with "morality" by many in this era.

As Leiter describes it, Nietzsche's goal is to speak to an elite group of human beings—to whom he often refers as "higher men"—to help them alter their conceptions about morality, to see the morality of the

---

2. Others have connected *Portrait* to Nietzsche. See David Major, "The Satirizing Superpowers: Stephen Dedalus and Zarathustra," *Colby Quarterly* 28:2 (1992): 115–22; and Sam Slote, "Stephen's Nietzschean Ethics," in *James Joyce: Metamorphosis and Re-Writing, ed. Franca Ruggieri* (Rome: Bulzoni Editore, 2010), 15–26. Slote philosophically connects Stephen's aesthetics to Nietzsche's ethics through the idea of self-creation.

3. Nietzsche also attacks Platonic metaphysics throughout his writings. He sees Plato as a precursor to Christianity in terms of idealism.

dominant culture as detrimental to the realization of their potential, and to accept their status as higher beings (40). Instead of defining the self and discerning its moral or spiritual status according to a larger narrative, as happens in Puritan hermeneutics, the higher man finds his "true self" by rejecting, escaping, and transcending all such larger narratives and associated moralities. The opening line of *The Genealogy of Morals* indicates that Nietzsche is interested in helping certain readers to discover their true selves: "We are unknown to ourselves, we men of knowledge— and with good reason. We have never sought ourselves" (15). He suggests that this text and its aphoristic form will not be accessible or understandable to all, for simply reading something does not equate with "deciphering" its meaning (23). Rather, he says aphorisms need to be interpreted through "the art of exegesis," something most readers are not patient enough to do (23):

> To be sure, one thing is necessary above all if one is to practice reading as an *art* in this way, something that has been unlearned most thoroughly nowadays—and therefore it will be some time before my writings are "readable"—something for which one has almost to be a cow and in any case *not* a "modern man"—*rumination*. (23)

Ironically, his text seems to have a purpose similar to that of many Puritan texts: in its style and content, it aims to lead certain readers—"men of knowledge"—to access their true selves. Of course, for Nietzsche the true self is something quite different than it is for the Puritans.

Nietzsche describes his project in *Genealogy* as a "revaluation of values." This implies that as he critiques and deconstructs the dominant morality, calling it "the danger of dangers," a new morality or a "metaethics" will take its stead (20). Yet although he is reacting against the moral and social categories that are seen to be generated by Protestantism, Nietzsche himself creates something of a character typology. There seem to be only two main "types"—higher and lower (or stronger and weaker). The *Genealogy* provides an historical account of the development of the weaker type, albeit not a scientific history such as would have been prevalent in Nietzsche's day. Nietzsche offers little proof or documentation for his by-now familiar narrative of how "slave morality" was developed by priests in revenge against the nobility. Here, I am not so interested in his historical and causal account, its fictionality or accuracy, but rather in the characteristics and qualities Nietzsche assigns to his higher and lower types; in how he views these types ontologically, epistemologically, and ethically; and in how he sees Christianity bringing negative changes to conceptions of the human subject.

Nietzsche certainly saw himself at the dawn of a new age in which Christian morality and its view of the human subject would pass away: "Christianity as a dogma was destroyed by its own morality; in the same way Christianity as morality must now perish, too: we stand on the threshold of this event" (*Genealogy* 161). Nietzsche suggests, as MacIntyre does, that morality and religion have separated over the course of modernity, and that while Christianity has lost its truth value, the remnants of its moral systems persist. Just as science and modern reason had destroyed Christian dogma, now the remnant of Christian modern morality would "bring about [its] own destruction" (*Genealogy* 161). At the center of this collapse would be the Christian conception of the human subject and the Christian conception of truth, for these are the cornerstones of Christian morality: "After Christian truthfulness has drawn one inference after another, it must end by drawing its most striking inference, its inference against itself; this will happen, however, when it poses the question 'what is the meaning of all will to truth?'" (*Genealogy* 161). Nietzsche claims to speak from a metaethical stance, examining the "herd's" assumptions for their truth value as if from outside them. He believes he can speak from the realm of the ethical, outside morality. He asks, "What meaning would our whole being possess if it were not this, that in us the will to truth becomes conscious of itself as a problem?" (*Genealogy* 161).

To Nietzsche, herd morality assumes truths about the human subject that he believes are false. This then leads to norms, values, and categories that simply are not true and do not apply to higher men. Leiter describes three things that Nietzsche disagrees with regarding the false self of lower men: 1) that human beings "possess a will capable of free and autonomous choice" and thus they can be held responsible for their actions; 2) that the "self is sufficiently transparent" such that one can distinguish actions based upon motives and then rank and evaluate those motives; and 3) that humans are "sufficiently similar" so that one moral code can be applied to all which is in the interests of all (2–3). Of course, these are three things that are assumed in Puritan hermeneutics.

I want to unpack these critiques further. Regarding the first point, Nietzsche finds false the modern ontological view of the self as autonomous, responsible, and able to make promises about moral principles from its own free will—what he calls the "sovereign individual" (*Genealogy* 59). Slave morality assumes "this power over oneself and over fate," a power that has "penetrated to the profoundest depths and become instinct" (*Genealogy* 60). Humans have made free will and moral responsibility into "instincts" that they refer to as the "conscience" or "soul" (*Genealogy* 60, 49). For Nietzsche, the Christian conscience is a "serious illness," for Christianity took ordinary, natural ideas of guilt in humanity, by which one could feel a diminishment of one's worth, and turned them into a "bad conscience" and a perverted sense of guilt (Reginster 57).[4] Forced socialization into Christianity's institutions turned man's natural instincts inward—instincts such as sex, violence, and freedom—and made them the problematic objects of analysis and criticism (Reginster 63). Man's state ever since has been to be at war with himself. The resultant guilt is perverted because through the constructed instinct of the conscience one feels responsible for one's natural instincts and constantly feels unable to live up to God's expectations regarding them. Guilt now involves moral judgment instead of merely a feeling of diminishment. The human subject who judges himself always feels he needs redemption but finds himself unable to provide it for himself (Reginster 77). The soul or will is in a constant state of dialectical contradiction.

Yet in Nietzsche's interpretation, "the doer," or the subject who has a free will and a conscience, "is merely a fiction added to the deed" (*Genealogy* 45). This fiction is in reality a false view of self that in a twisted way ultimately serves to hide one's *ressentiment* and one's desire to feel superior and powerful over others. Christian morality, in this light, develops as a way for the herd to feel superior to the nobility, to take revenge upon them, by holding everyone and their "free wills" to the same moral standards as they are co-opted into the church's institutions. Protestantism makes this scrutinizing of the self a much more individualized process and thereby centralizes even more authority in the self. This false view of the self–with its "bad conscience," perverted guilt, and sovereign individualism—continues into "secular" modern moralities such as Kantianism and utilitarianism.

The fiction of the "doer" and its need for redemption hinders life for Nietzsche, because the doer aspires to "a quite different type of existence," either in the afterlife or in a realm of ideals (Reginster 77). Moral practices and norms are developed within this fiction and are directed against the self in order to control its natural instincts. Similar to others, Nietzsche labels such practices and norms the "ascetic ideal." For him, asceticism is a process by which

---

4. Reginster suggests that Nietzsche's account of guilt is incomplete because he does not give us a full account of the pre-Christian "ordinary feeling of guilt" (57).

a few ideas are to be rendered inextinguishable, ever-present, unforgettable, "fixed," with the aim of hypnotizing the entire nervous and intellectual system with these "fixed ideas"—and ascetic procedures and modes
of life are means of freeing these ideas from the competition of all other
ideas, so as to make them unforgettable. (*Genealogy* 61)

Asceticism fixes as truths the notions of sin, good and evil, the conscience, the soul, free will, God. Yet to Nietzsche, the "ascetic life is a
self-contradiction: here rules a *ressentiment* without equal, that of an
insatiable instinct and power-will that wants to become master not over
something in life but over life itself, over its most profound, powerful,
and basic conditions" (*Genealogy* 118). To Nietzsche ultimately the self-
focus of ascetic evaluation by which "we cheerfully vivisect our souls"
is hubris, for the sovereign moral self who feels the need for redemption
ironically tends to believe he can cure himself if he only can become a
better and better "nutcracker of the soul" (*Genealogy* 113). The contradiction is that in trying to please God, the modern individual no longer
seems to need God. To Nietzsche, the modern philosopher is most prone
to such an illness. In the end, Nietzsche says the ascetic ideal of modern
moral man is a "will to nothingness, an aversion to life," but man is so
attached to the idea of his own free will that he "would rather will nothingness than not will" (*Genealogy* 163).

On the second and third of Leiter's points, Nietzsche reacts against
the epistemology and normativity of modern morality. Modern morality
assumes one can see into one's conscience or soul to determine motives
and that thereby one can pass moral judgment on human actions. The
false view of the self assumes that inner truth about oneself and about
others can be known, that the self can be identified. Charlotte Bartlett,
for example, at first believes she can identify and label the motives of
young George Emerson. Modern morality also assumes that every person
is structured in the same way, with an inner conscience, a free will, and a
rationality that governs choices. Because all humans are the same, there
are universal moral principles that should govern all humans. In modern morality the same moral code applies to all and is beneficial to all.
Nietzsche inverts this ontology, epistemology, and morality of the modern, Puritan self in order to free man's natural desires and instincts, in
order to emancipate the true self.

For Nietzsche, one's natural true self is largely unconscious, shaping one's drives and affects, and leading to one's ideas and images of the
world. Either a person is weak and accepts modern morality as the truth

that is needed, or one is higher and is able to think metaethically. According to Leiter, Nietzsche's higher and lower types are ontologically defined by particular "psycho-physical constitution(s)," what Leiter calls "type-facts" (5): "Each person has certain largely immutable physiological and psychic traits that constitute the 'type' of person he or she is" (Leiter 6). Most humans are unaware of their own natural constitutions that drive their actions or that cause them to develop certain ideas. The true self is *not* transparent, and motives for behavior are ultimately unknowable. Although he talks about the large classifications of "higher" and "lower" types, for Nietzsche all agents are essentially dissimilar, constituted by different "type-facts," and therefore no one universal morality can or should be applied to all (Leiter 7).

It seems that for Nietzsche the higher man is higher because he understands his true self and is able to access it. Nietzsche saw himself to be a higher man who could detect how moralities develop out of particular psycho-physical constitutions. The higher man is far more complex than were the original nobles of the genealogy, for modern higher men live at the end of the era of Christian morality and have to work through its effects. The higher man knows that the true core of man is unknowability and difference, and he can live comfortably with that uncertainty. A man's identity is not something that can be labeled, coded, or transformed from bad to good. As Mathias Rise outlines, for the Kantian man, the concept of the will allows the subject to think of himself as unified. For Nietzsche, on the other hand, unity is simply the "joint presence of desires or instincts in the same body, with shared memories and cognitive apparatus." There is not one "inner chooser" that shapes actions, but only "internal multiplicity," a "structure of many drives and affects" (77). Rather than trying to conform to what is similar and to believe human behavior and identity can be rationally known and understood, the higher man is conscious of being part of a "causal web" and can live comfortably with the conflicting impulses and drives constituting his makeup (Rise 80). He does not try to harmonize, control, or disown the disharmony of his constitution (Harcourt 278). He does not let inner multiplicity or conflict lead to *ressentiment,* guilt, or shame, but rather he has "physiological cofunctionality" by which everything can work together (Rise 77). He is healthy and sane, not ill, divided, and conflicted. By his very constitution, the higher man can live at peace with the multiple narratives, impulses, and instincts that shape him; he can rise above a need for unity or resolution; he can live with unknowability and contradiction; he can enjoy and be present in material life; he can achieve excellence.

In contrast, Christian morality to Nietzsche is antinatural, harmful to life, and condemnatory of the instincts, such as sexuality (Leiter 8–9). Modern morality denies the natural constitution of humans and tries to categorize and abstract human identity out of the body into some falsifying realm. For the herd, "man has evolved that queasy stomach and coated tongue through which not only the joy and innocence of the animal but life itself has become repugnant to him" (*Genealogy* 67). The higher man, on the other hand, is a person who lives in the body, who accepts his own physical-psychic constitution and does not try to deny it, and who is not always trying to conform to an abstracted ideal. Nietzsche ends his second essay in the *Genealogy* with this vivid description of the higher man:

> the creative spirit whose compelling strength will not let him rest in any aloofness or any beyond, whose isolation is misunderstood by the people as if it were a flight from reality—while it is only his absorption, immersion, penetration into reality, so that, when he one day emerges again into the light, he may bring home the redemption of this reality: its redemption from the curse that the hitherto reigning ideal has laid upon it. (96)

As Bruce Ellis Benson puts it, Nietzsche's higher man will find "redemption from redemption": redemption from all guilt, shame, and necessity, redemption from good and evil, redemption from a false reality and a false self (197).

The type of self idealized in many modernist novels seems to have much in common with Nietzsche's higher man: naturalness, presence in one's own body and in the world, affirmation of life, an easy commerce with unknowability and difference, an ability or desire to escape social-moral narratives and categories, and an ability to be sexually free. For the higher man there is no disjuncture between one's natural true self and one's presence, activity, and being in the world. The higher man translates his creative potential directly into action; he has no need to forge an intermediary identity that can be labeled in some way or to conform to moral norms. The higher man is metaethical in that he can "see through" modern morality and escape it. He can access his natural self that is able to exist outside society's moral codes, and he can live comfortably with conflicting influences by mastering them. Unlike Dorian Gray or Mrs. Emerson, the higher man does not have to succumb tragically to contradiction. Neither does he need a God to bring his conflicted soul to resolution.

Many modernists, like Wilde's Lord Henry, tended to label such a view of the self "aesthetic." This trend of using the term "aesthetic" to describe something that is not really about aesthetics but is rather about morality and the ethical has been perpetuated by literary critics as well. As Edward Harcourt points out, however, Nietzsche himself did not see the higher man as aesthetic and did not use that term to describe him. While he believed art was opposed to the ascetic ideal and elevated the artist figure, Nietzsche instead uses the term "healthy" to describe the higher man (Harcourt 279). The higher man's ability to give form to his life is not akin to the artist giving shape to his material, but rather is a reflection of his *virtu*, his innate power and constitution (Harcourt 280). The shaping of the self is not a permanent form as that achieved in the artwork, but rather is an ongoing healthy process. To Harcourt, then, it is crucial to distinguish between the aestheticism of the age, by which moral evaluation is suppressed in favor of aesthetic appreciation, from Nietzsche's metaethics. In this view, the categorization and supposed divergence of the moral and the aesthetic is actually part of the Puritan narrative Nietzsche intends to subvert. Metaethics, on the other hand, somehow supersedes the moral–aesthetic split. It is supposedly beyond the categories.

Some philosophers today speak as if Nietzsche's metaethical position is entirely possible. A recent anthology of essays on the *Genealogy*, for example, has on its frontispiece this goal: this book "illuminates what a post-Christian and indeed post-moral life might look like."[5] Interestingly, such philosophers also seem to be actively continuing Nietzsche's project of debunking and dismantling Christianity. As for many novelists and artists before them, for many modernists art and the ethical become the antidote to religion and morality.[6] This book, however, has been questioning whether such a metaethical stance is ever completely possible or valuable. Nietzsche's metaethics rebels against and believes itself to escape the Puritan narrative of self and history, attempting to free the desires and instincts from the prison of social and Puritan moralities. Yet just as with the other texts analyzed, in the end, metaethics is dependent upon and dialectically related to the Puritan narrative. Escape or full freedom from necessity seems impossible, for the ideas of escape and freedom are dialectically dependent on the very thing from which the escape is needed.

5. See May.

6. The idea that art is modernity's "antidote" to religion comes from the theologian, John Milbank.

Several scholars implicitly agree when they point out how Nietzsche did not succeed in escaping the morality discourse or the Christian narrative. Simon May points out that "The *Genealogy*'s success in undermining morality is limited by Nietzsche's conviction that suffering must be given a meaning—a conviction integral to the very tradition of morality he wishes to overcome" (10). Benson argues that Nietzsche never escapes the "logic of Christianity" because he simply moves from Christian religion and piety to developing a new Dionysian religion and piety (7). He does not give up the "mystical-God-Ideal" and hence is a "heretic in his own religion" (211). His desire for "redemption from redemption" merely repeats in a new form the Christian narrative of redemption (197). The true self still needs to emerge from the false self. In addition, when he assumes he can look at modern morality from an objective position outside it, Nietzsche could be seen as participating in modern scientific rationality and sovereign individualism. The higher man is autonomous and individual; there is no overt concern or care for others. Perhaps, too, becoming conscious of one's own free will as a problematic concept would inherently create an even more conflicted inner self and perpetuate in a new way the war within. Peter Berkowitz argues:

> Although the death of God broadly construed—the rejection of an external moral order that is independent of the human will—is fundamental to Nietzsche's thought, Nietzsche . . . has constant and critical resource to those things—truth, wisdom, the soul, will, right, virtue, justice, nature, the rank order, nobility, philosophy—which were bound up with the God that supposedly died and the host of traditional convictions about human nature that supposedly perished with him. (271)

Like many before him, Nietzsche is on a quest for what is "true," despite his debunking of the will to truth. Most central to his thought, according to Berkowitz, is "the intellectual conscience that compels Nietzsche to face up to God's death and to examine its moral and political significance for the good life" (271). His ideas do not eliminate the Puritan or Christian narrative, for any type of self built on a sense of escape necessarily involves memories and remnants of that from which the escape is made and is dependent on them for its own identity. The dialectic of necessity and freedom composes modern man. Nietzsche, and many modernists, simply leaned hard into the freedom end of that dialectic.

One has to wonder if Nietzsche's conception of the higher man and his rejection of Christian morality was inspired at all by his novel-reading, for his thought about the human self seems parallel in many ways to the novelistic dialectic this book has outlined. Indeed his style of writing, particularly in *Zarathustra*, seems highly influenced by novels (among other literary forms). Although Nietzsche read many novels, Stendahl was his particular favorite whom he read often and felt was highly influential for his philosophy. In the *Genealogy*, Nietzsche spends a few paragraphs comparing Stendahl to Kant and arguing that they differed over the idea of "disinterestedness" in aesthetic experience (104–5). Whereas Kant describes the beautiful as that "which gives us pleasure without interest," Stendahl "once called the beautiful 'A promise of happiness.'" For Stendahl, according to Nietzsche, this means that the beautiful "arouses the will" and involves "interestedness." Art is not a means of escape from one's natural instincts, as it was for Schopenhauer and Kant, but rather is a means of enhancing life and tapping into one's natural instincts. In a moment Joyce seems to capture in chapter 5 of *Portrait*, Nietzsche even has a little laugh at the Kantians who claim that "under the spell of beauty, one can even view undraped female statues 'without interest.'" Real artists, he says, as opposed to the philosophers, know that such beauty definitely involves "interestedness." Nietzsche asks: "Who is right, Kant or Stendahl?" But clearly he sides with Stendahl, who is not afraid to affirm life and its interests, to access his higher true self. In the end, Nietzsche's moral philosophy is a novelistic dismantling of a novelistic stereotyped Puritanism.

Joyce's Stephen Dedalus is perhaps the most influential modernist character who self-consciously desires and attempts to escape modern morality in a Nietzschean way. Yet at the end of *Portrait*, readers do not get to see whether he succeeds in his quest or not, just as they did not get to see Lucy Honeychurch and George Emerson in their life together in Forster's novel. Significantly, Joyce ends the narrative at the moment when Stephen could be said to have willed himself to be a higher man, but we do not see the ramifications or consequences of that decision. What the novel does give is the prehistory of the higher man's emergence. We are privy to Stephen's processes of revelation and insight regarding modern morality and thus are given a model of how the artist works through the false self. Like Nietzsche's higher man, instead of conforming to a larger narrative and thereby finding one's true self, only in the freedom found by escaping all larger narratives is the true self found. As Andrew Gibson has suggested, Stephen's *Bildung* or formation as an artist is inseparable from *Entbildung* or deformation (*Joyce* 97). The truth of the self emerges when the falsities of the self are dismantled and escaped. The logic of this conversion is the same as in Christian conversion, however, whereby the false self is broken down in order to let the true self participate in God's story. For Stephen, in contrast, the false self is broken down in order to let the true self take command of itself.

Stephen is widely accepted as a semi-autobiographical representation of Joyce. Both have boyhood Catholic educations; both have periods of early sexual activity and guilt; both have periods of religious fervor; both later oppose and leave the church; both are ambiguous when it comes to Irish politics; both become artists. Both strive for similar freedom from social-moral narratives, especially of the church, primarily to free their art and their sex lives from such constraints and to find a higher mode of being. Yet as seen in all of Joyce's texts, these social-moral narratives never go away. Narratives and languages of Catholicism and Protestantism, Irishness and Englishness, nationalism and imperialism, philosophy and theology, among others, all continue to inform his texts and his life. Much criticism and debate has focused on trying to determine Joyce's exact relation to these narratives. Was he a believing Catholic or not? What was his exact relation to Irish nationalist movements? Does he distort Thomas Aquinas in his use of him or not? Studies on each of these questions have ranged from answering "positively yes" to "positively no," to a range of qualified positions in between. Joyce seems to be a master of ambiguity. While this chapter is not interested in trying to answer any of these types of questions regarding Joyce, perhaps one view would be to see Joyce trying to be higher in a Nietzschean sense: not succumbing tragically to contradiction in his constitution but rather letting all the discourses, drives, affects, and narratives resonate in disharmony, finding a peace by not letting any one of them represent the truth of who he is or of human history. Like Stephen's, Joyce's only firm commitments seem to be to his art and to freedom.[7] Perhaps *Ulysses* can be seen as a textual representation of the higher man's constitution, a dismantling of all narratives and their associated moralities while at the same time a lasting recognition of their fragmentary presence and potential influence in forming human life. Joyce leaves us in *Portrait,* though, at the point of escape, and thereby ironically implies that the belief that one can completely escape is an adolescent idea, perhaps a necessary stage of progression but not yet a mature embodiment of the metaethical self.

---

7. For an argument that Stephen's concerns are not merely selfish but are interested in the Irish race and nation, see Pericles Lewis, "The Conscience of the Race: The Nation as Church of the Modern Age," in *Joyce through the Ages: A Nonlinear Vision,* ed. Michael Patrick Gillespie (Gainesville: UP of Florida, 1999), 85–106.

As Stephen Dedalus moves through childhood into adolescence into early adulthood, he works out his own aesthetic theory. Because Stephen strives to be a poet, this movement toward an aesthetic theory is also a movement toward a theory of himself. Stephen's theory of art and self strives for three inseparable things that nonetheless are discussed separately here: moral freedom, unity of body and soul, and stasis. Stephen's movement is toward freedom from necessity. At the end of the novel he says he wants to "discover the mode of life or of art whereby your spirit could express itself in unfettered freedom" (246). By encountering experience itself, Stephen wants to "forge in the smithy of [his] soul the uncreated conscience of [his] race" (253). He wants to find the language and truth of his soul, unshaped, uncreated by any narrative or force or power other than his own, and to forge that language in freedom. A distinction is made here between the pure inner self, which has its own true language, and the fetters of the falsifying and limiting languages that come from without. At the end of the novel, Stephen believes this absolute freedom from the power and authority of outer languages can be found. Each of the five chapters of the novel is structured to reflect this movement toward freedom. Over the course of them, Stephen moves from the imprisoning power of outside narratives and their associated moralities—especially those of the church, of Irish politics, and of his family—to discovering the creative potential of his self, his soul's own poetry.

As a child in the first chapter, Stephen is exposed to debates and disagreements among his family members about the church, politics, and public morality that reveal all three to be questionable narratives. The state of Ireland in Stephen's childhood is not conducive to engendering "belief" in any one institution, political party, or narrative. Even if Stephen does not fully grasp this yet as a child, the reader can identify the contradictions generated by these social-moral narratives. As a result, in chapter 1 conceptions of morality and truth are rendered ambiguous.

Central to this dismantling and to his family's arguments is the Parnell case, which ruins the Christmas dinner. In setting this argument on this particular day, Joyce renders questionable the idea that Christ's advent into the world transformed history and redeemed it. Ireland seems far from moving toward such an ideal. Stephen's father and the family's governess, Dante Riordan, argue at the dinner precisely over the issue of the proper relation of the Irish Catholic Church, politics, and social morality. The Parnell case brought such issues to a head, and in Joyce's boyhood, the ramifications of the case were still being worked out in Irish life. Interestingly, the role of English Protestantism was at the center of the

Parnell conflict, and in many ways, Puritanism and morality were under attack, both in real history and later in Joyce's novel.

Charles Stewart Parnell was a beloved Protestant leader of Irish nationalism and a Member of Parliament, serving from 1875. Beginning in 1880, he formed and was chair of the Irish Parliamentary Party. He had managed to form an alliance with Lord Gladstone and the Liberal Party, and together they had moved debates forward in the 1880s in favor of Irish Home Rule. In December of 1889, it became public knowledge that a divorce case was being pursued by William O'Shea against his wife, Kitty, and Parnell was named as the man with whom she had engaged in an adulterous affair. Gladstone broke off his alliance with Parnell, mainly for political reasons. The Irish Catholic Church condemned Parnell for his adultery and called for his resignation from politics. Various Protestant denominations in England made arguments to the same effect. The Irish Parliamentary Party ended up splitting over this case, with some siding with the church and others defending Parnell. His death in 1891 is documented in chapter 1 as Stephen lies sick in his school's infirmary (27). Parnell's case became the touchstone for much larger social and political issues. What was the role of personal morality in public politics? What was the extent of the church's authority in politics and in issues of social morality? At stake was the relation of church and state, public and private.

In *Portrait* Dante Riordan advocates for the church's position on Parnell, yelling out that "God and morality and religion come first" (38). Despite her being a staunch Irish Catholic in the novel, Peter Costello believes Dante is modeled on Joyce's own family governess, Mrs. Conway, who was an Evangelical Protestant. Mrs. Conway had deeply instilled into the Joyce children fears of end times and of judgment, and to Costello, had shaped young Joyce's views of Christianity and God in such a negative way that he never overcame them (64). Perhaps Mrs. Riordan's strong position on public morality is evidence of how to many, the Irish Catholic Church had become "too English" and "too Puritan." Paul Cullen, who was Archbishop of Dublin from 1853 to 1878, and Ireland's first cardinal, was often assigned most of the blame for this. While Cullen had countered British political influence, he also had reformed the church in the direction of what Gibson stereotypically calls "Anglo-Saxon, Protestant puritanism and Victorian-English cleanliness" (103). Sean Kay says Cullen is responsible for making the Irish Catholic Church "unified, structured, and puritan" (116). He rooted out all non-Romanist practices; he enforced strict adherence to papal doctrinal positions; he increased the standards for clergy (Cairns and Richards 63). This all helped a "devotional revolution" to occur that, according to David Cairns and Shawn Richards, stressed personal piety among the laity, made religious practices like confession much more actively pursued, and emphasized individual acts of devotion and attention to moral standards (63). Church attendance in Ireland became widespread under Cullen's leadership. To many, however, this meant the Irish Catholic Church had become more English and Puritan, having lost much of its original Irishness. It also meant the Irish felt a new sense of sexual repression and hindrances to freedom. After listing a litany of historical moments when he felt as if the Irish church had historically betrayed Irish independence, Mr. Dedalus adds: "O, by God, . . . I forgot that little old Paul Cullen! Another apple of God's eye!" (38).

Stephen's father, just like Joyce's own, idolizes Parnell and argues that the church should not have any authority in this matter. He and Mr. Casey at the Christmas dinner argue against Dante's view of the church, asking whether priests were "pastors" or "princes" (33), and suggesting that they would be loyal to the church when they "cease turning the house of God into a pollingbooth" (31). Mr. Dedalus argues that the church should "confine [its] attention to religion," but Dante responds: "It is religion. . . . It is a question of public morality. A priest would not be a priest if he did not tell his flock what is right and what is wrong" (31). Dedalus and Casey blame the Irish church for leading Parnell to his death and for doing the "bidding of the English people" (32). For Dante, in contrast, because Parnell was "a public sinner" he "was no longer worthy to lead" (32). The argument reaches potential heresy when Mr. Dedalus cries out that Ireland is "A priestridden Godforsaken race!" (37) and that "We have had too much God in Ireland. Away with God!" (39). Despite these statements, Stephen's father also claims to be a loyal Catholic through and through, just not to the Irish church in its current stance, which he believes is overextending its right to influence. To him, church and state should be separate entities: the church should not hold sway in politics, and private morality did not matter for public leadership, especially when Irish freedom was at stake. He echoes the sentiment of the Irish socialist James Connolly, who had accused the Catholic Church of being the "political accomplice of the British State in Ireland" (Gibson 24). For Dante, the church should be involved in and take precedence over the state and should speak out in public scenarios to lead its people. While she originally had been a Parnell supporter, even at one time beating a man over the head with her umbrella for playing "God Save the

Queen" (37), Dante shifted her allegiance to the church alone during the adultery case. To her, Irish freedom could not be built on sin. Poor young Stephen is left asking himself: "Who was right then?" (35). He could see value in both sides of the unresolved argument, partly because he loved all the people who were arguing. Stephen has to learn early on to hold contradictions together in his mind.

For Parnell supporters, Christianity, England, and social morality—in other words, Puritanism—were considered to be the enemies of Irish freedom and, by extension, of sexual freedom. Gibson believes such Parnellism shaped Joyce greatly and even modernism as a whole, fueling the creation of Stephen. Imitating Parnell, Joyce and Stephen both rebel against the church, which is associated with Puritan morality and England, as they seek their own sexual and artistic freedom.

Certainly in Stephen's mind, the church with its moral teachings is seen to be the enemy of sexual desire and its fulfillment. The first chapter, which ends with Stephen's successful "tattling" on the school priest who had unjustly punished him for not doing his schoolwork when his glasses were broken, depicts Stephen pushing back against authority (or necessity) for the first time. In the second chapter, Stephen exploits his personal ability to deny the authority of the church by indulging in sexual behavior. He sees the world through the language and imagery of the romantic authors he loves—Byron and Dumas. Literary texts typologically shape both his desire to seek and find the ideal beautiful woman (Mercedes) and to fulfill his darkest lusts. As the "constant voices of his father and of his masters, urging him to be a gentleman, above all things, and urging him to be a good Catholic above all things" begin to ring hollow, he frees himself from the fetters of power by descending into narcissistic sexual behavior, either alone or with prostitutes. Although he recognizes the seven deadly sins within himself during this time, "nothing was sacred" (98). He relishes in his indifference to his moral breach of church and society; he takes "pride in his own sin" (104).[8]

This rebellion is depicted as an immature though perhaps necessary stage in Stephen's trajectory toward freedom. His return to the asceticism of the church in chapter 3 is also depicted as being exaggerated and immature. Here, Stephen is required to attend a school retreat which consists of a series of powerful sermons on the "four last things": death, judgment, hell, and heaven. Father Arnall's stated purpose for the retreat

---

8. Joyce's narrative imitates in many ways Augustine's narrative in *Confessions*. For more on this, see Manganiello.

could easily have also been descriptive of a Protestant retreat: "to examine the state of our conscience, to reflect on the mysteries of holy religion and to understand better why we are here in this world" (109). The ultimate purpose was "to do God's holy will and to save our immortal souls" (110). In order to free himself from sin and guilt and shame, Stephen submits himself to the powerful narrative of the sermons and the theology of the self the sermons elucidate. When he finally confesses his sexual sins in a church far away from his school, he feels as if he has converted to a new life: "A life of grace and virtue and happiness! It was true" (146). For a while afterward, Stephen attempts to make the language of his inner self imitate the language of the social-moral and religious narratives by engaging in ascetic practices. He mortifies and disciplines his senses in his attempts to combat temptation and ascend toward holiness—he tries to sacrifice himself to God (150).

Gibson believes that Father Arnall's sermons are "vulgarly late Victorian" and represent the "puritanical morality" of English Protestantism rather than anything "intrinsic to Irish Catholicism" (103). Perhaps they reflect the Anglo-Puritanizing of the Irish church. Regardless of whether their moral lessons and rhetoric are more Irish Catholic or English Protestant, however, Gibson's phrasing exemplifies how English Puritanism has continued to be associated stereotypically in literary criticism with ascetic repression. The so-called Puritanism of social morality and religion was cause for rebellion for Joyce, and it has remained cause for rebellion for contemporary critics of Joyce as well as for many critics of modernism in general.

With stereotypes that were probably ingrained in him by Dante, who did not want him to play with Protestant children growing up, Stephen also does not have good things to say about Protestantism. When Cranly at the end of the novel asks whether Stephen is going to become Protestant because he has lost his faith in the church, Stephen replies: "I said that I had lost the faith, not that I had lost self respect. What kind of liberation would that be to forsake an absurdity which is logical and coherent and to embrace one which is illogical and incoherent?" (243–44). Stephen's and Dante's attitudes stem from a long history in which Catholics in Ireland feared and loathed Protestants. Especially in the wake of the post-famine Evangelical Revival at mid-century, Protestants had attempted to win more converts and make Ireland on "ideal society" through "a reformed faith based on a Protestant reading of the Bible" (Bowen 313). This extension of Protestantism was seen as the imperialism of British culture and authority. According to Desmond Bowen, these tensions and conflicts among the imperialist, Evangelical Protestants and the democratic, Ultramontantist Catholics in the mid-nineteenth century only "reinforced the identities" of each group and deepened "the sense of ethnic difference between them" (xiii). In Ireland, particular denominational identity did not matter as much as it did in England: one was either loyal to Protestantism or to Catholicism and was committed to the way of life that group promoted (xiii). Irish society was divided generally according to these two sets of religious, cultural, political, and ethnic bonds, then, and Joyce's novel clearly is a product of this history. When Stephen walks by Trinity University in Dublin, the dominant Protestant school, the college is described thus: "the grey block of Trinity on his left, set heavily in the city's ignorance like a great dull stone set in a cumbrous ring, pulled his mind downward; and while he was striving this way and that to free his feet from the fetters of the reformed conscience he came upon the droll statue of the national poet of Ireland" (180). The Protestant conscience and intellect has in Stephen's mind been a cumbrous weight at the center of Dublin and has hindered Irish poetry. It was a fetter from which he needed to escape.

Despite Stephen's intense and seemingly complete submission to his new religious fervor, soon the "insistent voices of the flesh" creep back in (152). He understands that they will not go away, that he will always feel guilt and shame in his endless quest for moral perfection (153). In chapter 4, Stephen frees himself from the fetters of asceticism, the church, and the Christian view of history when he rejects the priest's suggestion that he consider taking a religious vocation (157). Although he has spent much time imagining the power and secret knowledge that becoming a priest might give him, he has narcissistically always pictured himself as a priest "in a church without worshippers" (159). He has tried on the Catholic narrative for a while and has decided that it hinders life, expression, passion, and the body: "the chill and order of the life repelled him" (161). He cannot imagine hindering his own freedom for eternity. As he has the aesthetic vision of the girl at the seaside (172), he feels the ecstasy of flight (169), and he commits himself instead to art and self. "Yes! Yes! Yes! He would create proudly out of the freedom and power of his soul." He would not be constrained (170).

In the last chapter, Stephen has long conversations with the dean of his school and with his friend Cranly as he tries to work out his aesthetic theory, but he rejects their academically formed questions and inquiries as well, seeing them as holding no authority over the language and art he strives to devise. Stephen's final stance is reflected in what he once said to his friends when they were challenging his non-involvement in and ambivalence about Irish nationalism: "When the soul of a man is born in this country there are nets flung at it to hold it back from flight. You talk to me of nationality, language, religion. I shall try to fly by those nets" (203). He makes a conscious decision to "leave for ever the house of prayer and prudence into which he had been born and the order of life out of which he had come" (225).

This sought freedom from the power of language and narratives is especially a sought freedom from all senses of social and religious morality. Narratives from without, laden with moral norms and conventions, are always falsifying, "hollow," and abstracted for Stephen. When his classmates attack one of Stephen's favorite authors, Byron, because of his immorality and heresy, Stephen defends Byron's writings on other grounds (81). When the dean speaks to him of "moral beauty" and "material beauty" as two separate things, Stephen quickly becomes put off by his "dry tone" and abstract thoughts. He sees the English priest as living a limited life with a "mortified will" that sadly does not love in the least "the ends he served" (186). Stephen imagines the dean's dramatic conversion to Catholicism from his English dissenting background of sectarianism, schisms, "peculiar people, seed and snake Baptists, supralapsarian dogmatists," who had ingrained in him a rigid morality that hindered life while at the same time a language by which to dominate (189). When Cranly challenges Stephen's notion of freedom on moral grounds—would you steal, would you deflower a virgin, would you purposefully hurt your mother and cause her even more suffering by refusing to go through the motions of your Easter duty when you know it would please her—Stephen dismisses his questions as irrelevant to the purposes of art and self. "I will not serve," Stephen's famous line that echoes Father Arnall's sermons about hell (117) as well as Milton's Satan, has multiple meanings. I will not do my Easter service as my mother wishes I would; I will not serve the church; I will not serve any outside narrative or morality other than my own. The artist's self and the language of his soul are sufficient: "I shall express myself as I am," he tells Cranly (203). He seems to will himself to be a higher man, in a Nietzschean sense taking mastery of his true self amid all the potential contradictions.

Stephen sees the language of his soul as spiritual and material at the same time, and he wants to find the art form that allows him to express the simultaneous spirituality and materiality of this language in freedom. If he could do this, he believes he would create an inherently ethical art. In an exam paper written for a master's degree in Italy titled "The Universal

Literary Influence of the Renaissance" (1912), Joyce laments the evacuation of spirit from literary language in modernity: "The Renaissance . . . has placed the journalist in the monk's chair," he said, meaning that "it has deposed a sharp, limited and formal mind in order to hand the sceptre over to a mentality that is facile and wide-ranging . . . a mentality that is restless and somewhat amorphous" (188). In the Renaissance, a "poem would be reduced to an algebraic problem, put forth and resolved into human symbols in accordance with the rules" (189). Joyce felt this trend had worsened considerably in his day, as the "realists" dealt with endless trivial details and vague generalities rather than spiritual matters, becoming "amoral" and promoting what he called a "frenetic sensationalism." "We might say indeed that modern man has an epidermis rather than a soul" (189), he said. Joyce saw himself as restoring the ethical to literature by aspiring to write in a language that was spiritual and material at once. This proper restoration of the spirit to matter through language he felt was a recovery of the purest function and being of words. Joyce continues to use a word Nietzsche dismisses—the "soul"—as he seeks to recover a natural and original language and redeem it from the abstractions brought about by Puritan morality and Platonic metaphysics. Joyce and Stephen use rhetoric that implies they believe in an original language that has been corrupted by history.

This rejection of conventional language, categories, and norms can be further clarified by looking at what Stephen says about stasis. For Stephen, the language that rediscovers the unity of body and soul—proper art—produces in the viewer a state of stasis, not kinesis. If movement or kinesis does occur, then Stephen says the art is either "didactic" or "pornographic" (205), and is therefore improper art. "Pornographic" art and language cause movement in the body and do not attend to the soul, just like the realist literary authors Joyce denigrated in his "Renaissance" essay. Elaborating further, Stephen says pornographic art excites the desires of the body; it urges us to "possess," "to go to something" (205). *Portrait* plays around with this idea in several ways. In fact, we might label parts of the first two chapters "pornographic" in this sense, as Stephen experiments sexually and lets his body dictate the activity of his soul. Words in these chapters have the power to stimulate and affect his body: the word "suck" when he is a child, and later when he is a bit older, the word "foetus" carved into a desk at his father's old school, both move him physically (89). As a young teenager, Stephen produces "crude writing" and then lets his own words move him physically. Later, Cranly jokes that the Venus statue at the art museum inspired him to write his name on her buttocks in pencil. In seeming contradiction of Nietzsche's point about disinterestedness, Stephen responds by saying that Cranly's emotion was not the "esthetic emotion" because it was kinetic and "not more than physical" (206). These responses to pornographic art are depicted as early and immature stages in the artist's progression.

Although full of poignant and descriptive imagery, the language of the sermons in the middle chapter, on the other hand, is "didactic." Interestingly, the problem Stephen has with didactic art and language is not that it is too spiritual, but rather that it also is physical only. Didactic art moves the body by exciting in it not desire, but loathing. Didacticism urges us to "abandon, to go from something" (205), just as pornographic art urges us to "possess, to go to something." By moving Stephen's "diseased conscience" to fear (115), the sermons on hell and last things eventually cause Stephen to loathe the body entirely (or at least this is how Joyce depicts asceticism). Didacticism hinders life and abstracts the soul away from the body.

So what is the stasis that proper art evokes? Stephen says several things about it. Working from Aristotle, Stephen thinks aesthetic stasis is "tragic emotion," which is "a face looking two ways, toward terror and toward pity" (205). It involves holding contradictory feelings and views together as "the mind is arrested and raised above desire and loathing" (205). This state of stasis is produced by beauty and is beauty. Static esthetic apprehension "keeps away good and evil, which excite desire and loathing" (207). Thus, the normal moral sensibilities and categories of life are not a part of it. Aesthetic stasis is achieved when the artist perceives the *quidditas* of a thing—its "whatness," what Stephen says Aquinas means by "radiance" (213). The whatness of language Stephen wants to express is the word that is material and spiritual at once, radiant with beauty. Such language emerges from the artist's self, free of all external moral authority such that it causes no movement, but instead arrests the self in static aesthetic presence. It is uncreated by anything but the artist's own constitution and power. Only the true self can dissect and discern the falsity of outside narratives to discover the uncreated language of the human race.

Unlike Nietzsche but like Wilde's Lord Henry, Stephen uses the word "aesthetic" to describe the experience of escaping morality, finding the language of one's soul, and becoming present and unified in one's own materiality. The fact that he is developing an aesthetic theory means he still participates in the morality discourse Nietzsche is trying to overcome. Yet we can also associate aspects of Nietzsche's metaethics with Stephen's aesthetics. Just as Stephen had to learn to hold together contradictory narratives and values as a child, so now he can hold contradiction within himself. To answer Cranly's question about his belief in Christianity, Stephen says, "I neither believe in it nor disbelieve in it" (239). In the end, even though he is still in a theoretical stage and not yet a full, practicing artist, Stephen claims to use the language of specific narratives in the same way he admits to using Aquinas and Aristotle: "I need them only for my own use and guidance until I have done something for myself by their light. If the lamp smokes or smells I shall trim it. If it does not give light enough I shall sell it and buy another" (187). The self is the sole interpretive authority of the self. All narratives and languages are interpreted based only on the self. Stephen shows no concern for others.

Joyce leaves us with some open-ended ironies, however, and as a whole treats Stephen ironically. In the end, for example, Stephen is still a sovereign individual, perhaps even more of one, because he believes he can will his own rebellion and escape and take full responsibility for that choice. Stephen's narrative of self is still framed according to the logic of the novelistic dialectic, albeit on the escape or ethical side. Readers are left not to admire him fully. There is an element of pity for him in his rebellion as well as terror for what he has done. Stephen's friend MacCann has told him that he still needs to learn "the dignity of altruism and the responsibility of the individual" (199). While these are the exact terms Nietzsche attacks in the sovereign individual, Joyce leaves it open that Stephen may be too narcissistic in his rebellion. Certainly his mother's prayer at the end that he learn in his own life "what the heart is and what it feels" is also the reader's hope for Stephen as he seems to be headed to a life of loneliness (253). He has willed himself away from family, from human community, from love, from regard for others. Readers are not at all sure his aesthetic, ethical stance will be adequate, but they do not get to track his life further in this novel. Readers do not know if escape is sustainable or how Stephen will master the social-moral and religious narratives that will continue to surround him.

Joyce is ironically suggesting that the belief that one can escape morality completely in order to live aesthetically or in ethical experience is adolescent and limited. Unlike Dorian Gray, Stephen does not become tragically caught between contradictory narratives; he is more hopeful about transcending them. Yet the narrative implies that sheer rebellion and escape are not adequate, mature, or healthy. Full escape, in fact, may be impossible. One can imitate Stephen's momentous decision not to serve, but the remnants of church, politics, and morality will continue to be present in one's being and in one's society, potentially continuing to cause more conflict. Flying by the nets is a myth, but an alluring one. Stephen's "unbelief" can never be purely free, and he, in a Nietzschean sense, will have to master the lasting influence of the narratives he rejects.[9]

Some have wondered whether Nietzsche and Joyce were able to escape social morality and contradictory narratives to achieve a metaethical position in their own lives. Certainly both men seemed to face guilt and inner conflict throughout their lives. Benson surmises that for Nietzsche, madness was perhaps the only way to live what his philosophy demanded: "To be so transformed that one is literally outside of oneself is perhaps the only route left" (216). Perhaps the metaethical ideal and the higher man are things that can be achieved, if anywhere, only in a text and not in a life. Perhaps the contradictory and multiplicitous text of *Ulysses* or the aphoristic, literary-philosophical texts of Nietzsche come closer to the metaethical than their authors ever do. If this is true, then even the quest for the healthy, metaethical self is a quest for the otherworldly, a desire for an elsewhere. It is a quest generated within and through the novelistic grand narrative.

---

9. For a study that argues Joyce was entirely ironic in his portrayal of Stephen and that *Portrait* is in fact an "antimodernist" text, see Weldon Thornton, *The Antimodernism of Joyce's* Portrait of the Artist as a Young Man (Syracuse: Syracuse UP, 1994).

CHAPTER SEVEN

"I Leave It to You"

Church, State, and Morality in Ford Madox Ford's
The Good Soldier

*F*ORD MADOX FORD'S *The Good Soldier* has always been viewed as a novel that masterfully dramatizes epistemological uncertainty. Dowell appears to have the exact experience lauded by new ethical theorists: he is brought face to face with "unknowability" and has uncomfortably to recognize the limits of his own perspective. As he struggles to understand the truth about the last nine years and his own ignorance and blindness, a recurring phrase for Dowell is simply: "I don't know." The novel's scattered impressionistic form was radical in its day, breaking all the narrative conventions of fiction, and seeming to lead the reader, too, to a position of unknowability. Many prominent critics supported such a view of the novel and argued that for Dowell, epistemological and moral unknowability go hand in hand. Max Saunders calls *The Good Soldier* a "rendering without a comment" and says it "cannot be reduced to a moral message" (441). Hugh Kenner said the reader is left with "an impasse of sympathy for all sides" (54). And Mark Schorer: "*The Good Soldier* describes a world that is without a moral point."[1] Such critics seem to assume that dismantling narrative conventions is equivalent to dismantling morality and that moral unknowability is the

---

1. I am indebted to Jeffrey Mathes McCarty's essay for this collection of quotations. There are other major critics who value the novel's "amorality" or moral pluralism. See, for example, Samuel Hynes, "The Epistemology of *The Good Soldier*" in *The Sewanee Review* 69:2 (1961): 225–235, and also Michael Levenson's arguments in "Character" and *Modernism*.

reality of human life. Dowell's struggle for literary form represents, then, the human need for warding off a sense of meaninglessness. Ford himself might seem to support such a view, such as when he says that during his life he never developed a "fixed moral attitude" or "scheme of ethics" (qtd. in Mizener 21). As Jeffrey Mathes McCarthy has argued, however, such readings tend to "reproduce the limitations of autonomous aesthetics by justifying the process without measuring the results" (332). In other words, Ford's creation of Dowell in the novel is admired and reproduced in the criticism without an examination of whether this is an efficacious or good view of the self to hold. In a sense, modernism reads modernism into Ford's novel in order to justify its own aesthetics. This chapter argues that Ford's novel, while certainly a radical and groundbreaking experiment with characterization, is also concerned for the moral ramifications of Dowell's position.

Ford clearly links morality to England's religious and literary history, yet many proponents of the novel's moral unknowability ignore the historical religious references in the novel.[2] In contemplating Edward's character, Dowell ponders the English "Nonconformist Conscience," Anglo-Catholicism, Anglicanism, and novel-reading. Clearly the Irish Roman Catholicism of Leonora is pitted against the Protestant Reformation in the crucial scene at Marburg. Here, when Florence touches Edward's wrist, both Leonora and the reader know, but not Dowell, that an adulterous affair between them is about to begin. Ford's placement of this event in a significant early modern Protestant setting highlights the influence of Protestantism as a whole on shifting moral and political views of marriage and adultery.[3] The tension between the Nonconformist (or Puritan) background of Dowell and the Roman Catholicism of Leonora, as well as the relation of both of these to Florence's and Edward's Anglicanism, informs the entire novel. While recently more attention has been paid to such references, there is more to be said about how religious history relates to the novel's epistemological and moral concerns.[4] In its analysis of Puritanism and Puritan hermeneutics, this book has argued that religion, morality, history, and epistemology are integrally linked in the novel's form. This chapter argues that Ford was aware of and consciously manipulated these elements in *The Good Soldier*. In the

---

2. Saunders is an exception on this point.

3. Cheng was one of the first literary critics (beyond the biographers) to take the historical-religious references seriously; see "Religious Differences."

4. For other treatments of the religious references, see Cheng ("The Spirit of *The Good Soldier*), Mizener, Sutton, and also Stannard.

process, he renders Dowell's stance morally questionable and reveals its limitations. Debates in the 1900s and 1910s over the role of church and state in issues of marriage and divorce also influenced Ford's treatment of religious history, and so, as with the other novels analyzed in this book, readings of Puritanism in the novel are joined with those of the author's context.

As seen in chapter 3, battles between Anglo-Catholics and Protestants, and between Nonconformists and the Establishment, continued into the 1900s and 1910s, and certainly influenced Ford's perspective. Yet Ford's own religious identity has been a matter of some disagreement among his biographers. Ford was brought up "in the back rooms and nurseries of pre-Raphaelitism" (Mizener 6), with his famous grandfather, the painter Ford Madox Brown, and an atheist father who hailed from a German Catholic family. As a young man in 1892, Ford converted to Roman Catholicism while on the Continent, but the level of his commitment to practicing this faith over the course of his life is sketchy. Arthur Mizener argues that Ford was "scarcely Catholic in either feeling or conduct" most of the time and that his Catholicism was "essentially a by-product of his social and political views rather than a religious attitude" (20). Ford clearly put himself in the conservative camp, linking his "sentimental Tory" commitments to his Catholicism and "feudalism." Alan Judd calls Ford "a kind of Catholic, or agnostic, or a Catholic-agnostic—what he would have said would have depended upon his audience and when he was speaking" (1). Judd judges that Ford remained nominally a Catholic after his conversion, though "his practice was irregular and his belief at best ambiguous" (19). Judd believes Ford found the ceremony and tradition of Catholicism in line with his general worldview, but that Ford often had negative things to say about God and in general believed in a heretical "Albigensian Christ," one whose "redemptive work consisted only in His teaching" and not in his resurrection (20). Max Saunders gives Ford a little more credit for his belief, but argues that Ford's Catholicism had appeal because it "provoked the rationalist friends he was defining himself against," not because he was interested in any theological matters (54). It is probably safe to say that Ford's Catholicism did not play a vital role in his thinking about morality nor did it shape the way he lived. Interestingly, Ford's two daughters entered the church, and one even became a nun, much to Ford's dismay (Judd 20).

Ford's criticisms of English Nonconformity and Protestantism are well known, and one can only infer that Continental Roman Catholicism in part provided a means for him to rebel against his own culture.[5] While he voices an appreciation for his childhood experiences in the Anglican Church, suggesting that in church services there are "moments which are unsurpassable in this life" (*Spirit* 91), many of his writings are critical of the Reformation's influence on England. In his 1907 *The Spirit of the People,* and his 1911 *The Critical Attitude,* Ford analyzes the British "Puritan spirit," which he says is "the backbone of England" (*Spirit* 80). Like Arnold and Newman before him, Ford characterizes the Victorian era as the fulfillment of what the Reformation had started: it was a time in which Protestantism, individualism, "free speech, free thought, free trade, political economics" were all accepted as "unquestionable fact"—"firm, unquestionable, unshakeable" and certainly providential (*Spirit* 75). While this may have led to world ascendancy, Ford argues it also made the English religion "almost entirely a standard of manners" by which the Englishman "accepts an Anglicized Christ Jesus for his personal model" (*Spirit* 119, 169). This quote points to the idea that Puritanism had become merely an outer social morality while losing its religious and communal vitality. To Ford, the Protestant revolution "doomed England to be the land of impracticable ideals. Before that date a man could live without his finger upon his moral pulse: since then it has grown more and more impossible" (*Spirit* 81). Echoing Arnold, Ford felt that the Nonconformist conscience had created the British tendency to discourage "open and free expression," especially in religious and sexual matters, and to avoid one's feelings and passions (Cheng, "Spirit"). In terms reminiscent of Newman, such moral idealism leads to moral self-centeredness and a real "lack of sympathetic imagination" among Englishmen (*Spirit* 120). The Puritan Spirit also "availed itself of reason at the expense of intuition" (*Spirit* 115). Yet despite its rational nature, the Puritan Spirit squashed the "Critical Attitude" in England: "the Englishman has founded three hundred and forty-seven religions. And each of these religions is founded on a compromise. That is what the Englishman does to, that is how he floors—the critical attitude" (*Critical* 5). Using the example of Bible-reading, Ford describes Protestants as people who "take in its teachings from their births, and by its standards measure good and evil. . . . It is beloved, it is pored over, it is learned by heart, it inspires heroism, devotions, or cruelties" (*Critical* 7). Yet Protestants never examine the Bible critically. Roman Catholics, on the other hand, as well as free thinkers, have a more critical attitude toward the

---

5. For more on Ford and Continental Roman Catholicism, see Sutton.

Bible and can at times find it "a disagreeably realistic book" because it contains "barbarisms, crudenesses, disproportions, and revelations of sickening cruelties" (*Critical* 7–8). Clearly shaped by previous interpretations of Puritanism, Ford sees its negative influence on England in a fairly stereotypical light: it brought an emphasis on morality to the detriment of other aspects of being human; it elevated reason over feeling; it lacked a self-critical eye. Vincent Cheng suggests that Ford found in Continental Catholicism a society more open to the "instinctual, the sense of divine mystery, and the open expression of feelings" (Cheng, "Spirit"). This openness coupled with the "critical attitude" and a less rigid sense of morality, meant that Catholicism for Ford was "a religion that men can live up to" (*Spirit* 81), for it was based on the "sentiments and weaknesses of humanity" rather than on its quest for moral perfection (*Spirit* 115).

In his own time, Ford believed the Nonconformist denominations were waning, as Unitarians, Anglicans, Congregationalists, Quakers, and Methodists all seemed to have forgotten their original creeds and practiced instead a "faith of a vague and a humanitarian nature" (*Spirit* 99, 102). The established church's theology had likewise become fragmentary (*Spirit* 99), and overall the Puritan Spirit had lost its appeal, authority, tradition, and "popular comprehensibility" (*Spirit* 115). Like so many other modernists, Ford believed that because Protestantism had fragmented the modern world, making it "impossible to see [life] whole" (*Critical* 28), England would have to look to art to gain a knowledge of life (*Spirit* 111). Ford seems to find the wholeness Protestantism lacked in his quartet of feudalism, Toryism, Roman Catholicism, and art.

How Ford's characters—Nonconformist Dowell and Episcopalian Florence, Anglican Edward and Roman Catholic Leonora—fit in with such views of Protestantism seems confusing, for the novel does not paint a sympathetic picture of Catholicism in Leonora. It makes Dowell at least somewhat a victim and Edward the hero. Like Wilde, Ford seems to pit the moral, which is attached to Leonora, against the "ethical," which seems to be Dowell's attempted position. Yet interestingly, Ford reverses the stereotypical orientation of each: Leonora with her moral concerns is Irish Roman Catholic, and Dowell with his ethical unknowability is American Nonconformist Quaker.

It is important to remember these characterizations are all from Dowell's perspective. Ford clearly has in mind what Henry James said of the novel, "There is the story of one's hero and then there is the story of one's story." As he works through the information he has recently been given about the last nine years—the information about Edward's affair with his wife, Florence, as well as the history of Edward's multiple infidelities and final struggle to maintain an idealized love for Nancy—Dowell himself writes a novel. He does not merely offer incoherent conversational fragments to his listener as he claims, nor does he stay caught in an impossible quest for form. Rather, his novel takes a specific form: romantic tragedy. Readers should attend to Dowell not simply as a poor, repressed soul who is caught with horrible newfound knowledge and is trying to make sense of it. They should also attend to Dowell as a novelist and consider his choices and methods as a novelist. His epistemological uncertainty centers on ideas of morality and character, and the central question of his novel is a moral one: "How should we judge Edward Ashburnham on a moral level?" Dowell's novel begs a larger question, however, that readers should ask about Ford's novel: "How should we judge the novelist Dowell on a moral level?"

As Wilde did with Dorian Gray, Dowell depicts Leonora, Edward, and Nancy as being tragically caught between conflicting and seemingly irreconcilable, one-sided social-moral narratives about how one should live. According to Dowell, the story is tragically sad because the moral "normal type," Leonora, goes on to survive in society while the great souls—Edward and Nancy—are snuffed out (174–75). Leonora remarries and has a child, while Edward commits suicide and Nancy goes mad. Yet associating Dowell's position with what the reader is supposed to believe, or even with Ford's own position, is problematic. Certainly like Dowell, who claims he wants to be like Edward, Ford himself wanted to be free of, or at least struggled with, social-moral ideas about sex and marriage. Ford led a rather tumultuous sexual life, with several marriages, divorces, affairs, and longer extramarital relationships over the years. He told his publisher that *The Good Soldier* was a "serious . . . analysis of the polygamous desires that that underlie all men" (qtd. in Stannard 112). While it is difficult to know how seriously to take this line, in part this seems right. Dowell fairly successfully leads the reader to pity Edward as he imagines and identifies with Edward's "polygamous" desires. Yet the novel also purposefully considers Edward's desires in light of Great Britain's social structures, literary and religious history, and Christian ethos. While Dowell mournfully claims society does not allow people like Edward and Nancy to survive, it does not follow that this attitude should also be the reader's. Dowell's romantic tragic form and the position of unknowability he claims need careful analysis.

Examining Ford's historical context illuminates how and why he characterizes the religion and actions of his characters as he does. Ford sets up a clear difference in his British and American characters regarding the morality of marriage, divorce, and sex, despite the Protestant backgrounds of the Americans and the influence of Puritanism in both countries. Interestingly, Dowell never labels Edward's or Florence's adultery a "sin" like Leonora does. In parallel, Florence never seems to bear guilt in her conscience over her adultery like Edward does, or at least not to his extent. The novel attributes these different approaches in England and the United States to the different historical trajectories of church–state relations in both countries. When Florence touches Edward's wrist at Marburg to signal she is ready to sleep with him, she states:

> There it is—the "Protest." . . . Don't you know that is why we were all called Protestants? That is the pencil draft of the Protest they drew up. . . . It's because of that piece of paper that you're honest, sober, industrious, provident, and clean-lived. If it weren't for that piece of paper you'd be like the Irish or the Italians or the Poles, but particularly the Irish. (29)

In setting this scene at Marburg, Ford highlights the shift in church–state relations that the Reformation brought and the consequent effects on marriage and divorce law. In non-Catholic regions after the Reformation, marriage tended to become a civic contract governed by the civil courts, losing its status as a religious sacrament protected by church courts. Of course Protestants could individually maintain a sacramental, religious view of marriage, seeing it as indissoluble, but with the emergence of Protestantism appeals regarding divorce, adultery, and marriage are increasingly made to the state, not to the church. In this area, morality begins to separate from religion with the Protestant Reformation. This is what Leonora seems to express when she says to Dowell after the wrist-touching: "Don't you see that that's the cause of the whole miserable affair; of the whole sorrow of the world? And of the eternal damnation of you and me and them" (30).

In England, of course, Protestantism was founded on Henry VIII's break from Rome in order to get a divorce. The Church of England henceforth was bound to the state, and marriage, divorce, and adultery became the province of both church and state, which were intimately connected. The ecclesiastical courts of the Church of England still retained the power to dissolve marriages in the case of adultery, but an Act of Parliament also had to be granted. Because this was very expensive, divorce was largely open only to wealthy men. The English state was involved in religious and moral matters because it was part and parcel with the church. Even into Ford's day, England considered itself to be a Christian state. The Nonconformists emerged simultaneously in the Reformation period to combat this union of religion and nationalism, both theologically and politically.

Events in Ford's day were directly descended from the events of the Reformation. The relation of church and state, religion and morality, were dominant issues in Edwardian England; indeed, these issues constitute the crisis Wilde was dramatizing. In the wake of the Charles Stewart Parnell case, Nonconformists increasingly put pressure on the Establishment Parliament regarding moral matters. For example, one of these became the question of Sunday or Sabbath. When Prince Edward started playing golf on Sundays, a precedent was set for the "Victorian Sunday" to be violated, and the relation of religion and sport became a huge debate (Robbins 57–58). Nonconformists in particular put pressure on Parliament to protect the Sabbath. Bicycling, going to the theater, or participating in some other form of non-Sunday "play" was termed "going Continental" and seemed to be considered simultaneously nonnationalist and non-Christian (Robbins 58). At the Church of Ireland Conference in 1910, "The Secularization of Sunday" was debated at great length. With this issue, the relation of church and state in England was highlighted: should the state be expected to enforce religious, moral principles and practices? With the weakening of state protection of religious practices, increasingly Nonconformist churches formed organizations to combat irreligious patterns in society such as gambling, prostitution, and drinking (58). These organizations emphasized individual behavior, personal responsibility, character formation, and conversion as the ways to combat the larger evils of society (59). According to Robbins, while other types of Christians also participated in such tactics, including Catholics, this "zeal for respectable living" became associated primarily with the "Nonconformist Conscience" and the Puritan emphasis on morality which emerged and intensified in the wake of the Parnell case (59). Such endeavors were often seen as "hangovers from the nineteenth century" and "as an essentially middle-class moral crusade" (Munson 1). The "Nonconformist Conscience" came stereotypically to mean "a selective application of rigid rules" pressured onto others but not onto one's self (Munson 241).

Yet as Munson argues, there was more to the Nonconformist conscience than this stereotype. Methodists were interested in making sure public political figures were also morally upright (108). This trend is reflected in Dowell's treatment of the Kilsyte case, Edward's first infidelity:

> You see, the servant girl that he then kissed was nurse in the family of the Nonconformist head of the county—whatever that post may be called. And that gentleman was so determined to ruin Edward, who was the chairman of the Tory caucus, or whatever it is—that the poor dear sufferer had the very devil of a time. They asked questions about it in the House of Commons; they tried to get the Hampshire magistrates degraded; they suggested to the War Ministry that Edward was not the proper person to hold the King's commission. Yes, he got it hot and strong. (41)

For the Baptists and Congregationalists, politics and religion had always been more thoroughly related. These denominations felt responsible for ensuring and maintaining English liberties: freedom and hope for all citizens, not just the elite (Munson 220).

With the success of Nonconformity in politics in the 1900s, however, according to Munson, Nonconformist religion, just like Anglicanism, simply became absorbed into "mainstream urban life" (304). Nonconformist prosperity in politics did not aid its cause, for just as in the Anglican Church, others could simply see the divergence of public and private forms of Christianity, mistrusting the alliance of religion and politics. Perhaps this is what Ford observed when he said the Protestant forces were waning in England. Even some Nonconformists felt the weakening of their current influence and of their historical position as social and political gadfly. The Baptist leader, J. H. Shakespeare, advocated for ecumenical unity instead of denominational solidarity, saying in 1918: "so far as England is concerned, the era of division has spent its force and lost its moral appeal" and that "the gains do not outweigh the losses" when it comes to "Puritanism" (71–72). In addition to this weakening of the Nonconformist position, Ireland, Scotland, and Wales were all in their own ways exerting pressure on the "religion" versus "nation" question, such that as the state wrestled with unity so did the Anglican Church (Robbins 87). Despite all this, however, Robbins still sees the period leading up to the Great War as one in which the established church was "part of the fabric of the State" (103). In fact, when the war began, many of these religious-national tensions receded as other matters became more important.

Ford would have witnessed and read about, as well as been person-
ally affected by, extended political debates over laws regarding marriage,
divorce, and adultery that occurred in the 1900s and 1910s. In these years
divorce law reform was a hot topic of debate. Divorce law had not been
modified in England since 1857. In that year, Parliament had passed the
Matrimonial Causes Act, which allowed ordinary people, and not just
the wealthy, to divorce under certain conditions. Men could divorce on
grounds of adultery, but it was much harder for women to initiate and
secure a divorce. Not only did women need to prove their husbands were
unfaithful, but they also had to prove at least one additional fault such as
cruelty, rape, incest, sodomy, bestiality, bigamy, or two years of abandon-
ment. If another fault were not present, women could not divorce on the
basis of adultery. Well into the twentieth century, then, women in Britain
had little recourse against abusive husbands. This means that Leonora,
who late in the novel offers to divorce Edward in order that he can be
with Nancy, really could not have attained a divorce, for there was no
other fault she could prove. In her case, both her Catholic Church and
the state would have prevented a divorce. Any divorces that did occur
in Ford's day would likely have been widely publicized and considered
scandalous, such as the Brand case Nancy reads about in the newspaper. In this case the courts are able to prove on behalf of Mrs. Brand that
Mr. Brand committed adultery and that he was physically abusive to her
when he was drunk. The paper Nancy reads is probably a popular tabloid, which often dramatized open court divorce proceedings and revealed
"scandalous details" to please and draw in curious readers (Harris 35).
E. S. P. Haynes, a leading proponent of divorce law reform, blamed the
popularity of divorce court publicity specifically on the Puritans:

> We are suffering from the type of Puritan whom Macaulay described
> as putting down bear-baiting not because it gives pain to the bear, but
> because it gave pleasure to the non-Puritan spectator. Our Puritan of
> today not only enjoys the spectacle of the Divorce Court but also the sat-
> isfaction of knowing that it gives pain to a vast number of persons, and
> particularly to those who, however foolishly or innocently, have strayed
> from the path of Puritan conventions. (99–100)

Because divorce was so publically scrutinized, often it was a matter of
honor for the man to take the blame. Perhaps this is why Edward does
not consider divorce an option, for it would bring dishonor to Leonora

as well. Dowell reflects this fact when he says "it was only by [Edward's] making it plain that a divorced lady could never assume a position in the county of Hampshire that he could prevent [Florence] from making a bolt of it with him in her train," for she had constantly offered to divorce Dowell (68).

In the 1900s, books, articles, editorials, and novels were widely published on the topics of marriage and divorce. Among other things, at issue were unequal rights for the poor, who could not afford a divorce; unequal rights for women; and the bawdy publicity allowed in tabloids and other venues. In 1910, debates heated up so much that King Edward established a Royal Commission on Divorce and Matrimonial Causes, whose purpose was to consider these issues.[6] The Commission was made up of fourteen commissioners, including two women, the first ever to serve on a Royal Commission. They sat from February 25, 1910, to December 1912, and heard 246 witnesses from all walks of life and from various institutions and organizations. Janice Harris puts forth four reasons for why the Royal Commission was established: an English sense of vulnerability within Europe; fear of a declining population or "racial" degeneration; anxiety over the increasing numbers of marital separations and consequent extramarital relationships and illegitimate children; and David Lloyd George's agenda of social welfare (16). In the latter case, Lloyd George argued that the state should take an interest in the welfare of its people by establishing various social programs to support them. This policy went against England's established tradition of seeing public and private moral and economic responsibility as separate things. Harris believes such policies opened the way for the state to enter into family issues, opening marriage in England to more public scrutiny (23).

An issue Harris addresses only briefly in her study of Edwardian divorce is one that is central to the debate and to Ford's novel: the relation of church and state and their proper roles in moral issues. The Commission's recommendations called for changes in the civil law including: court reduction of costs so poor people could have equal access to divorce; the establishment of equity between men and women in divorce proceedings; and curbing of divorce case publicity (Harris 67). The Commission on the whole split over the issue of whether grounds for divorce should be broadened beyond adultery, and so did not make a recommendation regarding it. The minority report formulated and distributed

---

6. The proceedings of the Commission are well documented in *The Times* as well as in most of the major journals of the period.

widely in opposition to the majority report was written mostly by church-men who did not agree with the Commission's recommendations. The minority report continued to cause much debate in the ensuing years, and perhaps caused such a divide at the time that essentially nothing was done to make the changes for which the Commission had called. Only after the Great War in 1923, were more laws passed making divorce slightly easier for women in England, although the essentials of the law remained unchanged. Only in the 1950s was another Royal Commission established on this topic.

Most fundamentally at stake in the Royal Commission debates was the nature of marriage. Is it sacred or secular? Sacramental or merely a legal contract? In England it historically had been both as church and state were closely linked. As one writer in the *Times* put it, the Commission arises recognizing the "increased difficulty of correlating the civil and the ecclesiastical factors of marriage" and that "since the Reformation the tendency had been more and more to exalt the civil and depress the ecclesiastical aspect of marriage." In England, this writer says, "the Church's control of marriage had never been complete."[7] This ill-defined relation of church and state regarding marriage law stemming from the Reformation consistently fueled the Edwardian debates. Although they had some differences on how to interpret the Bible on moral issues, church leaders—Anglican, Roman Catholic, and Nonconformist—all essentially agreed that the Christian view of marriage was sacramental and that marriage was therefore indissoluble, except perhaps in the case of adultery. The Nonconformists actually tended to favor equal rights for women and men, but vehemently argued for the sanctity of marriage and against law reform.

In arguing this question of marriage's nature, various other sub-questions were debated during the Commission between churchmen and secularists. These included: What exactly did the Reformers believe in England about marriage and divorce? Was Thomas Cranmer's *Reformatio Legum,* which allowed for more causes for divorce, actually acted upon, or was it a mute document with little effect historically? Haynes, one of the dominant voices for secularizing marriage, claimed the church did not know its own history as well as it should. He argued:

> It is fairly common knowledge that Cranmer and others recommended a law of divorce that would have given liberty of remarriage in the case of

---

7. *The Times,* June 28, 1910, p. 2.

adultery, cruelty, and desertion, and abolished permanent separation as opposed to divorce. At the Reformation the doctrine of a sacrament in marriage was abandoned, and this revived the controversy whether marriage was of its nature indissoluble. (739–40)

Haynes argued that the church had never upheld the position for which it currently was standing. The man most responsible for the minority report, Sir Lewis Dibdin, Dean of the Arches, on the other hand, argued that not only was Cranmer's document not made law, it was not instituted at all in the Reformation and "never had any operative force" ("English Church Law" 904). Related questions argued over were: Is the Church of England more Catholic, Protestant, or a mixture of both? If more Catholic, as surely it is, because the English church adhered more to Catholicism's "rigorous state of things than other Protestant countries" did, can't it get around this issue by establishing a practice of annulment, as the Roman Catholic Church has done?[8] Another line of argument asked: Despite the Church of England's stance on the sanctity of marriage, what have its practices actually been in the past? Have not there been times when the church has looked the other way, so to speak, and allowed aristocrats to buy divorces through Parliament? One writer suggests that even if the upper classes divorced and remarried through private Acts of Parliament or in "defiance of the law" from the Reformation onwards, even if the "national conscience had fallen away from the Catholic ideal of marriage, the law alike of Church and State still stood for the higher morality" and should continue to do so ("Divorce and the English Reformation" 21). Debaters argued over whether divorce reform would actually lead to more social immorality or not. Some saw England's being so far behind the rest of the West on this issue an embarrassment and a sign of England's decline. They wanted England to overcome its Puritan history on this topic.

Numerous churchmen and women, officials and laity, gave testimony before the Commission on these topics, and many articles and essays were published in journals arguing for all sides. The marriage question like no other seemed to bring to the forefront of national discussion the potential effects of the separation of church and state on religious and moral issues. Many could not understand the church's upholding of the sacramental view of indissoluble marriage to the detriment of women and the poor, who might be stuck in abusive situations or who might cohabitate

---

8. See Haynes, "The Church."

and establish families outside of marriage in light of having little other option. They wondered why the civil law had to uphold the sacramental view of marriage, even more so if since the Reformation marriage had been primarily a civil contract. Clearly, while not ever in danger of having to change its position, the church saw as the most crucial issue the need to maintain the law's alliance with Christian teachings. In the terms of this book, at stake in the marriage debate was this question: should the law uphold Puritan morality as it currently stands, or not?

In the time Ford writes, then, while the state's governance over moral and religious issues is debated in response to the Royal Commission as well as in other areas, the state nevertheless upholds what the church had upheld for centuries: it was very difficult to get a divorce in England. The effect of such laws, which Dowell specifically links to religious attitudes and beliefs, is the reason Dowell sees Edward, Leonora, and Nancy as trapped and tragically doomed. English marriage laws still assume and speak to the inner conscience and to ideas of sin, good and evil, and God; they are still informed and shaped by both Puritan religious belief and Puritan social morality. In Dowell's novelistic view, which is very similar to Nietzsche's, the laws and religions of England inhibit the freedom and passions of the natural true self by causing religious guilt, social shame, and inner conflict.

In the United States, on the other hand, where the terms "dissent" and "nonconformist" held little meaning, church and state were constitutionally separate entities and always had been. Marriage and divorce laws more quickly lost their religious grounding. By 1880, one in sixteen marriages in the United States ended in divorce, the highest rate in the world. By 1910, the United States had by far the most divorces in the world. The skyrocketing divorce rate and looser legalities against adultery paralleled increasing American affluence, a trend Ford reflects in his American characters. Quite simply, the transition of marriage from a sacrament to a civil contract occurred much more quickly in the United States than it did in England, even if the full opening of the law to no-fault divorces in both places came at similar times (1960s and 1970s). Ford's novel clearly implies that the more liberal American morality was a function of the separation of church and state and hence of religion and morality, while the slower pace of England was due to the fact that church and state, and hence religion, morality, and the law were one and the same Protestant Establishment.

Ford's stance in this seems contradictory, however, for Tory–Catholic–Feudal Ford held disdain for Protestantism, yet he and his character Dowell seem to want the freer sexual morality it historically enabled. England had been slow to find this sexual freedom, as the union of church and state maintained the guilt and shame cultures longer than in other Protestant nations. Ford in his own life certainly identifies with the impulse found in so many modernist texts to escape the "Puritan" idea of the self. Yet what Ford knew, but his character Dowell seems not to know, is that the relation of Puritan social morality to sexual freedom and romantic desire is in large part the dialectic of the novelistic narrative. *The Good Soldier* explores and manipulates this dialectic.

In the novel, American Protestant concern over adultery and extramarital sex seems to be retained only by Florence's old spinster aunts, who were thoroughly imbued with the "New England Conscience" (9), but who nonetheless could not actually use the word "sacrament" when describing marriage (56). The sisters Hurlbird are characterized by Dowell as the old-fashioned keepers of an old-fashioned religion and morality that no longer applies in the world. Although they are Episcopalian, they are among the last remnants of what emigrated as the English Puritan Spirit to the United States and manifested itself, according to Dowell's stereotypical view, in the form of a rigid work ethic and a rigid morality. They were the Hurlbirds of Stamford, Connecticut, "where, as you know, they are more old-fashioned than even the inhabitants of Cranford, England, could have been" (2). The family came to America from Fordingbridge in 1688, presumably before the Glorious Revolution during the months when it appeared as if England was headed for an extended Catholic monarchy. As Dowell sees it: "on the strength of that [Florence] was going to take her place in the ranks of English country society" (55). Dowell claims that: "when I called in on Florence in the little, ancient, colonial, wooden house . . . the first question [the aunts] asked me was not how I did but what did I do" (9). Because Dowell does "nothing," they used to say he was "the laziest man in Philadelphia" (9). This concern for a work ethic is also seen in Florence's father, who, when he retired from being a manufacturer, decided to take a world tour in order that he not be called "the laziest man in Waterbury" (11). The aunts were emotionally and stereotypically repressed. When Florence announces her intent to marry Dowell, the aunts "could not say one single thing direct" but merely wrung their hands, got tears in their eyes, and tried indirectly to warn him because they knew of Florence's premarital affairs (56). On the morning after Florence and Dowell's elopement, her father reads to Dowell a "full-blooded lecture, in the style of American oration, as to the perils for young American girlhood lurking in the European jungle" (59).

Dowell hails from a different branch of American Nonconformity: he is a Quaker of Philadelphia, "where, it is historically true, there are more old English families than you would find in any six English counties taken together" (2). He carries around the world with him the title to his family farm, deeded by the Indians to the "first Dowell, who left Farnham in Surrey in company with William Penn." This deed he keeps "as if it were the only thing that invisibly anchored [him] to any spot upon the globe" (2). In fact, Dowell claims he has traveled so much that "the whole world for [him] is like spots of colour in an immense canvas," and he reflects that "perhaps if it weren't so [he] should have something to catch hold of now" (9). Proclaiming himself to be a "wanderer upon the face of public resorts," Dowell has absolutely nothing to do and has "no attachments, no accumulations" (13–14). He does nothing because he never saw "any call to do it": "Why does one do things? I just drifted in and wanted Florence" (9).

As Americans, then, both Dowell and Florence are detached from the religious narratives of their family histories. There is no connection in their minds between religion and marriage, and in fact, they seem to have little religious sensibility at all. At one point, for example, when discussing Leonora's consternation over any future children not being raised Catholic and Edward's insistence they be raised Anglican, Dowell says: "I don't understand the bearing of these things in English society. Indeed, Englishmen seem to me to be a little mad in matters of politics or of religion" (101). Florence appears to flit from experience to experience with little to motivate her except her aesthetic interests and economic and social drive. She is all "culture," always reading guidebooks and instructing her companions on European history and art, "always an Anglomaniac" (22). It would appear, then, that the Americans Dowell and Florence, although different, attempt to live life entirely on the surface without religious or moral grounding and without a narrative to live by: a life of supposed freedom.

Yet Dowell's Quaker heritage perhaps plays a vague role in shaping him, for it is the Puritan view of the self that he ends up struggling with in his moral assessment of Edward. Dowell's central concern for the moral judgment of Edward is remarkable, given the pain and anguish Dowell's newfound knowledge must generate in him. He has learned that his own marriage was built on lies; that his best friends whom he thought constituted a model couple, instead had a terrible marriage and didn't speak to each other in private; that his hero was a frequent adulterer, including with Dowell's wife; that his wife committed suicide; that his hero also was desperately in love with the same woman Dowell was in love with; and that this woman loved Edward, not him. Dowell also learns that he has been ignorant of all of these facts. Yet unfathomably, Dowell's storytelling, while occasionally showing signs of anger, centers on the epistemological problem of how to understand Edward on a moral level.

Dowell's first shock from his new knowledge seems to be the idea that there is a divide between the depth and surface in people's character, that the Puritan view of the self may be true, or at least that it appears to be true with English people. He realizes he "had never sounded the depths of an English heart" but had "known only the shallows" (1). He thinks: "After forty-five years of mixing with one's kind, one ought to have acquired the habit of being able to know something about one's fellow beings. But one doesn't" (23). Dowell is frustrated with the split he now sees between surface and depth, between social convention and inner passions or sentiments. In this frustration, Dowell echoes much of what Ford himself believed about the Englishman. Dowell says that "this state of things," in which there is such a divide between outer and inner personhood, in "only possible with English people" (1). He goes on to describe that

> the whole collection of rules applies to anybody. . . . You meet a man or a woman and, from tiny and intimate sounds, from the slightest of movements, you know at once whether you are concerned with good people or with those who won't do. You know, this is to say, whether they will go rigidly through with the whole programme from the underdone beef to the Anglicanism. (24)

There is a social-moral establishment built entirely on the surface and this surface is so strongly embedded in the English character that it masks or even makes it impossible to access the inner self: "with all the taking for granted, you never really get an inch deeper than the things I have catalogued" (24).

Yet ironically, Dowell has himself been incapable of accessing his inner desires or intuitions about people. Like Ford's "Puritan-spirited" Englishman, Dowell has been satisfied entirely with the surface and hence has been blindly optimistic his whole life, despite the moral trespassing occurring beneath his very nose. He may have lost his religion, but Dowell's stereotyped Nonconformist heritage has been passed on nonetheless: he has lacked "the critical attitude" as well as the ability to intuit and to express the feelings of his true self.

To Dowell, Edward's virtues were always clearly evident on the surface: Edward was a good soldier, a good "feudal" landlord to his tenants, a sentimental and generous person. Leonora's divulgences about Edward's affairs makes Dowell wonder, however, whether the entire idea of forming judgments of people based on the appearance of their virtue should be dismissed forever. He wonders if one should change one's view of someone and of their virtue if one finds out things that do not comply with one's previous judgment. Perhaps there is the outward person whom one sees, whom one judges to be "good people" based on conventions and experience, but then also the inner person who is more inscrutable, hidden, who might have passions and desires not detectable on the surface but which point to a person's "real" self. As did Wilde's Lord Henry, Dowell questions the Puritan idea of "character" itself, asking: "For who in this world can give anyone a character? Who in this world knows anything of any other heart—or of his own?" (107). He goes on to say that one cannot predict a person's behavior all the time but can only form "average estimates" about how people will act (107). Just as Florence's longtime trusted maid all of a sudden stole a ring, so Edward had aberrations in his behavior that resulted in extramarital affairs. At first Dowell says "It was nothing in her [or Edward's] "character," nothing fixed in their natures that caused these breaches. But then immediately, Dowell backtracks, thinking it may have been Edward's character after all, but then he leaves the discussion saying, "It is difficult to figure out" (107). In the end, Dowell is unwilling to assign Edward a permanently or even temporarily corrupt or malformed inner character, as might be done in Puritan hermeneutics.

Instead, Dowell ends up lauding Edward's inner desires as being "natural" in a novelistic, Nietzschean sense: his multiple affairs are merely the product of Edward's inner sentimental and emotional, passionate self. Edward is heroic for Dowell because he is able to access and live out these desires. Yet unlike Wilde's Lord Henry, Dowell does not dismiss the surface elements of social morality. Rather, Dowell admires both Edward's outward social-moral virtues and his inner passions. To him, the aristocratic–feudal ideals of "courage, loyalty, honour, constancy" are not misaligned with Edward's inner sentimentality and romantic drives (17). Ideally, they could work together, and Dowell admits to wanting to be just like Edward. Rather than pass definitive moral judgment on him, identifying Edward as an immoral character type and establishing in the reader a negative judgment of him, Dowell says: "It is impossible of me to think of Edward Ashburnham as anything but straight, upright, and honourable. That, I mean, is, in spite of everything, my permanent view of him" (78). For Dowell, the Puritan view of the self is not capable of providing full and accurate knowledge about Edward's true nature. Such questioning and dismantling of Puritan epistemology is, as we have seen, part and parcel of the British novelistic tradition. Dowell himself adheres to what this book has been outlining as the novelistic narrative: the view in which natural human passions or the true self are in conflict with the Puritan narrative of morality and truth. These natural passions preside outside society's moral codes and any narratives that establish those codes.

From the beginning to the end of his novel, Dowell sets up a romantic, tragic framework by arguing that there is not a universal narrative that provides us with the categories by which to make moral judgments: "Madness? Predestination? Who the devil knows?" (19). The absence of a directing narrative or a God at work in human history particularly seems a problem for interpreting moral matters, especially sexual ones: "I don't know. And there is nothing to guide us. And if everything is so nebulous about a matter as elementary as the morals of sex, what is there to guide us in the more subtle morality of all other personal contacts, associations, and activities? Or are we meant to act on impulse alone? It is all a darkness" (7). If there is a motivating force in the universe, for Dowell it is cruel and impersonal, and the story is sad to him because he does not see how anyone could have done anything differently (161). He claims to pity Edward that he "should be so tormented by blind and inscrutable destiny," and says there "is no priest that has the right to tell me that I must not ask pity for him, from you, silent listener beyond the hearthstone, from the world, or from the God who created in him those desires, those madnesses" (33). Dowell also refers to the events of the last nine years as a "monstrous and incomprehensible working of Fate" (123); as a "merciless trick of the devil that pays attention to this sweltering hell of ours" (146), and as Providence's "sinister jokes" (36). The only truth is that "the record of humanity is a record of sorrows" (143). Even the coincidence of the dates—all of the major events in Florence's life occur on August 4—is an ironic reversal of the coincidence of dates in *Robinson Crusoe*.[9] In Defoe's novel, the coincidence of dates would have been recognized by Puritan readers as an indication that God's Providence is at work, guiding history with a purpose. In contrast, Dowell does not

---

9. Florence's birth, her world tour, her first time being a mistress, her marriage to Dowell, the beginning of her affair with Edward, Maisie Maidan's death, and Florence's own death, all occur on August 4 (82). Similarly, in *Robinson Crusoe*, many of the key events occur on the same date.

know if this "curious coincidence of dates is one of those sinister, as if half-jocular and altogether merciless proceedings on the part of a cruel Providence that we call a coincidence," or whether it was "the superstitious mind of Florence that forced her to certain acts, as if she had been hypnotized" (53).

In Dowell's novel, then, there is no telos for human life other than the satisfaction of one's desires. Because there is no narrative by which to make moral judgments, and because all religious narratives restrict human nature, Dowell explicitly and purposefully leaves most moral points open for the reader to judge, especially toward the end of his novel. When reflecting on Edward's long struggle to stay away from Nancy as well as Leonora's behavior during that time, Dowell wonders if Edward was "unfortunate" because of Leonora's lashings, or whether he is fortunate "because he had done what he knew to be the right thing" (146). He does not pass judgment, and says, "I leave it to you" (146). He repeats this phrase again when he discusses whether Nancy really loved Edward or not after learning of his affairs, and also when discussing whether Edward was selfish or not in making Nancy move to India: "I can't make out which of them was right: I leave it to you" (170). In this light, Dowell appears to be an "ethical self," a person who exists outside social-moral concerns and categories, beyond good and evil. He explicitly puts himself and the reader in the position of unknowability. In this view, moral judgment is made to be radically individualist—each reader must form a moral judgment of any given case for him- or herself. Michael Levenson explains Dowell's lack of moral direction by arguing that Dowell is an "impressionistic" self: a subjectivity "before doing, feeling, and knowing takes shape" ("Character" 120), before experience, norms, and conventions put the limits on his judgment. Levenson calls Dowell a subject without a "character," an innocent man who has "performed no act that would place him beyond the moral pale" (*Modernism* 110, 116).

On one level, this seems true: by giving seemingly random and hodge-podge memories and impressions and by avoiding making judgments, Dowell supposedly imposes no interpretive framework on the reader nor does he seem have an interpretive framework for himself. Yet there are too many inconsistencies and troubling moments in his narrative to believe he is entirely original or "pre-form." Despite his repeated denials and claims to the contrary, Dowell imposes, albeit subtly, the genre of romantic tragedy upon the reader and clearly wants the reader to agree with his placement of the characters into this form. When Dowell argues that he hopes he has not given the wrong impression of Edward, that all of Edward's life was not taken up by affairs despite the time they receive in his narration, and that really these were just brief moments when one considers Edward's whole life and everyday activity (104), Dowell is saying that life is not like a novel. On the flipside, though, he is also admitting that his narration of Edward *is* more like a novel because his text focuses mostly on Edward's desires, affairs, and romantic ideals, just as many novels tend to do. Additionally, Dowell is constantly giving us information that he could never have had. The only way he can explain his newfound knowledge is to imagine these people as characters in a novel. His characterizations become the types seen in novels. Dowell depicts Edward and Nancy as the tragic heroes whose lives, like Dorian Gray's, challenged the Puritan categories of social morality in order to live their natural, passionate desires, but in the end were tragically eliminated from society. Female novelistic types are exploited: Nancy is depicted as the ideal, pure, virtuous woman; Florence as the conniving harlot; and Leonora, by the end, as the villain.

Similar to Wilde's tragic Hegelian structure, Dowell portrays Edward, Leonora, and Nancy all as "shuttlecocks," to use the word Nancy is prone to yell out in her insanity at the end of the novel. They are tragically torn between conflicting yet mutually constitutive narratives. Edward is caught between the narrative of the Anglican Establishment and his sentimental novelistic passions. Nancy's Catholicism conflicts with her sentimental novelistic passions. Leonora, the "normal type," is also torn between conflicting narratives—Catholicism and English social morality—but she is able to survive because in English society, according to Dowell, these are compatible with each other. Yet inconsistencies in Dowell's narration of these conflicts should cause readers to question his choice of narrative form and his own position within that form.

The character with whom Dowell wants his readers to sympathize the most is Edward, the hero of the tragedy. Edward's outward character and virtue are clearly linked to his position in the Establishment. He is descended from the "Ashburnham who accompanied Charles I to the scaffold" (2). His virtues are mostly social and outward, but he does feel regret and remorse with each marital infidelity that seem to be shaped by his Anglican conscience. When Edward is on his quest to stay away from Nancy and to keep his love for her idealized, it is to the Anglican prayer book that he returns, hoping to find the strength to remain "pure" in his desire (91). Edward's sense of Anglicanism is not helpful to him, however, and his character reflects what Ford writes about the Establishment in *The Spirit of the People*:

> What distinguishes the worshippers belonging to the Established Church is a frame of mind and not a religion—a frame of mind in which, though the ethical basis of Christianity is more or less excellently preserved, the theological conditions remain in a very fragmentary condition. Thus the devout and carefully practicing Churchman is apt to awaken and find the state of his mind to be singularly chaotic. (99–100)[10]

Edward is the product of a long-standing family and religious tradition in which the theology is disjointed from the social-moral behavior he is supposed to uphold. Dowell describes Edward as trying to work through both his "passions and his shame for them" as well as "the violent conviction of the duties of his station" (38). For Dowell, it is the religious narrative and its expected morality and sense of conscience, especially regarding sexual matters, that hinders Edward's passions. In the end, according to Dowell's novel, it is Edward's religious sense of guilt, however fragmentary, in conflict with his novelistic desire for pure and ultimate love for Nancy, that causes his final tragic fall. The two cannot be reconciled.

Ironically, however, Dowell does not seem to catch that the romantic ideals Edward gains from his novel-reading might be just as limiting, and perhaps just as false, as Edward's Establishment religion and social-morality. As an Anglican, Edward does not hold the Puritan fear of novels, yet novel-reading typologically shapes him in the ways Puritans feared it could: novels orient Edward's passions toward a sentimental, idealistic view of love and women that ironically seems to cause and shape his marital infidelities. Dowell suggests that for Edward life imitates art. As Levenson has brilliantly argued, Ford's novel dismantles social values *and* reveals romantic passion to be just as much a convention (116). Saunders identifies this, too when he says that "Edward and Nancy are acting out the ultimate romantic clichés" (429). Novels tend to say that romance and sexual desire—the supposed stuff of man's natural true self—is what can be accessed if one is able to escape and dismantle Puritan social-morality. Dowell buys into this narrative and clearly elevates Edward's romantic sentimentalism as noble. When describing Edward's "sentimental view of the cosmos," Dowell remembers how Edward "would say how much the society of a good woman could do toward redeeming you, and he would say that constancy was the finest of the virtues" (17). Dowell points out how ironic this is, given Edward's own marital inconstancy, but he justifies it as an influence of novels: "I must add that poor dear

---

10. For elaboration on this point, see Cheng, "Spirit."

Edward was a great reader—he would pass hours lost in novels of a sentimental type—novels in which typewriter girls marries Marquises and governesses Earls. And in his books, as a rule, the course of true love ran as smooth as buttered honey" (17). Edward talks like a novelist (75), and Dowell has seen "his eyes filled with tears at reading of a hopeless parting" (17). Dowell describes Edward's desire that "the girl should go five thousand miles away and love him steadfastly," providing "moral support" from afar, as something one finds in "sentimental novels" (168). Yet even though he says it is silly at times, Dowell does not condemn Edward for this influence. In fact, in the end Dowell claims he is "just as much of a sentimentalist as [Edward] was" (175). Dowell's tragic novel, like so many novels, shows the incompatibility of novelistic romantic passion with Puritan social morality and leads the reader to sympathize with Edward for his noble goals, entrapment, and unfulfilled love. Dowell writes a novel fully conforming to the dialectic of the novelistic narrative and sees it to be the truth about human life.

Yet there is a glaring inconsistency in Dowell's narrative if this is the narrative by which readers should judge Edward, for he also narrates Florence as being driven by novelistic role-playing and yet he condemns her behavior. Unlike Nancy, whom Dowell always describes in idealistic terms and who is impassioned by novels in the same idealistic ways Edward is, Dowell sees Florence modeling herself after great erotic characters. Clearly there is a connection between Florence and Flaubert's Emma Bovary: both commit adultery multiple times, both take prussic acid to kill themselves. Dowell says Florence "wanted to be a great lady" (80), to be "like one of the great erotic women of whom history tells us" (81). He even suggests that Florence never told Edward about the fabrication of her heart condition because the fiction made her seem more romantic (90). In the end, Dowell says Florence "wasn't real, she was just a mass of talk out of guidebooks, out of fashion plates"; she had the "personality of paper" (83). Unlike with Edward and Nancy, Dowell passes judgment on Florence, suggesting that "perhaps she deserved all that she got" (76), and he admits to hating what Florence did "with such a hatred that [he] would not spare her an eternity of loneliness" (47). To Dowell, Florence acted only out of self-interest: she wanted to live on an English estate and be an English lady, and Edward provided the means to this. But Dowell's hatred is curious. One would think he would hate Florence for lying throughout their marriage and for cheating on him with his best friend. But ironically this is not the case, for Dowell hates Florence not for her dishonesty and adulterous behavior, but rather for "cut[ting] out that poor imbecile of an Edward" from her own "sheer vanity" (47). She used sex for economic and social gain as well as for developing a certain sense of her own image, according to Dowell, and she thereby disrupted and denigrated Edward's quest for true love. Dowell has Florence play the novelistic type of the fallen, vicious harlot, and Dowell condemns her for wanting to be this type.

Dowell's treatment of Leonora is only slightly better. He does show some sympathy for her position of being stuck in a marriage with an unfaithful husband, but he clearly shows disdain for her church and blames it for pushing her toward unrealistic moral ideals regarding marriage. In some ways Dowell reflects a typical Nonconformist hatred of Catholicism that was still prevalent in Ford's day. Debates between Nonconformists and Anglo-Catholics had peaked in the 1890s, and both camps felt historically and presently abused by each other (Munson 228). Nonconformists described themselves as suffering particularly at the hands of Catholics and invoked much "anti-Popery" rhetoric (Munson 265). Well into the twentieth century, Roman Catholicism in the British Empire was still seen to be the enemy of democratic values (Robbins 14). Anglicanism's relation to Roman Catholicism was no better. In 1895, Pope Leo wrote *Ad Anglos,* which called for the conversion of England but never mentioned the Church of England. As Robbins says, "Rome pronounced Anglican orders to be null and void; Canterbury pronounced Nonconformist orders to be null and void" (19).

Yet, ironically, Dowell despises Leonora's Catholicism not so much because it is Catholic, but more because it is particularly English and Nonconformist in its concern for morality:

> Leonora was a woman of a strong, cold conscience, like all English Catholics. (I cannot, myself, help disliking this religion; there is always, at the bottom of my mind, in spite of Leonora, the feeling of shuddering at the Scarlet Woman, that filtered in upon me in the tranquility of the little old Friends' Meeting House in Arch Street, Philadelphia.) So I do set down a good deal of Leonora's mismanagement of poor dear Edward's case to the peculiarly English form of her religion. (39–40)

Dowell goes on to say that her "English Catholic conscience" was "all wrong" in this case because

> she quite seriously and naively imagined that the Church of Rome disapproves of divorce; she quite seriously and naively believed that her

church could be such a monstrous and imbecile institution as to expect her to take on the impossible task of making Edward Ashburnham a faithful husband. She had, as the English would say, the Nonconformist temperament. (40)

The Nonconformist Conscience was imposed on the Anglo-Catholics, according to Dowell, through

centuries of blind and malignant oppression, of ostracism from public employment, of being, as it were, a small beleaguered garrison in a hostile country, and therefore having to act with great formality—all these things have combined to perform that conjuring trick. And I suppose that Papists in England are even technically Nonconformists. (40)

On the Continent, a simple bribe would have secured Leonora a divorce, says Dowell. According to Dowell, Leonora responds to Edward's infidelities with a harsh asceticism, enduring self-denial, and working with such a "purposeful efficiency" to manage the estate that she loses her ability to feel, to access her desires, as well as to relate sympathetically to her husband (99). By the end of the novel, Edward's infidelities and final fall appear to be her villainous fault.

Leonora feels like a shuttlecock between her Roman Catholicism, by which she sees marriage as a sacrament, and her English social role, which did not expect divorce or even marital troubles of a gentlewoman, between her own guilt and shame. While she always maintains her social façade, Leonora also participates in religious practices. Both Leonora and Nancy attended the same convent. A fairly common practice in Ford's day, by 1900, 10,000 Roman Catholic women in England were in 600 houses. At these convents women performed both domestic tasks and typically "male" tasks such as managing property (Robbins 75). Leonora's experience in the convent gave her the skills to take over the estate when Edward was squandering it and having to pay blackmail. While she doesn't seem to attend church on a regular basis, Leonora does seek advice from her "spiritual advisers," and she attends retreats periodically. Dowell thinks the advice she gets from her spiritual advisers to be pretty bad, however. They encourage her to give Edward a fun time in Monte Carlo, but this is where his affair with La Dolcequita begins (109). In response to her concern for Edward's affairs, her advisers simply tell her, "Men are like that. By the blessing of God it will all come right in the end" (129). This makes Dowell state that in the Catholic Church, "the lot of women was patience and patience and again patience" until God should reward them (129).[11] Indeed, Catholic women in Ford's day tended to see Protestant women as "disturbed" as they worried about suffrage and divorce rights (Robbins 74). Dowell sees Leonora's passion to get Edward back as one that she felt would be a victory for her church, and he does not understand it (129). The whole situation causes her great consternation, something for which Dowell has some sympathy, but in the end it seems he despises her, too, for her Nonconformist morality intervened in and prevented Edward's happiness. With her Nonconformist temperament Leonora "had read few novels," and this, along with her Anglo-Catholic view of marriage, meant she had never been exposed to "the idea of a pure and constant love succeeding the sound of wedding bells" (129). Dowell implies that Leonora thus would never have been able to provide what Edward sought. His novel considers her to be the "normal type" because her outward social role, even though Catholic, and her essentially Nonconformist inner self, although in tension with each other, coincide enough to be acceptable in English society.

The only other character Dowell is sympathetic toward is Nancy, who is eventually caught between a Catholic understanding of marriage (it was "one of those blessed things . . . contemplated with reverence by her church") and a novelistic view of romance (77). The tension arises for Nancy when she reads of the Brand divorce case in the tabloid. This article shifts her thinking: she realizes that marriage was not a thing that always lasted forever or was necessarily based on love, and so it was possible Edward could love someone else. She also sees for the first time the hatred between Leonora and Edward. Leonora reminds her that the permanent sacramental view of marriage is the "law of the church. It is not the law of the land" (153), and that Protestants, if there is due cause, could secure a divorce. Nancy gradually summons in her imagination the versions of love and passion she has read about in novels, in which love is described as "a flame, a thirst, a withering up of the vitals" (154), in which love could "render a hopeless lover's eyes hopeless," causing drinking and sighing (155). Gradually, she realizes this description of the lover type matches Edward and his condition exactly. Ironically, she interprets Edward's inner state typologically as life imitates art. Through this identification of the "truth" of Edward's soul, Nancy comes to

---

11. One distinctly gets the sense with Leonora that Ford is consciously making her situation parallel to that of Augustine's mother, Monica, in the *Confessions*. Here, Monica endured abuse and infidelity from her husband with patience and prudence, until he saw the errors of his ways and late in life converted to the faith.

understand both that he loves her instead of Leonora, and that because he is Protestant, he might do so more readily. When Leonora intervenes with her "talk," however, it puts Nancy's soul in conflict: What was her Catholic duty, and what did her heart, as shaped by novels, desire? As it was for Edward, her inability to reconcile the contradictory narratives is the end of her, causing her to go mad. Dowell describes Nancy as someone who could have matched Edward's passion and returned the idealized love he sought because she believed, as Edward did, in the novelistic narrative of confinement and escape (169, 77).

Interestingly, in Nancy's madness, as she repeats over and over again in Latin: "I believe in God the Father Almighty" (162), Dowell claims "it is a picture without a meaning" (176). It appears that Dowell leaves the reader in a similar position as Wilde's novel does: which one of these is the truth about life—the Christian narrative or the dismantling of it? To Dowell, all the pain and anguish caused by and in these characters as they are batted back and forth among conflicting religious and social narratives, has come to nothing. Dowell derives no lesson from this tale other than his novelistic one: the norms and types exist to perpetuate society while those who are "the passionate, the headstrong, and the too-truthful" are condemned (175). He conveniently ends with a scene he has forgotten to include earlier: Edward's suicide scene—the final fall of the tragic hero. The romantic tragic novel is complete, and all the characters have fulfilled their novelistic roles.

And yet this ending should not sit well with the reader because it raises an explicit moral question that Dowell seems to avoid: Why would Dowell let Edward kill himself? Putting this scene at the end leads the reader to see it as the end of Edward's misery, perhaps the only option left as he succumbs to tragic contradiction, as Dowell claims it is. In fact, this is the excuse Dowell gives for not stopping Edward from killing himself:

> I guess he could see in my eyes that I didn't intend to hinder him. Why should I hinder him? I didn't think he was wanted in the world, let his confounded tenants, his rifle-associations, his drunkards, reclaimed and unreclaimed, get on as they liked. Not all the hundreds and hundreds of them deserved that that poor devil should go on suffering for their sakes. (177)

Dowell seems all the more impotent when he finds he has nothing to say to Edward's last words: "I wanted to say, 'God bless you,' for I also am a sentimentalist. But I thought perhaps that would not be quite English good form, so I trotted off with the telegram to Leonora" (177). In the novel Dowell writes, Edward's suicide is the necessary escape from the torments and contradictions of the world, and Dowell does not want to hinder this dramatic, romantic ending. The reader sees at some level that Edward has been pushed to this point. Yet what kind of person would let his friend commit suicide? If they have not already, at this point readers should begin to question Dowell's moral position, for the scene Dowell ends with is not the ending of the real story in terms of chronology. At the time of Edward's suicide, Nancy is still fully sane and potentially available to Dowell, though she is on her way to India. Dowell has not heard of Edward's infidelities yet from Leonora, including with his wife, Florence. He has not heard of the despicable state of Edward and Leonora's marriage. All he knows at this point is that Edward loves Nancy desperately, for Edward himself has confessed this to him. Might not Dowell have simply wanted Edward out of the way in order that he might have Nancy? Might his tragic narrative be constructed in order to hide the immoral nature of his own character? These are certainly possibilities that the reader ought to consider.[12]

There is also some incoherence on Dowell's part about the telegram Edward receives in this moment. Edward commits suicide shortly after reading a telegram from Nancy, who is at Brindisi. Earlier, however, we are told that Edward responded to the telegram with the belief that Nancy still loved him "underneath the official aspect of hatred," and that "her quite atrocious telegram from Brindisi was only another attempt to do that—to prove that she had feelings creditable to a member of the feminine commonweal" (170). He does not respond with suicide, but rather with a continued hopefulness that Nancy was just confused with her own conflicted soul and was trying to irk him. This inconsistency might simply be an error on Ford's part, but it also might be an error on Dowell's part, revealing how much he constructs his story into a tragic ending and fictionalizes events. There are plenty of other inconsistencies that previous scholars have pointed out that bring his reliability into deep question.[13]

---

12. The number of different ways Dowell's moral character and his response to Edward's suicide have been interpreted is intriguing. Some downplay Edward's suicide or try to justify Dowell's passivity in some way (see Sutton, and also McFate). Others believe Dowell undergoes moral growth or moral education over the course of the story (see Hood, and also Lynn). For other views, see Poole, Hawkes, Snitov, and also Bailin.

13. See, for example, Patrick A. McCarthy, who also lists other studies of Dowell's inconsistencies: "'In Search of Lost Time': Chronology and Narration in *The Good Soldier*," *English Literature in Transition* 40:2 (1997): 133–49.

That Dowell simply wanted Edward out of the picture does not seem so far-fetched when one looks back to Dowell's behavior in Florence's death scene. Although he believes at the time Florence died of her heart condition and is thus ignorant of her suicide, Dowell is still amazingly passive in this scene. He says he had little feeling for her at the time of her death (even though he did not know of her affair with Edward at the time): "I thought nothing, absolutely nothing. I had no ideas; I had no strength. I felt no sorrow, no desire for action, no inclination to go upstairs and fall upon the body of my wife" (75). In fact, he even says, "Florence didn't matter" (83), and that since that time he has had "no regret" and has considered her merely to be "a problem in algebra" (82). After he learns from Leonora years later of Florence's suicide, he says: "It is even possible that, if that feeling [of Florence not being real or mattering much] had not possessed me, I should have run up sooner to her room and might have prevented her drinking the prussic acid. But I just couldn't do it; it would have been like chasing a scrap of paper—an occupation ignoble for a grown man" (83). She didn't matter, the reader can infer, because Dowell's interests were with Nancy. The singular utterance he makes when told of Florence's death is to Leonora: "Now I can marry the girl" (71). Although he tells readers they should not think negatively about him for this and that he doesn't know why he said it at the time, it is hard to ignore. While Dowell claims he did not know he loved Nancy until that moment, readers also have to see that he is capable of not caring enough about people to intervene in life and death situations. He cannot act in real life, and he believed his intervention in two suicide cases would have been too "ignoble" or not quite "good English form."

Dowell tries to maintain a detachment from the world that disbelieves in the Puritan notion of the self and tries to exist outside social morality, but he has no ability, resolve, or convictions to act morally in the world. In fact, in this light he exemplifies the corruption of following only one's inner "natural" desires without a narrative or set of categories to guide one morally. As Dowell pursues his desire for Nancy, other humans become dispensable. It is entirely possible that Dowell constructs his passive and impotent "unknowable" stance and his tragic romance in such a way as to hide from his readers and even possibly himself his own moral emptiness and his despicable moral position. Extremely ironically, then, one possible ending for the reader is to judge Dowell's Puritan self typologically.

As it foregrounds the constructed nature of the novelistic narrative, Ford's novel asks its readers to consider how narratives form moral sensibilities and shape the self. It shows how the romance narrative and its elevation of human passion is itself a set of conventions perpetuated by the dialectic of Puritanism and escape in the novel. In Dowell's mind, romance novels tap the more real and natural desires and passions of the human being. In typical novelistic fashion, he pits religious and social-moral narratives—English Roman Catholicism, Nonconformity, Anglican Establishment, each of which is thoroughly imbued with the "Puritan Spirit"—against the romance narrative. Not surprisingly, he finds all the religious narratives lacking, false, and imprisoning, tragically hindering the ability to live out one's desires. The romantic genre Dowell chooses allows him to relegate real moral issues and judgments to the background as he assumes he has attained an ethical position and experience of life that is more representative of man's nature and human truth. Yet disturbingly, the romance narrative and Dowell's fragmentary form that hides it, also become Dowell's excuse for ignoring and hiding his own questionable social-moral position in regards to others. In the end, Dowell claims not to find meaning in the story or in Nancy's madness—it merely was inevitably fated to occur. Yet this explanatory narrative of tragic romance itself constitutes a moral position: one does not have to worry about morality because one is inevitably trapped in a fate that is beyond one's control. The novel thereby self-reflexively reminds readers that all narratives, even the narrative of escaping the Puritan narrative to achieve an ethical, natural self, embodies a moral stance.

Levenson argues that Dowell is an impressionistic self who at the end of the novel can begin to construct himself from scratch, so to speak, and begin to make moral judgments not based on norms but individually (117). This complies with the view in new ethical theory that morality can only be individualized. In Dowell, Levenson says, we see "morality, degraded by convention and thwarted by passion, hesitantly reappear[ing] in the simple judgments of a mind struggling to weigh its preferences" (121). When Dowell decides to favor Edward and Nancy, Levenson says, he may not "know, but he decides, and in so deciding, he gives a picture of morality in its nascent state, founded not on inherited norms but on original judgments of value" (121). Although this seems in many ways to be true, this chapter contests that argument. First, although Levenson shows how *The Good Soldier* reveals the constructed nature of both social-moral norms and romantic passion, he also seems to buy into Dowell's portrait of himself and neglects to question its moral validity. His argument focuses on the story of the hero and less on the story of the story. Ironically, in putting forth the idea that moral judgments can be derived individually and originally, Levenson and new ethical theorists promote an even more radical individualism than what the Puritan social-moral narrative was purported to do. Second, it fails to discuss the fact that when Dowell chooses Edward and Nancy it is not only at the end; he chooses them and the tragic romance genre throughout the novel. Additionally, Dowell's choice of a conventional narrative seems far from original. This leads one to ask: are there ever choices that are original and individual? Is there ever a nascent moral stance to be had? Not only does Ford make Dowell at least morally questionable if not reprehensible, he also shows the inadequacy, the lack of care, the self-focus, of the subject who believes he can be ethically sovereign as an individual. The ethical self is radically liberally individualist, and this is an asceticizing—and dangerous—limitation. In Ford's novel, the ethical self is *not* an adequate telos.

Rather than simply admiring Dowell's premoral ethical stance and Ford's construction of this personality, I believe that as with Wilde's novel, readers are also forced to consider the ramifications of this stance. Generating a frustration and disdain for Dowell, the novel forces readers to ask whether moral unknowability is really an adequate position for living in human community. "I leave it to you" might be what one feels like saying because of the complexity or ambiguity of many situations, but for humans to live in community and to value each other, seeing and connecting across the boundaries that separate groups and races, there has to be common ground, meeting points and norms of some kind. Leaving all moral judgments up to the individual—or believing the individual can exist outside or "before" morality—allows all individuals to remain sovereign individuals and is a great contradiction. Dowell seems to be the epitome of an uncaring radical individualism, unattached to society, and even unattached to his friends, who are expendable when they conflict with his desires.

To say all this, however, does not mean Ford did not see value in escaping Puritan social morality. Obviously he, too, longed for sexual freedom and furthered the social norm that stereotypically defined Puritanism as ascetic and repressed, as something in need of surpassing. Like many modernists, he also believed in art's ability over institutional religion's to speak truth about human life. Yet by exposing the modernist ethical self's link to novelistic conventions, he shows how this need for escape is conventional in itself and can never, or should never, be untied from social-moral concerns. While Dowell elevates novelistic romance over English religious narratives, Ford does not dismiss religion entirely and knows a mere dismantling of the Puritan framework is inadequate and itself limiting. Indeed, this book argues that achieving freedom from Puritan morality is an impossible stance to achieve, for ethical unknowability and Puritan morality are dialectically dependent upon each other in the novel's form. In shifting the idea of the self toward the ethical, as many modernists did, one can never escape the moral. In fact, as Ford's novel and Dowell's novel show, one can never fully escape a Puritan approach to morality and the self, one can never deconstruct it away, at least when one is writing a novel, for the novel is built upon this very foundation. Any sense of self, no matter how impressionistic or ethical, involves a form of asceticism. In this case, while the ethical subject seemingly finds more pleasure and less conflict in life, he occupies a morally questionable position, for he elevates his own desires and status over those of others and of society and assumes an even more sovereign individualist position of interpretive authority.

In making England's moral and religious history a theme, Ford returns us to the roots of the novelistic dialectic of Puritanism and its dismantling as well as to the roots of England's church, state, and morality debates. The status of marriage law in Ford's day is tied to this history. His novel stresses that Puritanism is a historical thing in England that should be historicized and analyzed. The church and state in England could separate; the state did not necessarily have to uphold religious principles or Puritan morality. Yet Ford's text also shows how the novel is a part of England's moral and religious history. Through pointing out the limitations of Dowell's novel and perspective, Ford's novel asks: How much have attitudes about marriage and romance and passion been shaped by religious belief, and how much by novels? Even more, how much have attitudes toward Puritanism been shaped by novels? Ford seems to know both that history shapes the novel and that the novel shapes history and at least in part, determines how the modern self thinks of itself and others. Like Wilde, Ford depicts a crisis point faced by society, a crisis over the relation of religion and morality, church and state, the freedom of the individual and the law. But bound up in this crisis is a crisis faced by the novel, for in modernity its dialectic has become a grand narrative that shapes how people think about these topics. The ideas that religion and morality do not have to cohere, and that man's natural desires and passions are opposed to Puritan morality, such that this morality must be escaped in order to achieve freedom, are ideas perpetuated by and constitutive of novels. One implication of Ford's novel may be the idea that this novelistic dialectic has run its course. While Ford obviously wants Puritan influences to be overcome in England, he also does not condone an "ethical self" such as Dowell who claims unknowability on all issues and is entirely aloof from and unable to act in the social-moral realm. Complete autonomy to pursue one's own natural desires, and to let others "be" in order that they can pursue their own, cannot be an adequate moral position. Although to Ford it needed overhaul, the realm of the social-moral must never and can never be neglected or escaped, especially in an art that claims to seek truth.

Conclusion

*M*ODERNISM in large part is a reaction against Puritanism. Modernist novelists reacted against both Puritan Christianity, which
assumes the presence of an inner conscience in the human subject and the
reality of a universal moral order governed by God; and Puritan social
morality, by which the assumed religious truths are discarded and only
an ungrounded surface morality remains. Historically literary critics have
narrated the modernists as successfully escaping both forms of Puritanism to become a new type of self, one who is free at last. Such a trend
is perpetuated by the new ethical theorists. This study has argued, in
contrast, that in reality a complete escape is ultimately impossible, for
the novel is still a novel, Christianity is still Christianity, and society is
still society. To various degrees, some early modernist novelists knew
this as they engaged with both sides of the Puritan dialectic that shapes
the novel: the biblical hermeneutics that shape its typological narrative
form as well as the ironizing of or rebellion against Puritan morality that
often shapes its narrative content. Modernists lean hard into the freedom,
doubt, and irony side of the dialectic as they question more thoroughly
than any other era the necessity, belief, and fundamental side of it. Some
such as Wilde and Ford highlight the impossibility of escape. They show
how the ethical self, which is constitutionally dependent upon the Puritan self, is itself a limited type formed through asceticism. Joyce leaves
us wondering ironically about the efficacy of the ethical self in Stephen
Dedalus, while only Forster finds a way to marry some elements of both

sides of the dialectic in Mr. Emerson. Nietzsche attempts to bypass the dialectic entirely by theorizing the higher man who learns to master its lasting influences, but even his formulation of "redemption from redemption" cannot escape morality and the logic of the Christian and novelistic narratives.

Modernist novelists and their characters question and doubt the truth of the biblical narrative and its view of history, as well as the idea of a universal moral order. Wilde seems to believe such an order is possible, but finds the expressions of it in his present context—Puritan morality and aestheticism—unacceptable and contradictory. Forster's characters have debates over what guides history, but in the end, only the "now" matters as Mr. Emerson promotes joy and bodily life in the present. Stephen Dedalus consciously removes himself from the Christian narrative, saying he both believes and disbelieves. Ford makes a theme of Protestantism's historical emergence. Like Wilde's, his novel reveals that the novelistic dialectic of Puritan morality and romantic escape has itself become a grand narrative that shapes how modern people think of themselves and their lives, especially regarding love and marriage. Many modernists and their critics view life through the novelistic narrative, by which escape from morality, religion, and rationality is achieved through art, the aesthetic, and the ethical. The novel emerges historically in the midst of early modern Puritan cultures, but it also goes on to shape history, influencing how people think of themselves in relation to what becomes a stereotyped Puritanism. The question Wilde was so fond of pointing out rings true throughout the novel's history: does life imitate art, or does art imitate life? This study sees the novel's retention of or dialectical dependence upon the Christian formulation of history and plot not as secular, but as still embodying a religion and a morality. The dialectic of belief and doubt, Puritanism and its dismantling, that forms the novel always leads the reader to believe in some sort of truth and to inhabit some form of morality, no matter how much a novel self-reflexively highlights its own fictionality.

Ironically, the ethical self who reacts against Puritanism in these texts because Puritanism is perceived to involve labeling, individualist interpretation, certainty, knowledge, otherworldliness, asceticism, and narrow one-sidedness, is itself individualist and autonomous. The ethical self is the sole interpreter of the self and society; the self is the sole source of the moral; the self is its own master. Yet the individual ethical self occupies a questionable moral position. Except for Mr. Emerson, the characters treated here have little regard or care for others, if any, as they pursue their natural inner desires and think of themselves as outside the conventional categories of morality, the remainder that cannot be contained by them. Some die tragically while others live only in solitude. They withdraw from human community and detach themselves even from those closest to them. In many ways, as it seeks an elusive freedom, the ethical self becomes even more of a liberal, sovereign individual than the Puritan self was. In fact, in creating and perpetuating the stereotype of the Puritan, one could even say that some modernist characters, novelists, and critics are just as "Puritan" as the Puritans, for ironically they do what they condemn the Puritan of doing. They limit Puritanism through imposed categories and assumed knowledge in order to justify their own position. Pericles Lewis argues that many modernist novelists searched for a spiritual type of community that could replace the diminishing relevance of the churches. This seems right, but it may describe more a fictional longing than a reality, for many modernist writers and characters are unwilling to submit themselves to any sense of communal identity. They tend to see all cultural narratives, except for the ones based on art, as inadequate. Dowell, Stephen, Lord Henry, and Dorian are unwilling to meet even part way those whom they reject, and they egoistically see themselves to be superior. Dismantling dangerous categories and forms of judgment is needed, but rebellion, escape, and passive tolerance do not lead to community or to lasting societal change.

So where do these revelations get us? For one thing, this study points to the necessity of moving beyond the novelistic narrative as it shows how the ethical self is dialectically dependent on a stereotypical definition of Puritanism and a typological narrative that participates in that which it condemns. It calls for renewed attention to the moral side of human life within modernist studies. The ethical experience of epistemological uncertainty to which modernist novels are purported to lead their readers no doubt has some positive value, but if we really want to establish community, a shared life, and to overcome the limits of typecasting and its categories that lead to violence, racism, sexism, oppression, brutality, and hatred, we have to find a way to carry ethical experience into practice in ways that create community rather than reject it. This calls for literary critics to look at modernist novels anew, to be open to the modernists' own attention to and concern for the moral and the religious, as well as to the novel's embeddedness in Puritan hermeneutics, as this study has shown them to have. Some modernists warn about and mourn the escape into the ethical, seeing it as an excuse for an impossible position of "amorality" and autonomy. Others point out the limitations of the position so many literary critics ever since, including the new ethical theorists, have glorified. In turn, literary critics could be willing to reexamine Puritanism, Protestantism, and Christianity anew and become more open to attending to their realities rather than to perpetuating the ways in which they have been stereotyped historically in novels, in criticism, and otherwise. In turn, as is happening in theology already, Christian believers might attend to what the modernists and the Catholics historically claimed about Puritanism and vice versa, which surely contains some truth, for it may help the church to develop more faithful, biblically derived practices, modes of reading scripture, and new relations with others. The individual must dialectically both submit to and critique the social-moral and religious discourses that compose the self, always striving for a better communal life and practice. Ideally such interpretation, submission, and critique would be practiced in community.

This study should make us also rethink the novel and its dialectical nature, seeing it not as a product of the religious–secular divide in modernity, but instead as perpetuating the narrative in which religion separates from morality, and in which the ethical (or aesthetic, in some cases) is thought to be an escape from morality. The novel's dialectic is Puritan first, deriving from the dialectical, typological process of Puritan Bible-reading in which a contradictory inner self is repeatedly drawn into a larger anagogical reality and made new, such that the self recognizes its epistemological limits, over and over again, hoping for the not yet while also concerned for moral practice in the present. The novel throughout its English history both believes in and doubts that narrative, holding belief and disbelief in tension. Hegel alters the Puritan conversion dialectic and applies it to his concept of world history, which itself becomes a helpful model for thinking about the novel. As seen, some novels such as Wilde's and Dowell's explore the tragic collisions of one-sided, contradictory truth claims. Some novels lead the reader to believe the dialectic can be transcended by the individual self, just as Stephen Dedalus, Lord Henry, and Nietzsche strive to do. Wilde, Forster, and Ford, on the other hand, as interpreted here, see a need for dialectical engagement in which both moral categories that are knowable and an ethical "letting be" of what is unknowable are constantly negotiated.

Let us briefly return to *Atonement,* the novel discussed at the beginning of this book as one that brings into question the value of epistemological uncertainty and much of modernism. At the end of *Atonement,* the reader receives the revelation that the text she has been reading is actually written by Briony herself. It is the novel Briony has been trying to write for fifty-nine years, ever since the rejection of her original draft which did not have enough plot and character development. Readers also learn that Briony, now an elderly woman, has just received a diagnosis of vascular dementia, which further brings her reliability into question. Briony admits to the reader she has altered the truth in her novel, not giving us the real historical ending but instead letting her characters, who are based on real people, live on to have a happy fictional ending. Readers are left with questions similar to those with which Dowell leaves them in *The Good Soldier:* How should readers judge the novelist, who is an imaginary character, on a moral level? Is the resultant novel a true struggle with conscience, or is it an attempt at self-justification through the fictionalizing of reality? Unlike Dowell, however, who seems to think the novelistic dialectic tells the truth about the human subject, that Puritan morality and law always hinder natural romantic desire, Briony willingly admits she has altered reality to fit a novelistic romance form. Does this difference lead to a different moral judgment of Briony than of Dowell?

At this ending point of the novel, readers are led to understand that Briony, who has become a famous novelist over the years, has continually struggled with how to tell her story. Presumably, her struggle to write has also been a struggle with her own conscience and guilt, and with her own moral position in the plot. Briony's childhood "crime" involved making a false accusation against Robbie, the boy she had seen with her sister when her sister had undressed and submerged herself in a fountain. Later that night, based on Briony's evidence, Robbie is accused, arrested, and jailed for his supposed attempted rape of Briony's cousin, Lola. Yet this accusation was neither certain nor based on facts, but only on Briony's imaginative piecing together of the things she thinks she saw and the placement of those impressions into a simple plot of good and evil.

Part I of her finished product is presumably the Woolf-like narrative upon which Cyril Connelly commented, in which Briony attempts to produce an amoral novel by telling the fountain scene from multiple perspectives. She tries to capture the way in which a child might imagine a false reality based upon the types of stories and morality tales a child knows. Briony as a child is a "Puritan," interpreting everything according to knowable and rigid moral categories, even more so because a sexual act is at stake of which she knows little. Briony in this section both wants to attribute such Puritan interpretation to a child, who thus might not be fully culpable, and at the same time recognize that guilt and error should nevertheless be assigned. This first section depicts Briony's accusation as immature, and her mode of storytelling in which facts are placed simply into moral categories and received plots as similarly immature. Real life, morality, and human character are more complex than a child can envision. Briony seems to be confused about her actions and her lack of forthrightness, especially when she has the chance to retract her statements. Part I also reveals, then, the powerful position of the novelist or storyteller who has the ability to influence how others interpret reality. Such influence can even come from an immature child.

Briony's "amoral" tale, in which the level of her moral culpability is uncertain or even ignored, was rejected for not having enough plot and character development. This means any sense of character or plot development in part I may be later fictionalizations, including Briony's own sense of guilt. It also means parts II and III are probably attempts at writing a novel that would please a publisher as well as the reader who expects moral and spiritual development of a novel's characters. Like Dowell, Briony tries to understand reality and the past by imagining its actions and people as if they were in a novel, but she admits she has created a fiction, whereas Dowell does not.

Part II moves out of Woolf-like epistemological uncertainty and is instead an intensely realistic yet fragmented portrayal of Robbie's experiences in World War Two at the Battle of Dunkirk. In this section, Briony seems to justify herself in part by leading the reader to understand that all humans are guilty. Just as in the war all parties participate in evil such that individuals are morally culpable not only because of their own choices but also because they are trapped in larger societal circumstances, so Briony is a product of society and culture at large. She did not choose the childhood stories and their moral categories that led to false judgment—these were given to her by English literary history. Fiction and history have mutually shaped each other. This section also implicitly asks how a story with plot and character development could be written when human reality is so far removed from such simplicity, when war can smash all previous notions of what is right and wrong and render the human subject lost in a violent and overwhelming reality. Part III returns to typical narration and depicts Robbie reunited with her sister, Cecilia. It even depicts a scene in which Briony, now a war hospital nurse, goes to their apartment and takes some steps toward amendment of her childhood "crime." Yet with Briony's revelations at the end, readers learn that Robbie did not survive the war to be reunited with Cecilia. His death at Dunkirk means the war section of Briony's novel is essentially historical fiction, rendered "realistic" through her research at the war museum and obviously not relayed to her directly by Robbie. Readers also learn that

Cecilia died in London during a bomb raid, and that Briony never went to her apartment, never met with the pair, never was reconciled to her sister, and never confessed her crime to anyone.

Her novel-writing, then, has simultaneously been her way of atoning for her crime and for achieving a justice for Robbie and her sister that was rendered impossible because of the war and their deaths. On the latter point, Briony sees the best justice for Robbie and Cecilia to be a fictional, romantic ending in which they are reunited. She justifies her fictionalization of Robbie's and Cecilia's lives by arguing that telling of their deaths would not have served any purpose:

> How could that constitute an ending? What sense or hope or satisfaction
> could a reader draw from such an account? Who would want to believe
> that they never met again, never fulfilled their love? Who would want to
> believe that, except in the service of the bleakest realism? . . . When I am
> dead, . . . no one will care what events and which individuals were mis-
> represented to make a novel. (351)

Briony claims that creating the romantic ending in which the lovers are reunited after the brutal war, which she has only in her last draft decided to do, serves a higher purpose for the reader by giving hope and satisfaction: "I like to think that it isn't weakness or evasion, but a final act of kindness, a stand against oblivion and despair, to let my lovers live and to unite them at the end. I gave them happiness, but I was not so self-serving as to let them forgive me. Not quite, not yet" (351).

Here, Briony argues that readers want romantic endings in which love triumphs over false moral judgment, over war, and over history. Yet in this case, the reader also knows that even if she is establishing Robbie and Cecilia in an eternal happiness that is entirely fictional, Briony is somehow in that process giving a better outcome than were the actual consequences of her childhood misrepresentation of the facts. Her childhood storytelling, in which Robbie played the villain, had real moral consequences in real life, ruining Robbie's life and prohibiting his love relationship with Cecilia. Further, what is one to think when Briony at the end admits she has returned purposively to where she began with her childhood play-writing—to romance and a fictionalization of the facts? Whereas the childhood plot-making had drastic moral consequences, she believes her current plot-making is a means of achieving justice for Robbie and Cecilia, to let them have a happier ending than their real lives did and to let the reader also have an idealistic escape experience. Robbie and Cecilia's imaginary love breaks free of the moral categories that led them to tragedy; their desires find satisfaction. In the childhood case, Briony does not know how she is fictionalizing reality while in the latter she does, and she has now decided that the fiction of romance is better than attempting to portray reality. She assumes romance is needed for readers in a world that is bleak and full of tragedy caused by the conflict of one-sided truth claims. For Briony, the novel with a happy ending provides hope for escape and a higher ethical experience and thereby plays a vital role in human life. If the novel ended only with this happy reunion, one could judge Briony in a way similar to Dowell, seeing her denying her moral culpability and justifying her own moral position by reworking reality into a novelistic form and into the ethical realm of letting the lovers simply "be."

Yet unlike Dowell, Briony does not simply dismiss the moral questions raised in her story, and in fact, she confesses she has fabricated much of the story in order to serve Robbie, Cecilia, and the reader. She is unwilling to write a scene in which she is granted full forgiveness. She recognizes as a truth the Puritan notion that the novelist is both creator and exegete, and she highlights this fact explicitly. The reader begins to realize the limiting nature of the novelistic dialectic. Briony admits the novel cannot provide atonement:

> The problem these fifty-nine years has been this: how can a novelist achieve atonement when, with her absolute power of deciding outcomes, she is also God? There is no one, no entity or higher form that she can appeal to, or be reconciled with, or that can forgive her. There is nothing outside her. In her imagination she has set the limits and the terms No atonement for God, or novelists, even if they are atheists. It was always an impossible task, and that was precisely the point. The attempt was all. (351)

Fulfilling what Puritans believed, Briony knows the novelist is the highest being with the most authority in a particular novel, but also that a novelist cannot provide atonement for herself because she is the creator of the narrative. It is not that she could *not have written* a story in which she was repentant and forgiven; that was a possibility all along. She could have created her own conversion and redemption, but she did not. Instead she highlights her own fictionalizing and does not let the reader romanticize her moral position or believe she has escaped it.

In the end, she says her attempt to seek atonement in the novel was enough. In fact, this seeking is all that is actually possible in a novel. She carried her past with her throughout her life and never closed off the memory of it by creating a plot that resolved everything. She narrates herself as a child who could not recognize that simple Puritan morality was not adequate to tell complex human stories. Fifty-nine years later, Briony seems to recognize also that the human subject and human storytelling cannot escape completely the realm of the moral and the social, and she wants to remind both readers and herself of this. To complete this particular novel without this confession would be to deny her unresolved guilt and moral culpability in the story. Elements of the Puritan moral side of the dialectic remain and help explain the events and stories of human life, but they never, perhaps, tell the full story.

Her novel ends, then, with neither a Puritan conversion of the self nor a Hegelian resolution of the tragedy. But it also does not leave readers in a position of saying that epistemological uncertainty is of utmost ethical value or the final truth about human life. We are left both with the fictionalized romance plot and its satisfaction of desires for escape and letting be, and with the ongoing moral quest undertaken by Briony. Like so many postmodern novels, Briony's novel self-reflexively brings into question the power and function of novels and storytelling in real life, continuing to play with the relation of art and life upon which Wilde was so focused. Briony denies the power of a novel or novelist to provide either final moral resolution or atonement for any human situation. Likewise, however—and this is key—she denies the power of a novel to provide a means of total escape from human moral situations. She retains a moral value for storytelling, as she sees the processes of trying to make sense of reality through storytelling to be a way of working out the moral complexities of life, even if those stories—and life itself—cannot provide complete redemption or resolution. One always has to recognize the limitations of the novelistic narrative.

All of this, of course, raises the question of whether atonement would be possible for Briony outside the novel. Perhaps, and perhaps Briony or McEwan leaves that as a possibility. But there is not much sign of religion in the novel, and Briony clearly believes the novel does not reflect a universal moral order. To her, no God but the novelist can intrude into the text. In the end, McEwan may be highlighting for us how the novel is trapped in the logic of the Puritan dialectic, finding itself unable to imagine anything different. On the one hand, this view could lead to pessimism and debunking, to the doubting side of the dialectic, to a modernist sort of rebellion and a longing to be outside the limits. It could also lead to seeing idealized romantic escape as the only life-giving function of the novel, as so many postmodern novelists do. These views see the novelist as Briony does, as the only reigning sovereign over storytelling, the novelist as God. Perhaps McEwan's novel opens the view a little wider, however, acknowledging there are moral realities that do not go away, that are beyond the power of the individual self to resolve, that nonetheless command communal attention, action, and effort. Perhaps the novel can only justify the sovereign self and its limitations while not leading to anything new, but perhaps there are more possibilities for it than modernism as a whole has led us to think.

Finally, then, this study is a call for new novels, ones that can incorporate more fully the dialectic of the moral and the ethical, just as Augustine's Bible-reading did, giving us characters and narratives that might lead us out of the limitations of the sovereign ethical type and the sovereign moral type, and toward a more complex, communal, and active humanity, one that can negotiate both the now and not yet, the moral and the ethical. It is not enough to escape the present and its categories and to await passively a future atonement or redemption that may never come, as the new ethical theorists tend to do. We have to attend to the now, submitting to the valid truth claims of the Other while at the same time actively engaging with them in light of the valid portions of our own truth claims. Like Augustine and the early modern Puritans, we have to believe in change and be open to it—that we can change, that others can change. To believe that no moral truths or judgments can be spoken or that no moral reconciliation or resolution of seemingly contradictory positions can occur, to believe that tolerance and pluralism are the best ideals, puts one in a lonely, impoverished, and self-focused position, one that limits the path to human flourishing.

Like Dorian, Stephen, and Dowell, Briony is alone. Her dementia will trap her forever in this loneliness, no matter how famous she is. She has been limited by her own years of doubting and searching within the confines of the novelistic narrative. There is much more to life than being an ethical self who rebels against, attempts to escape, or merely sees the self above and outside Puritan morality, just as there is much more to life than being a Puritan self who assumes certainty and thereby potentially places limits and debilitating categories upon others. Each side of the dialectic is incomplete in itself, but if some form of dialectical reading can be achieved in community that is willing to negotiate repeatedly the realms of the moral and the ethical, and to sacrifice the self's sovereignty, perhaps we can find new ways to serve each other well. The seventeenth-century

Puritan pastor, Thomas Watson, called on Christians to become "walking Bibles." The modernist novelists analyzed here warn readers that the modern need for escape and "letting be," as well as the practices of using labels and categories with assumed ultimate certainty, are both one-sided truth claims of the novelistic dialectic. In this light, becoming "walking novels" without a full sense of the dialectical relation of the moral to the ethical may be very dangerous indeed. This is one moral lesson some of the early modernist novelists were interested in pointing out.

✑ WORKS CITED

Albert, John. "The Christ of Oscar Wilde." *Critical Essays on Oscar Wilde*. Ed. Regina Gagnier. New York: G. K. Hall, 1991. Print.

Altieri, Charles. "Lyrical Ethics and Literary Experience." *Mapping the Ethical Turn: A Reader in Ethics, Culture, and Literary Theory*. Ed. Todd F. Davis and Kenneth Womack. Charlottesville: UP of Virginia, 2001. 30–58. Print.

Anger, Suzy. *Victorian Interpretation*. Ithaca: Cornell UP, 2005. Print.

Ardis, Ann. "Hellenism and the Lure of Italy." *The Cambridge Companion to E. M. Forster*. Ed. David Bradshaw. Cambridge UP, 2007. 62–76. Print.

Armstrong, Nancy. *How Novels Think: The Limits of British Individualism from 1719–1900*. New York: Columbia UP, 2005. Print.

Arnold, Matthew. *Culture and Anarchy* [1869]. In *Culture and Anarchy and Other Writings,* by Matthew Arnold. Ed. Stefan Collini. Cambridge: Cambridge UP, 1993. Print.

———. "Equality" [1878]. In *Culture and Anarchy and Other Writings,* by Matthew Arnold. Ed. Stefan Collini. Cambridge: Cambridge UP, 1993. Print.

Augustine. *Confessions*. Trans. F. J. Sheed. Ed. Michael P. Foley. Second edition. Indianapolis: Hackett, 2006. Print.

———. *On Christian Doctrine* [excerpt]. *Critical Theory Since Plato*. Ed. Hazard Adams. Revised edition. Fort Worth: Harcourt, Brace, 1992. Print.

Bacon, Ernest W. *Spurgeon: Heir of the Puritans*. London: Allen and Unwin, 1967. Print.

Bailin, Miriam. "An Extraordinary Safe Castle: Aesthetics as Refuge in *The Good Soldier*." *Critical Essays on Ford Madox Ford*. Ed. Richard A. Cassell. Boston: G. K. Hall, 1987. Print.

Benedict, Ruth. *The Chrysanthemum and the Sword: Patterns of Japanese Culture*. Boston: Houghton Mifflin, 1946. Print.

Benson, Bruce. *Pious Nietzsche: Decadence and Dionysian Faith*. Bloomington: Indiana UP, 2008. Print.

Bercovitch, Sacvan, ed. *Typology and Early American Literature.* Boston: U of Massachusetts P, 1972. Print.

Berkowitz, Peter. *Nietzsche: The Ethics of an Immoralist.* Cambridge, MA: Harvard UP, 1995. Print.

Bowen, Desmond. *The Protestant Crusade in Ireland, 1800–70: A Study of Protestant-Catholic Relations between the Act of Union and Disestablishment.* Dublin: Gill and Macmillan, 1978. Print.

Bridgewater, Patrick. *Nietzsche in Anglosaxony: A Study of Nietzsche's Impact on English and American Literature.* Leicester: Leicester UP, 1972. Print.

Bruce, William. *The Formation of Christian Character: A Contribution to Individual Christian Ethics.* Edinburgh: T & T Clark: 1902. Print.

Butler, Judith. "Values of Difficulty." *Just Being Difficult? Academic Writing in the Public Arena.* Ed. Jonathan Culler and Kevin Lamb. Stanford: Stanford UP, 2003. 199–215. Print.

Cairns, David, and Shawn Richards. *Writing Ireland: Colonialism, Nationalism, and Culture.* Manchester: Manchester UP, 1988. Print.

Cambers, Andrew. *Godly Reading: Print, Manuscript, and Puritanism in England, 1580–1720.* Cambridge: Cambridge UP, 2011. Print.

Cheng, Vincent J. "Religious Differences in *The Good Soldier*: The 'Protest' Scene." *Renascence* 37:4 (1985): 238–47. Print.

———. "The Spirit of *The Good Soldier* and the Spirit of the People." *English Literature in Transition, 1880–1920* 32:3 (1989): 303–16. Print.

Cormack, Alistair. "Postmodernism and the Ethics of Fiction in *Atonement*." *Ian McEwan: Contemporary Perspectives.* Ed. Sebastian Groes. London: Continuum, 2009. 70–82. Print.

Cornell, Drucilla. *The Philosophy of the Limit.* New York: Routledge, 1992. Print.

Costello, Peter. *James Joyce: The Years of Growth, 1882–1915.* London: Papermac, 1994.

Cunningham, Valentine. *Everywhere Spoken Against: Dissent in the Victorian Novel.* Oxford: Clarendon P, 1975. Print.

———. "The Novel and Protestant Fix: Between Melancholy and Ecstasy." In Knight and Woodman, 39–57. Print.

Damrosch, Leopold. *God's Plot and Man's Stories: Studies in the Fictional Imagination from Milton to Fielding.* Chicago: U of Chicago P, 1985. Print.

D'Angelo, Kathleen. "To Make a Novel: The Construction of a Critical Readership in Ian McEwan's *Atonement*." *Studies in the Novel* 41:1 (2005): 88–105. Print.

Davis, Thomas M. "The Exegetical Traditions of Puritan Typology." *American Literature* 5:1 (1970): 11–50. Print.

Defoe, Daniel. *Robinson Crusoe.* New York: Modern Library, 2001. Print.

"Divorce and the English Reformation." *The Saturday Review of Politics, Literature, Science and Art* 116 (July 5, 1913): 20–1. Print.

"English Church Law and Divorce: A Review of Sir Lewis Dibdin's *English Church Law and Divorce Reform*." *The Contemporary Review* 102 (1912): 904–6. Print.

Finney, Brian. "Briony's Stand against Oblivion: The Making of Fiction in Ian McEwan's *Atonement*." *Journal of Modern Literature* 27:3 (2004): 68–82. Print.

Ford, Ford Madox. *The Critical Attitude.* London: Duckworth, 1911. Print.

———. *The Good Soldier: A Tale of Passion*. New York: Penguin, 1999. Print.

———. *The Spirit of the People: An Analysis of the English Mind*. London: Alston Rivers, 1907. Print.

Forster, E. M. *A Room with a View*. New York: Bantam, 1988. Print.

———. "What I Believe." *Two Cheers for Democracy*. New York: Harcourt Brace, 1938. 67–96. Print.

Foster, John Burt, Jr. *Heirs to Dionysus: A Nietzschean Current in Literary Modernism*. Princeton: Princeton UP, 1981. Print.

Frei, Hans W. *The Eclipse of Biblical Narrative: A Study of Eighteenth and Nineteenth Century Hermeneutics*. New Haven: Yale UP, 1974. Print.

Frye, Northrop. *The Great Code: The Bible and Literature*. New York: Harcourt Brace, 1981. Print.

Galdon, Joseph A. *Typology and Seventeenth-Century Literature*. The Hague: Mouton, 1975. Print.

Gibson, Andrew. *James Joyce*. London: Reaktion, 2006. Print.

———. *Postmodernity, Ethics, and the Novel: From Leavis to Levinas*. London: Routledge, 1999. Print.

Gillespie, Michael Patrick. "Ethics and Aesthetics in *The Picture of Dorian Gray*." In Sandulescu, 137–55. Print.

———. *Oscar Wilde and the Poetics of Ambiguity*. Gainesville: UP of Florida, 1996. Print.

Gordon, David J. "Two Anti-Puritan Puritans: G. B. Shaw and D. H. Lawrence." *Yale Review* 56 (1966): 76–90. Print.

Greenhough, J. B. *Half Hours in God's Older Picture Gallery: A Course of Character Studies from the Old Testament*. London: Stockwell, 1903. Print.

Guy, Josephine, and Ian Small. *Studying Oscar Wilde: History, Criticism, and Myth*. Greensboro: ELT Press, 2006. Print.

Hale, Dorothy J. "Aesthetics and the New Ethics: Theorizing the Novel in the Twenty-First Century." *PMLA* 124:3 (2009): 896–905. Print.

———. "Fiction as Restriction: Self-Binding in New Ethical Theories of the Novel." *Narrative* 15:2 (2007): 187–206. Print.

Harcourt, Edward. "Nietzsche and the 'Aesthetics of Character.'" In May, 265–84. Print.

Harris, Janice. *Edwardian Stories of Divorce*. Rutgers UP, 1996. Print.

Hawkes, Rob. *Ford Madox Ford and the Misfit Moderns: Edwardian Fiction and the First World War*. New York: Palgrave, 2012. Print.

Haynes, E. S. P. "The Church and Divorce Law Reform." *Fortnightly Review* 86:520 (1910): 736–41. Print.

———. "The Difficulties of Divorce Law Reform." *Westminster Review* 170:5 (1908): 516–24. Print.

———. *Divorce Problems of Today*. Cambridge: W. Heifer, 1912. Print.

Hegel, G. W. F. *Hegel on Tragedy*. Ed. and intro. Anne and Henry Paolucci. New York: Doubleday, 1962. Print.

Henderson, Heather. *The Victorian Self: Autobiography and Biblical Narrative*. Ithaca: Cornell UP, 1989. Print.

Henn, Silas. *Religion in Earnest: Designed to Aid in Forming and Perfecting the Christian Character.* London: E. T. Whitfield, 1851. Print.

Hennegan, Alison. "'Suffering into Wisdom': The Tragedy of Wilde." *Tragedy in Transition.* Ed. Sarah Anne Brown and Catherine Silverstone. Malden: Blackwell, 2007. 212–31. Print.

Hildalgo, Pilar. "Memory and Storytelling in Ian McEwan's *Atonement.*" *Critique* 46:2 (2005): 82–91. Print.

Hinojosa, Lynne Walhout. *The Renaissance, English Cultural Nationalism, and Modernism.* New York: Palgrave, 2009. Print.

Hofer, Matthew, ed. *Oscar Wilde in America: The Interviews.* Urbana: U of Illinois P, 2010. Print.

Hood, Richard. "'Constant Reduction': Moderns in the Narrative Structure of *The Good Soldier.*" *Journal of Modern Literature* 14:4 (1988): 445–64. Print.

Hunter, J. Paul. *The Reluctant Pilgrim: Defoe's Emblematic Method and Quest for Form in Robinson Crusoe.* Baltimore: Johns Hopkins UP, 1966. Print.

Jacox, Francis. *Traits of Character and Notes of Incident in Bible Story.* London: Hodder and Stoughton, 1873. Print.

Jameson, Fredric. "The Experiments of Time: Providence and Realism." In Moretti, vol. 1, 95–127. Print.

Jeffrey, David. *Houses of the Interpreter: Reading Scripture, Reading Culture.* Waco: Baylor UP, 2003. Print.

Johnson, Dale A. *The Changing Shape of English Nonconformity, 1825–1925.* New York: Oxford UP, 1999. Print.

Joyce, James. *A Portrait of the Artist as a Young Man.* New York: Penguin, 1976. Print.

———. "The Universal Literary Influence of the Renaissance." *James Joyce in Padua.* Ed. Louis Berrones. New York: Random House, 1977. 43–49.

Judd, Alan. *Ford Madox Ford.* Cambridge, MA: Harvard UP, 1991. Print.

Kay, Sean. *Celtic Revival?: The Rise, Fall, and Renewal of Global Ireland.* London: Rowman & Littlefield, 2011. Print.

Kenner, Hugh. "Conrad and Ford: The Artistic Conscience." *Shenandoah* 3 (1952): 54. Print.

Kermode, Frank. *The Sense of an Ending: Studies in the Theory of Fiction.* London: Oxford UP, 1966. Print.

Kern, Stephen. *The Modernist Novel: A Critical Introduction.* Cambridge: Cambridge UP, 2011. Print.

Killeen, Jarlath. *The Faiths of Oscar Wilde: Catholicism, Folklore and Ireland.* New York: Palgrave, 2005. Print.

Knight, Mark, and Thomas Woodman, eds. *Biblical Religion and the Novel, 1700–2000.* Aldershot: Ashgate, 2006. Print.

Korshin, Paul. *Typologies in England, 1650–1820.* Princeton: Princeton UP, 1982. Print.

Kort, Wesley. "Calvin's Theory of Reading." *Christianity and Literature* 62:2 (2013): 189–202. Print.

Landow, George P. *Victorian Types, Victorian Shadows: Biblical Typology in Victorian Literature, Art, and Thought.* Boston: Routledge and Kegan Paul, 1980. Print.

Langland, Elizabeth. "Forster and the Novel." *The Cambridge Companion to E. M. Forster.* Ed. David Bradshaw. Cambridge UP, 2007. 93–103. Print.

Larsen, Timothy. *Contested Christianity: The Political and Social Contexts of Victorian Theology.* Waco: Baylor UP, 2004. Print.

———. *A People of One Book: The Bible and the Victorians.* Cambridge: Cambridge UP, 2011. Print.

Leiter, Brian. "Nietzsche's Moral and Political Philosophy." *Stanford Encyclopedia of Philosophy.* 2007. http://plato.stanford.edu/entries/nietzsche-moral-political. Accessed 1.20.2010. Online.

———, and Neil Sinhababu, eds. *Nietzsche and Morality.* Oxford: Clarendon P, 2007. Print.

Levenson, Michael. "Character in *The Good Soldier.*" *Twentieth Century Literature* 30:4 (1984): 373–87. Print.

———. *Modernism and the Fate of Individuality.* Cambridge: Cambridge UP, 1991. Print.

Lewis, C. S. *The Screwtape Letters.* Revised edition. New York: MacMillan, 1961. Print.

Lewis, Pericles. *Religious Experience and the Modernist Novel.* Cambridge: Cambridge UP, 2010. Print.

Lynn, David. "Watching the Orchards Robbed: Dowell and *The Good Soldier.*" *Studies in the Novel* 16:4 (1984): 410–23. Print.

Lyttelton, Edward. *Character and Religion.* London: Robert Scott, 1912. Print.

MacIntyre, Alasdair. *After Virtue: A Study in Moral Theory.* Second edition. Notre Dame: U Notre Dame P, 1984. Print.

Manganiello, Dominic. "Reading the Book of Himself: The Confessional Imagination of St. Augustine and Joyce." *Biography and Autobiography: Essays on Irish and Canadian History and Literature.* Ed. James Noonan. Ottawa: Carleton UP, 1993. 149–62.

Manning, Stephen. "Scriptural Exegesis and the Literary Critic." In Bercovitch, 47–66. Print.

Mather, Samuel. *The Figures or Types of the Old Testament* [1705]. Intro. Mason I. Lowance. New York: Johnson Reprint Corporation, 1969.

May, Simon, ed. *On the Genealogy of Morality: A Critical Guide.* Cambridge: Cambridge UP, 2011. Print.

McCarthy, Jeffrey Mathes. "*The Good Soldier* and the War for British Modernism." *Modern Fiction Studies* 45:2 (1999): 303–39. Print.

McEwan, Ian. *Atonement.* New York: Anchor Books, 2001. Print.

McFate, Patricia. "*The Good Soldier*: A Tragedy of Self-Deception." *Modern Fiction Studies* 9 (1963): 50–60. Print.

McKeon, Michael. *The Origins of the English Novel, 1600–1740.* Baltimore: Johns Hopkins UP, 1987. Print.

———, ed. *Theory of the Novel: A Historical Approach.* Baltimore: Johns Hopkins UP, 2000. Print.

Miller, Andrew. *The Burdens of Perfection: On Ethics and Reading in Nineteenth-Century British Literature.* Ithaca: Cornell UP, 2008. Print.

Miller, J. Hillis. *Literature as Conduct: Speech Acts in Henry James.* New York: Fordham UP, 2005. Print.

Miner, Earl, ed. *Literary Uses of Typology from the Late Middle Ages to the Present.* Princeton: Princeton UP, 1977. Print.

Mizener, Arthur. *The Saddest Story: A Biography of Ford Madox Ford*. London: The Bodley Head, 1971. Print.

Moretti, Franco, ed. *The Novel*. 2 volumes. Princeton: Princeton UP, 2006. Print.

Munson, James. *The Nonconformist: In Search of a Lost Culture*. London: SPCK, 1991. Print.

Newcomb, Harvey. *Youth and Its Duties: A Book for Young Gentlemen, Containing Useful Hints on the Formation of Character*. London: [n.p.], 1873. Print.

Newman, John Henry. *Lectures on the Present Position of Catholics in England*. London: Burns and Lambert, 1851. Print.

Nietzsche, Friedrich. *On the Genealogy of Morals* and *Ecce Homo*. Trans. Walter Kaufmann and R. J. Hollingdale. New York: Vintage, 1967. Print.

O'Malley, Patrick R., "Religion." In Roden, ed., *Palgrave Advances*, 167–88. Print.

Oser, Lee. *The Ethics of Modernism: Moral Ideas in Yeats, Eliot, Joyce, Woolf, and Beckett*. Cambridge: Cambridge UP, 2007. Print.

Pan-Anglican Papers, Being Problems for Consideration at the Pan-Anglican Congress, 1908. London: Society for Promoting Christian Knowledge, 1908. Print.

Pater, Walter. *Studies in the Renaissance: Studies in Art and Poetry* [1893]. Ed. Donald L. Hall. Berkeley: U of California P, 1980. Print.

Pease, Allison. "Aestheticism and Aesthetic Theory." In Roden, ed., *Palgrave Advances*, 96–118. Print.

Pettella, Tera H. "Devotional Reading and Novel Form: The Case of *David Simple*." *Eighteenth Century Fiction* 24:2 (2012): 279–300. Print.

Phelan, James. "Narrative Judgment and the Rhetorical Theory of Narrative in Ian McEwan's *Atonement*." *A Companion to Narrative Theory*. Ed. James Phelan and Peter J. Rabinowitz. Malden: Blackwell, 2005. 322–36. Print.

Poole, Roger. "The Unknown Ford Madox Ford." *Ford Madox Ford's Modernity*. Ed. Robert Hampson and Max Saunders. Amsterdam: Rodopi, 2003. 117–36. Print.

Preus, J. Samuel. "Secularizing Divination: Spiritual Biography and the Invention of the Novel." *Journal of the American Academy of Religion* 59:3 (1991): 441–66. Print.

Prickett, Stephen. "From Novel to Bible: The Aestheticizing of Scripture." In Knight and Woodman, 13–23. Print.

———. *Narrative, Religion, and Science: Fundamentalism versus Irony, 1700–1999*. Cambridge: Cambridge UP, 2002. Print.

———. *Origins of Narrative: The Romantic Appropriation of the Bible*. Cambridge: Cambridge UP, 2005. Print.

Qualls, Barry V. *The Secular Pilgrims of Victorian Fiction: The Novel as Book of Life*. Cambridge: Cambridge UP, 1982. Print.

Reginster, Bernard. "On the Genealogy of Guilt." In May, 56–77. Print.

Rise, Mathias. "Nietzschean Animal Psychology versus Kantian Ethics." In Leiter and Sinhababu, 57–82. Print.

Robbins, Keith. *England, Ireland, Scotland, Wales: The Christian Church 1900–2000*. Oxford: Oxford UP, 2008. Print.

Robinson, Marilynne. *Absence of Mind: The Dispelling of Inwardness from the Modern Myth of the Self*. New Haven: Yale UP, 2010. Print.

————. *The Death of Adam: Essays on Modern Thought*. Boston: Houghton Mifflin, 1998. Print.

Roche, Mark W. "Introduction to Hegel's Theory of Tragedy," *PhaenEx: Journal of Existential and Phenomenological Theory and Culture* 1:2 (2006): 11–20. Web. 8 August 2011. Online.

Roden, Frederick S. "Introduction." In Roden, ed., *Palgrave Advances*, 1–6. Print.

————, ed. *Palgrave Advances in Oscar Wilde Studies*. New York: Palgrave, 2004. Print.

Sandulescu, C. George, ed. *Rediscovering Oscar Wilde*. Volume 8 of *The Princess Grace Library Series*. Gerrards Cross: Colin Smythe, 1994. Print.

Saunders, Max. *Ford Madox Ford: A Dual Life. Volume One: The World before the War*. Oxford: Oxford UP, 1996. Print.

Schorer, Mark. "An Interpretation" [1951]. In *The Good Soldier*, by Ford Madox Ford. New York: Vintage, 1955. Print.

Schuchard, Ronald. "Wilde's Dark Angel and the Spell of Decadent Catholicism." In Sandulescu, 371–96. Print.

Seidel, Kevin. "Pilgrim's Progress and the Book." *ELH* 77:2 (2010): 509–34. Print.

————. "*Robinson Crusoe* as Defoe's Theory of Fiction." *Novel: A Forum on Fiction* 44:2 (2011): 165–85. Print.

Shakespeare, J. H. *The Churches at the Crossroads: A Study in Church Unity*. London: Williams and Norgate, 1918. http://babel.hathitrust.org/Record/008918109. Accessed 8.24.12. Online.

Shusterman, David. *The Quest for Certitude in E. M. Forster's Fiction*. New York: Haskell, 1973. Print.

Sinclair, William, Ven. *Influence of Religion on Character: A Lecture Delivered before the Ethiological Society*. London: Ethiological Society, 1908. Print.

Smith, Philip E., and Michael S. Helfand, eds. *Oscar Wilde's Oxford Notebooks: A Portrait of Mind in the Making*. New York: Oxford UP, 1989. Print.

Snitov, Ann Barr. *Ford Madox Ford and the Voice of Uncertainty*. Baton Rouge: Louisiana State UP, 1984. Print.

Spurgeon, Charles H. *The Autobiography of Charles H. Spurgeon, completed from his diary, letters, and records by his wife and his private secretary*. Volume IV. Cincinnati: Curts and Jennings, 1878–1892. Print.

Stannard, Martin. "Reformations: Ford Madox Ford and Transubstantiation." *The Poetics of Transubstantiation: From Theology to Metaphor*. Ed. Douglas Burnham and Enrico Giaccherini. Aldershot: Ashgate, 2005. Print.

Starr, George. *Defoe and Spiritual Autobiography*. Princeton: Princeton UP, 1965. Print.

Stewart, Carol. *The Eighteenth-Century Novel and the Secularization of Ethics*. Burlington: Ashgate: 2010. Print.

Sutton, Timothy J. *Catholic Modernists, English Nationalists*. Newark: U of Delaware P, 2010. Print.

Thatcher, David S. *Nietzsche in England, 1890–1914: The Growth of a Reputation*. Toronto: U of Toronto P, 1970. Print.

Trilling, Lionel. *E. M. Forster*. New York: New Directions, 1943. Print.

Warner, William B. "Realist Literary History: McKeon's New Origins of the Novel." *Diacritics* 19:1 (1989): 62–81. Print.

Watson, Thomas. *A Body of Divinity: Contained in Sermons upon the Westminster Assembly's Catechism.* London: Banner of Truth Trust, 1965. Print.

———. "How We May Read the Scriptures with the Most Spiritual Profit." In *The Bible and the Closet: or How We May Read the Scriptures with the Most Spiritual Profit, by Rev. Thomas Watson, and Secret Prayer Successfully Managed, by Rev. Samuel Lee.* Ed. John Overton Choules. Boston: Gould, Kendall & Lincoln, 1842. Print.

Watt, Ian. *The Rise of the Novel: Studies in Defoe, Richardson, and Fielding.* Berkeley: U of California P, 1957. Print.

Wells, Amos R. *Bible Miniatures: Character Sketches of One Hundred and Fifty Heroes and Heroines of Holy Writ.* London: Fleming H. Revell, 1909. Print.

Wilde, Oscar. "The Decay of Lying." *Critical Theory since Plato.* Ed. Hazard Adams. Fort Worth: Harcourt Brace, 1992. Print.

———. *De Profundis.* Ed. Robert Ross. Second edition. New York: Putnam, 1909. Print.

———. *The Picture of Dorian Gray.* New York: Penguin, 1962. Print.

Wright, Thomas. *Oscar's Books.* London: Chatto and Windus, 2008. Print.

LITERATURE, RELIGION, AND POSTSECULAR STUDIES

Lori Branch, Series Editor

Literature, Religion, and Postsecular Studies publishes scholarship on the influence of religion on literature and of literature on religion from the sixteenth century onward. Books in the series include studies of religious rhetoric or allegory; of the secularization of religion, ritual, and religious life; and of the emerging identity of postsecular studies and literary criticism.

Puritanism and Modernist Novels: From Moral Character to the Ethical Self
Lynne W. Hinojosa

Conspicuous Bodies: Provincial Belief and the Making of Joyce and Rushdie
Jean Kane

Victorian Sacrifice: Ethics and Economics in Mid-Century Novels
Ilana M. Blumberg

Lake Methodism: Polite Literature and Popular Religion in England, 1780–1830
Jasper Cragwall

Hard Sayings: The Rhetoric of Christian Orthodoxy in Late Modern Fiction
Thomas F. Haddox

Preaching and the Rise of the American Novel
Dawn Coleman

Victorian Women Writers, Radical Grandmothers, and the Gendering of God
Gail Turley Houston

Apocalypse South: Judgment, Cataclysm, and Resistance in the Regional Imaginary
Anthony Dyer Hoefer